D1346256

TRAVELS OF A
CAPITALIST LACKEY

TRAVELS OF A
CAPITALIST LACKEY

*

FRED BASNETT

THE COMPANION BOOK CLUB
LONDON

This edition is issued by arrangement with
George Allen and Unwin Ltd., London

© George Allen and Unwin Ltd., 1965

Made and printed in Great Britain
for the Companion Book Club (Odhams Books Ltd.)
by Odhams (Watford) Limited
Watford, Herts.
S.267.V.

Author's Note

At the time of this trip Khruschev seemed
to be firmly in power. He had just screwed
up the courage to have Stalin's body
removed from the Red Square mausoleum,
and he was making more and more of his
heavy Ukrainian jokes. Now that he has
been ousted by Brezhnev and Kosygin, what
changes would one notice in Russia? Professional kremlinologists apart, I think the
answer must be—very little. Jokes, Ukrainian or otherwise, will not be popular around
the Kremlin; you only have to look at the
faces of B. and K. to realize that. Possibly
the Khruschev sartorial style of voluminous
trousers and turned-up trilby will be
dangerously out of fashion. But the country
and its citizens will be much the same as
they were in 1961.

The museums will still be full, the
churches empty, the restaurants slow, the
trains slower, the police alert, Intourist
inert, and the people will remain the most
unpredictable, the most generous-hearted a
traveller of any persuasion could hope to
meet. And, although the Soviet is keeping
ahead in the space race, they still don't make
ball-point pens.

F. B.

CONTENTS

	PAGE
Author's Note	5
10,000 Miles on an Overdraft	11
Guys and Trolls	14
Sibelius was Right	34
Leningrad Baroque	50
A Public Brush with the Secret Police	65
Moscow, tu n'as pas changé, worse luck	78
Very Flat, the Ukraine	98
Limping Through Georgia	108
Idolatry in Erevan	131
There's a Little Railway Station to the South of Azerbaijan	143
In a Common Market, Persian Style	157
The Yashmak Strikes Back	174
The Golden Whore of the Bosphorus	204
Map	10

List of Illustrations

facing page

The Arctic Circle, Norway — 64

Peasants at Vishny Volochek — 65

The Winter Palace, Leningrad — 65

St Basil's, the Alvis and me — 96

The road to Orel — 97

The Georgian Military Highway — 97

Stalin on a plinth of tufa — 160

Peasant on a pile of melons — 160

Through our barred window at Djulfa — 161

Camel, driver and car, Iran — 161

A ford in central Turkey — 192

The hat-seller at Khoi, Iran — 192

Istanbul, from the fish market — 193

Acknowledgements

My grateful acknowledgements for all sorts of assistance are due to Roy Adnams; Alvis; the Automobile Association; Brown Bros; Champion Sparking Plugs; Delaney-Gallay; Dunlop; Tim Godfrey; Goodlass Wall; Grundig; Interlock; Lambretta-Trojan; Mike Lauderdale; Lesney Products; Lord Montagu; Pneumatic Tent Company; Postland Engineering; Roll-tip Pens; Tip-Top Vulcanizing. Without their help the trip would have been ill-advised, poorly equipped and highly expensive. In fact, it might not have happened at all.

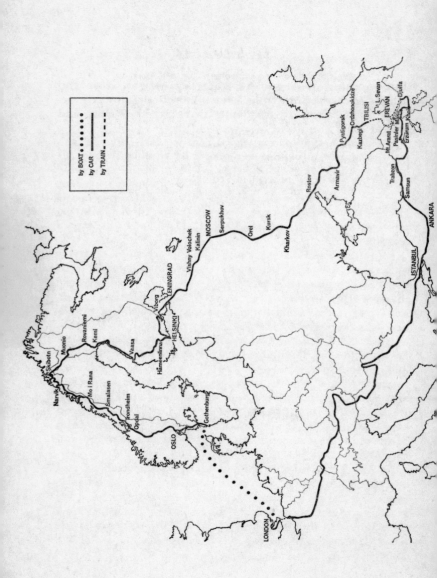

10,000 MILES ON AN OVERDRAFT

THE morning of August 22, 1961, was bright, clear and heavily streaked with panic. I was committed, quite irrevocably, to going on a 10,000-mile drive across Russia, and several other countries, in a very old car.

If anyone had asked me why, I couldn't have given a convincing answer. I could remember only how it had all happened. Like many idiot ideas, it was born in a pub. Some clown suggested to Paul Redfern, an ex-colleague and boozing companion of mine, that he drive to Moscow in his vintage 1926 Alvis. In turn, Paul canvassed me as navigator, photographer, co-driver and linguist. My refusal was a reasoned one.

Although I could read a map and use a camera, I didn't own either; I had no driving licence, and my total Russian vocabulary was *da, niet* and vodka; I had no burning desire to see Moscow—certainly not by racing there and back rally-style; I could hardly ask for a holiday from a brand-new advertising job; I had no money.

Undeterred, Paul tapped me again a couple of weeks later. By this time the trip had expanded. Instead of a straight in-and-out to Moscow, the plan was to cross to Sweden, shoot up to the Arctic Circle, from there drive south to Leningrad and Moscow, and then home via Poland and Germany. Paradoxically, this appealed to me much more, and I found myself saying, 'If I went on this trip I'd carry on from Moscow to the Caucasus and return through Turkey and the Balkans.'

As soon as I said this, I knew there was no if about it. I was in. Even when the jaunt swelled to a 10,000-mile marathon across a dozen countries in as many weeks. My reasons for not going were reduced to a short-list. This I then ignored, and Paul and I met one evening to decide what we would need in the way of essentials.

Not being outdoor types we had nothing in the way of camping or cooking equipment. Even the clothes we had would cope with nothing more than a stiff breeze in Oxford Street.

Paul had already collected several offers of items or services to do with the car, and had also had a generous offer of sponsorship from Lord Montagu, who was keen on unearthing a Russian car from revolutionary times or before. But this still left a mountain of stuff to be begged, borrowed or, as a last resort, bought. Naturally we nobbled all the people we knew in advertising to pass on any free samples of their products, but there is a limit to the amount of creamed rice and bath cubes you need, let alone can carry, on a trip like this. Solid, down-to-earth things like ground-sheets and thick socks just didn't seem to be advertised.

So each evening was spent with a trade directory and *What's where in London,* sending out a steady bombardment of letters requesting inflatable tents and collapsible buckets, sleeping bags, pep pills and string vests, cameras and survival kits, stoves, fire extinguishers, language courses, money, a kind word, cast-off clothing, anything. My style varied widely —from the bluff, no-nonsense approach one might expect from a leather-tough explorer who's no damned good with words to a wheedling flow of honey that I didn't dare re-read.

My targets were just as widely spread—from the Gulbenkian Foundation to a firm which made bullet-proof waistcoats. Although I played up the bandits in Anatolia, there was a very polite refusal from the latter, ending with the crushing flourish, 'Actually, these Waistcoats are made to order, and are such that when worn they would be soiled and unsaleable.'

At a liberal estimate only one out of ten letters hit the button. Some people didn't bother to reply. Others had a world-weary note: 'We get so many requests of this nature that it is impossible . . .' The quest for commissions from newspapers, magazines, radio and TV drew the whitest of blanks. They all said much the same thing: 'Sounds interesting. Let's see your stuff when you get back.'

Perhaps I'm breaking some unwritten law concerning

expeditions by mentioning finance. Certainly I can't remember reading of any traveller who seemed to have the slightest difficulty raising money. Surely they can't *all* have private means? Or is there some esoteric club where you merely mutter something about the Matto Grosso to a lean, tanned secretary in an impeccable Glen Urquhart suit and are immediately handed a shoe-box full of fivers? I wish I knew. I do know that by the time we'd paid for boat tickets to Gothenburg, settled for camping tickets and hotel bookings in Russia (these have to be paid for in this country) and bought the items we couldn't beg, we were both suffering from acutely swollen overdrafts.

GUYS AND TROLLS

August 22

Although we'd had one-and-a-half rehearsals of packing the back of the car (the rear seats had been ripped out and a sort of coffin lid fitted), when it came to the actual performance there was a small mountain of essentials left over. Everything had to be whipped out, a sub-stratum of carriage springs, brake drums and boxes of assorted nuts and bolts flung away, and the whole arrangement reshuffled and hammered in with a madman's strength. I was still left with a bulging brief-case, three cameras in my lap and various boxes of things under my feet.

Moving cagily to get used to the unaccustomed weight, we drove round to the 'Lamb' in Lamb's Conduit Street, for the send-off. The jam of cars outside indicated that the stirrup cup was going to take rather longer than expected. Naturally, we'd invited a few friends along but Tim Godfrey, a colleague of Paul's, had done a splendid PR job and collected a large selection of reporters from the Press, ITV and BBC. I managed to order lunch (a sausage roll and half a bitter) just as a reporter said 'You are Mr Bissett, aren't you?' Before I could spell the name correctly he vanished in a swirl of people. Two more reporters also disappeared in mid-flow and it was a relief to be called outside by the photographers. Here we had to pose with car, on the bonnet, on the seat-back, raising our glasses to toast each other, Lord Montagu, the car, even occasionally drinking the beer, which was getting flatter all the time.

There was a quick TV interview in a nearby mews, a pretend start for the photographer's benefit (our friends were dragooned as unpaid extras to cheer us off), and then we were really on our way, through the City and on to the A13.

The time to reach Tilbury had been cut fairly fine, and we

had to push along a little. This plus the cruel load started a mutinous mutter in the engine, which Paul nursed as frequently as possible with shots of Redex. At this point I'd have given quite ridiculous odds against the chance of making the whole trip under our own steam. The first of a long series of joking unbelievers was a woman attendant at a garage: 'Russia? You'll be lucky if you make Tilbury.'

The dock, dealing in people rather than goods, had the clean unreality of a large toy—the sweep of blond wood underfoot, Meccano-like passageways in bright, lawnmower green, the gleaming paintwork on the ship tied alongside. Some mobile friends had driven down for a farewell drink on board the ss *Britannia*, and our cabin was soon jammed with people drinking bottled beer out of plastic mugs. The car was driven on to a very casual sort of rig, and swung, equally casually, on deck. 'All ashore that's going ashore' in precisely Scandinavian English, and then we were staring at a line-up of our friends' faces across a marbling channel of water.

The big Swedish boat took its big Swedish time about lurching round in the river and getting up speed, and our shouted exchanges and farewell remarks seemed to go on and on. Small talk sounds even smaller when it has to be bellowed. It was a relief when we could stop shouting and start waving.

We went below to have one for absent friends while waiting for dinner. The public address system was relaying tunes of the 'twenties. I remember a beautiful period rendering of 'That's my weakness now' which fitted perfectly into the atmosphere on the boat, and suggested that the ship's radio was one of those monolithic jobs with a sunset fretworked over the speaker and a dusty, dimly glowing dial.

After dinner I began to notice what a remarkable number of young, unattached girls there were about the ship. At first it seemed like a holiday camp raised to the power n, but after a time the procession of uniformly fair faces became disturbing, slightly inhuman.

A pink Finnish youth who'd seen the Alvis being loaded came over to ask questions about it, and within two minutes had invited us to stay at his home in Vaasa if we passed that way. Were all Scandinavians as friendly? I went up to the sharp end of the boat to think about this. The Kent bank of the river was receding greyly, the Essex bank still strung with lights. In the dusk the gulls drifted in our wake like soot flakes, silent until a pan of garbage was thrown out of the galley, when they plummeted in a screaming dog-fight. By the immaculate white funnel, its red star staring blankly at the saucily winking lightships, a couple of youths in jeans and winkle-pickers were hotting up 'There is a tavern in the town' on guitar and muted trumpet for some Swedish girls who jived with stiff, unsmiling precision. Their cool eyes betrayed nothing.

August 23

The next day the sea was getting up and hitting us with monotonous regularity. I had to lie down on the bunk twice while dressing, and I've never found tying my shoelaces quite so hazardous. The vulcanized egg and tightly curled bacon rasher looked revolting. Weakly I asked for a soft-boiled egg, but when it came I couldn't face the surgery of cutting off the top. Paul offered to show me the part of the boat which moved about least, but half-way there I sloped off and had a quiet half-hour in the heads. I spent a convalescent afternoon on the breezy promenade deck swaddled in blankets watching the sea heave its slow, hesitant way up the rails and back again. By this time Paul had taken to his bunk and was occasionally sipping a little grapefruit juice or light broth.

My dinner was almost spoiled by a mountainous man opposite who wolfed through his courses, as he disarmingly explained, to try and keep them down. Fortunately he'd disappeared when the biggest wave of all hit us. Plates crashed and bounced; coffee sluiced across the tables; apples and oranges rolled wildly about the floor. The fact that my stomach survived this was due entirely to a girl from Stockholm who was enthusing about the modern jazz she'd heard in London. It was her pronunciation which gripped me. She called it 'yazz', which sounded much more raffish, and

16

kept referring to a delightful instrument called the 'wibes'.

August 24

The ship docked at some mind-numbing hour of the morning, yet everybody was not only up and about but cheerful. Remembering I hadn't collected my duty-free bottle of whisky, I wandered about until I found the chief steward. Five minutes too late; one apparently had to see him *before* six o'clock. The car looked in great shape as it was swung ashore, the paintwork as glossy as a beetle and the brass flashing in the glittering morning air. The dockers didn't have the earthiness of a true working class. There was no roar of disbelief when we explained that we intended crossing Russia; merely politely raised eyebrows.

For some reason I'd pictured Gothenburg as a city of old, grey stone with cloaked students walking in absorbed debate down cobbled streets. Instead, there was a pervasive tang of smoked fish, and a main square trellised and creepered with neon advertisements. Before starting north, we bought an axe big enough to tackle a Douglas pine, and an arty-looking black anorak to replace my old golf-jacket, which was about as wind-resistant as a fishing net.

Made the Norwegian border, a lonely fjord full of cold shadow, at sunset. The Customs weren't interested in anything we might have to declare, but obligingly changed our Swedish loose coins. The only place that seemed open in Halden was a cafeteria, which also combined the functions of pub and teenagers' coffee house. A lad on a motor bike guided us to the youth hostel, where the weary warden explained in a sleepwalker's monotone that watches have to be put on an hour when one crosses the border. Unfortunately I mentioned the trip, and he was suddenly disposed to yarn all night. Between yawns that were almost tearing my head off I made my excuses, and was asleep before I'd finished putting my watch right.

August 25

My eyes opened on a ceiling painted with scutcheons, acanthus leaves and what looked like swags of cigars. It turned out that they were cigars. The house, now belonging to the Town Council, was built by a merchant who made his pile out of the Norwegian passion for cigars. The floor mats also puzzled me for a time. They were of *leather*, and punched with oddly familiar-shaped holes until they were like lace. I realized that there must be a local shoe factory when my heel fitted so neatly into one of the holes that I almost took a sharp dive over the banister. When I untangled myself and got down the stairs less dramatically, I found the local Press waiting—a pimply, embarrassed youth with a polaroid camera and no English. The interview consisted of spelling out our names, and then he was delightedly banging off photos.

The warden called out his wife for a group portrait. I asked her if I could buy a thick sweater in town, and she told me that a friend of hers was having a sale, and wasn't I lucky? I wish she'd have told me she was Scottish before I complimented her on her grasp of English. The sale was pretty good, and for about £2 I collected a sweater, gloves and a hat—all classic Norwegian designs, of course, and liable to give eyestrain if looked at for long, but I thought that they'd tone down with a bit of dirt.

While Paul was having a guard fitted to the car sump to protect it from bouncing stones, I climbed up to the castle where Christian IX walked into a musket ball in 1760. From the ramparts, thick-barrelled cannons pointed suspiciously at the placid harbour and the quiet, pine-dark hills. The trunnions were freshly painted, and each pyramid of cannon balls looked as if it had a daily dusting. In the museum two delightfully unflattering portraits of long-chinned kings stared disgustedly at the spiky clumps of rapier-bayonets hurriedly stacked by departing soldiers. The whole place seemed to be brooding rather than dead, an atmosphere that kept me longer than I intended. When I picked my way down the cobbled slope from the castle, the car had been ready for the road for some time, and we reached Oslo late in the afternoon.

The sheer bulk of Oslo town hall is overbearing to the point of discomfort. Although there is really lots of space in front, the dominating façade seems to push you much too close to the waterfront—an impression strengthened by the long line of various craftsmen in bronze, who menace you from the top of the steps like a meeting of strong Trade Unionists about to advance on a blackleg. The square itself is densely populated by even larger bronzes and monolithic granite sculptures of huge, very naked women.

The rest of the day dithered away in a miserable series of mishaps. After driving out to Bygdehoy (and losing nearly an hour by getting into the wrong traffic lane), we found that both the Kon-Tiki and the Fram museums were closed. Back to the centre, tried to book an hotel; full. To the railway station where they have a hotel-booking service known as Kvartering; wrong station. Found the right station, asked for a central hotel, given one in the suburbs. It is called Helsfyr. Reached it after following a tram track for about a hundred miles. Had a bath, changed into a suit, went down for a meal willing to forgive and forget. Waited half an hour to order only to find that the cook went home ten minutes ago. Settled for a sandwich and a beer and took a taxi into town to catch some jazz in Akersgate. We arrived in time to see the last stragglers leaving. Returned to Helsfyr in the same taxi.

August 26

Although we were supposed to be moving on the next day, we were in two minds about giving Oslo another chance. The decision was made for us by Rasmus Thime, an advertising contact of Paul's, who gave us a mosquito spray, insisted we stay the night at his house and phoned up the newspaper *Aftenpost* to send a reporter and photographer round. A pleasantly chubby girl reporter appeared with a Hungarian photographer in tow. Her English was good; his apparently limited to an unsmiling 'Hello'. After a couple of shots of the car, which we found under a deep drift of Norwegians, we moved over to the Hotel Viking, a rather severe thirteen-storey job outside, but warm with lots of good-looking wood inside, and studded with modern motifs in riveted copper.

The interview started off formally enough, but after a few

strong Export beers the girl's English disappeared in waves of giggles, and she seemed to be having difficulty with her writing. When he heard we were going to Budapest, the Hungarian joined in with a bizarre but understandable variety of English. He explained that he'd found his way to Norway after the abortive rising, and would I please look up his sister at this address, and give her this note because he hadn't heard from her since? He also archly passed me another note in Hungarian, which he assured me said, 'I wish to love you, Hungarian woman.' His heavy winks indicated that this was a powerful stimulant not to be used lightly. When I asked him to put an identifying mark on the note to his sister, so that I wouldn't get them mixed up, he was vastly amused. When we left to go to Bygdehoy he was very happy, and the girl was weakly wiping her glasses. As far as I know the interview never appeared.

The museums were open this time. The Kon-Tiki sparingly lit in a dim hall, with a glass panel showing various denizens of the deep beneath the balsa raft, looks stagy and unbelievable. And why was the log written in English?

The Fram, on the other hand, is entirely believable, and everything about it breathes its period—cramped cabins strewn with a manly array of sealskin parkas, harpoons and meerschaum pipes; a ferocious clutch of surgical saws and scalpels looking as if they were specifically designed for amateur operations by the light of a swinging oil-lamp; an antediluvian movie camera; a box of Horlicks made long before night-starvation was invented. It was easy to picture the hold alive with the kind of high-minded, clean-limbed lads who once strode through the *Boys' Own Paper*.

The Fram is indoors. The Vigeland Sculpture Park is outdoors, but it doesn't seem like it. There's the feel of a brisk, salty breeze about the Fram, but the avenue of Vigeland's disordered fantasies was like an airless corridor in a lunatic mansion. Few artists can have had it so good as the sculptor Vigeland. His undoubted talent was recognized early, and the State set aside a site for a park to contain as many sculptures as he cared to produce. So, in his early thirties, Vigeland was made for life. No expense was to be spared in producing his works, all of which were assured of an honoured place in the capital, and he had ten models strolling around his garden waiting for him to be inspired. This must be an artist's dream of absolute power, and we all know what absolute power does. Without any discipline except that imposed by his materials, he worked like a maniac for forty years. His enormous output is now displayed in a spacious park at Frogner, and, in my eyes, it represents one of the most expensive courses of psychiatry in history.

Beyond the huge gate a wide bridge is lined with dozens of bronzes of rather lumpish men, women and children in almost every attitude of love, hate, fear and anger that their dull faces and stocky bodies can express. Over to the left is a circle of child bronzes, with a centre-piece of a full-term foetus on its head. Following your nose you come to a fountain with a large, square basin decorated with some very stunted and tortuous trees in which figures writhe and twist and peer in highly unadjusted ways. The Frieze of Life goes a little further round the bend. This is a series of plaques which are like stills from dream sequences which would have put Freud in a fever. The giants holding up the fountain bowl can be seen only dimly through falling water. The mind boggles at what a failure of the water supply would reveal. Terraces lead from here to the feature which dominates the whole avenue, a column of closely entwined, pulsating figures. It is cagily referred to as the 'Monolith' in the guide-book, which goes on: 'This gigant [sic] is chiselled out of a single block of stone and meassures [sic] 17 meters in height.' Well, to me this gigant is a monumental phallus. Several granite groups placed around it are engaged in activities ranging from the barely imaginable to the unfathomable. The Wheel of Life that closes the avenue could be the biological complement to the Monolith, but I won't press the point. A final mad flourish; on top of four columns some very scaly dragons are knocking the daylights out of two men and molesting two women.

There is a Nietszchian air about this vigorous, peasantish race of Vigeland's creation. The men obviously tear up trees in their wrath; the women could crack coconuts between

21

their thighs; any of the babies could survive a week on a Spartan hillside. Their life is brutish and short, their sex savage and open; and any less brutish idiot caught painting on rocks or making up an alphabet would probably have been used as a football by his healthier contemporaries.

It began to rain softly on the park. The tribe of hardy naturists looked completely at home under the grey, ragged sky, water gleaming on their hard thighs and patterning their thick, straight backs with streaks, raindrops glistening from their fingers and noses.

I was relieved to find that Norwegians didn't practise Vigeland's version of the Life Beautiful. Of course they're an outdoorsy lot. Those who don't work in the open quit the towns in droves at week-ends to go ski-ing, hunting or berry-picking. Their long, saw-edged strip of mountains, forests and fjords is two-and-a-half times as big as England and, with a total population only a third that of London, they have no need to jockey for a place to drop a haversack.

But this doesn't make them mindless; everyone seems to read furiously, often in English or German, and modern art is not a joke. When we went to Rasmus Thime's home, the place was full of books (in four languages) and Chinese prints, African carvings and Norwegian oils, all of them original. The exotic objects came from different members of his family who were scattered around the world. The paints were by artists he knew personally, and they sounded a lively crew. One had started a radish farm because he liked their colour. Another was credited with pulling down a train-blind in Italy because he couldn't take any more sensations. Perhaps the most original was the one serving a prison sentence for wounding a pursuer after a bank robbery committed in the sacred name of art.

Over a delicious supper of local shrimps dipped in remoulade and washed down with cold beer, the conversation had a global range, from China (where Rasmus had lived until he was fourteen) to the Cameroons where a relative was a missionary; from a youthful hitch-hike through England (Birmingham came in for as much praise as Cornwall) to the atrocious roads we'd meet in the north of

Norway. I suppose I must have been getting tired when I remarked to Mrs Thime how much I liked the use of timber for walls and ceilings. It does give vigour to a room, but to comment on this in Norway, where wood is everywhere you look, is the equivalent of complimenting a housewife in Penge on her exquisite taste in bricks.

August 27

Although next day was Sunday, the whole family was up with us for an early breakfast—two young daughters who bobbed solemn curtsies on being introduced and a small son who hid his head in his mother's lap. A Norwegian breakfast is the sort of spread that would have made the pen of Dickens dribble. The only hot thing you eat is a boiled egg, but the variety of cold plates is huge. Large platters of beef, mutton, salami and ham, and, on the side, a smoked leg of sheep. This dense, ox-blood red meat is cut sparingly in curling leathery snippets, and the taste has to be acquired. There is a board of different cheeses, including the soft, brown goat cheese which had the consistency of fudge and a blandly elusive flavour without the slightest suggestion of cloven-hoofed rankness. We had dishes of herring and anchovies; bread in rolls, twists and cobs, bone-hard rye biscuits, pumpernickel; tall creamy glasses of milk, big cups of strong coffee and earthenware pots of jams—rich, dark cherry and translucent amber cloudberry.

The family sang a lively grace before eating. Rasmus explained that the children would have sung it in canon for us if they hadn't been shy. He carefully drew a map to get us by the shortest way on to the Trondheim road, and pressed a bottle of home-made rosehip wine on us, and everyone waved us out of sight, ignoring the steady drizzle.

The sun burst through as we came in sight of Mjosen, Norway's largest lake. We drove along it for hours, with the lake disappearing and then reappearing vaster than ever. The far side never came in view at all. Mjosen didn't drop behind until Lillehammer, the big centre for ski-ing, which was sullen and deserted under a snowless sky. A polite policeman came over as we stopped, with a request to move the car to the other side of the completely empty street.

The road meandered pleasantly along the Gubransdal, never far from the sound of water, to Otta and Dombas, where a rambling shanty of a restaurant was advertising *varmer polser*. This sounded like something to be applied to boils, but turned out to be hot dogs. While we were wolfing a couple of these, a lone English holidaymaker with an earnest W.E.A. face raced over to talk to us. He wanted to tell us not to miss visiting a lonely farmhouse five miles off the road where they sold delicious milk. I was more interested in where he'd picked up his deep tan. 'Yorkshire,' he said bleakly.

The small sun glowed like a frost-nipped nose as we climbed up to the high, sweeping moors of the Dovre plateau, already showing the first rich stains of autumn. The wattle fences on the bleaker stretches of road, presumably to protect animals in snow, had no effect on the cutting edge of the bitter wind, and I saw none of the travellers' rests which the saga says King Systein built around here.

My face burned like a bonfire for an hour after reaching the hutted warmth of the hostel at Opdal. The warden, a woman built like a sparrow, was shortening her old life by lugging buckets of water about. She was watched with mild interest by a few hostellers. Apparently the plumbing had failed, but this was regarded as the warden's sole concern. The little woman was almost shocked when we relieved her of the buckets. When a beefy English girl appeared to inquire peevishly, *'Isn't* there any water yet?' my homicidal look sent her hurrying back to her postcards.

August 28

There is a spare tough feel about Trondheim, which makes it a fitting start for the Arctic Highway, the Great North Road of Norway. The market in the main square is no effete, sheltered affair with roof-heaters. The stalls are open to the low, grey sky, and the muffled owners stamp around in the cold rain stoically. The cathedral, too, has an austere look. There is little suggestion of a fat living for rosy bishops

24

in its echoing interior, barely illuminated by stained-glass windows which the thin daylight hardly penetrates. A long, open-sided shed rang with the hammering of stone-carvers chipping at cornices and man-size niche figures. Glistening blackly under the rain, two stone seals seemed ready to bark for herring.

We followed the Trondheim Fjord out of town and climbed the Faetten defile to the Skogn valley. I will not provide set-pieces about conifered crags and breath-taking vistas. Norwegian scenery *is* great, but there's so much of it. I often had the feeling that I was seeing the same reel again. Panoramas which, anywhere else, would have had me reaching convulsively for my camera simply failed to register after a time. I think that perhaps one has to walk through such country to be perpetually charmed.

At Levanger the Arctic Highway began to take on a more rugged character, with ruts and pot-holes scarring the surface of water-bound gravel. Snaasa Lake loomed up on our left, a lonely, noble stretch of water with darkly humped, boat-shaped islands bristling with pines right down to the water-line.

Considering the road surface, we'd covered a respectable distance by the time we reached Grong, but the name put me off. So we pushed on another fifty miles to Smalasen. Not, I grant you, an entirely innocent name, but obviously less under the sway of the trolls than Grong. In case you are docketing me as an over-sensitive plant I would like to mention that among the reading matter we carried was J. R. R. Tolkein's trilogy *The Lord of the Rings*. It's one thing to skim through this in the agnostic atmosphere of Hampstead but quite another thing to read it in the brooding environs of Grong. It would take a brash man to say there's no such place as Mordor when it might easily crop up on the next signpost. Although I didn't mention it—no point in causing unnecessary panic—I kept a keen watch on the sky-line for signs of the Black Riders, and my ears were often ringing with the strain of listening for harsh Orc laughter. It's as well for my heart that Norwegian country-folk are not great horse-riders or harsh laughers.

For the last couple of hours, driving was in the dark, and we could see the headlights of anything approaching, even round a bend, so that for long stretches we could hog the middle of the road and avoid the larger varieties of pot-hole and stone which favour the sides. We overshot the lonely hostel, and tracked it down only just before official closing time. The place looked as if it had been closed for a year. A light sprang up after ten minutes' hammering and, after another ten minutes of sliding bolts, lifting latches and rattling chains, the door opened. It was a small, old woman; it seems as if all old women below a certain height are given preference for wardens' jobs.

According to the book, we were the first visitors for over a week, but if the old woman was delighted to see us she kept her emotions well under control. She led us to the kitchen, and stolidly read a newspaper at arms' length (her arms were only just long enough to get it into focus) willing us to hurry our frugal supper.

August 29

I surfaced from a dream in which I was the clapper in a big bronze bell. In fact, the noise came from the field outside my window. Cow-bells. Not sounding with an occasional melancholy tonk but clanging away like fire-alarms. The racket was caused by just three young cows, who were gaily bucketing about trying to get their cursing herdsman to join in a bit of a romp. One mild-eyed, creamy animal waited until the man had caught her halter, and then raced him off his feet around the field with the other cows excitedly tearing alongside. I wish I could have stayed to watch them being milked; it promised to be a riot.

We started off in a steady, cool drizzle, which smoothly increased to a downpour as we came into Mosjoen. Although it modestly takes little credit for either, Mosjoen has two claims to fame. It is bang in the middle of Norway and has the best downpours in the country. The townspeople are very blasé about any rainstorm that doesn't actually fell you to the ground. They walk around in normal rain without hats, without raincoats, without even a token bending of the head. Umbrellas are a concession allowed only to the sick and the aged.

Paul went to have the car brakes adjusted, and I sloped off to try and buy a bottle of *akvavit*. The Vinmonopolet, the shop where all liquor is sold, was closed for the day. One slat of the Venetian blind was inched apart to look at my hooded, dripping figure, but whoever it was went back to drinking the stock. I went into a stationer's to buy some writing paper, and came out with the stationer who had appointed himself as my guide. He took me along to the local newspaper office to get the paper punched to fit my clip-file, and introduced me to everybody *en route*—the teacher, the petrol-pump attendant, the shopkeeper, the editor—with a cosy, provincial intimacy. And, of course, we had to be interviewed by the Press, and have our grainy photograph taken in the rain. It was here that I learned the real reason why we were such irresistible press-bait in Norway. There are over 200 newspapers in this thinly-populated country (some of them with circulations of only 5,000), and the reporters are often desperate for a filler. Suitably chastened, we shook hands with the total able-bodied population of this small, friendly, wet town and set course for Mo i Rana. I almost wrote 'set sail'; a lyrical, palm-fringed name like Mo i Rana should be a dot on a Pacific chart not threaded on the cold, twisted line of the Arctic Highway.

Under the persistent rain the road was bogging down nicely. The springs and shock-absorbers were taking a terrible beating from an infinite series of pot-holes. These had become a linked system of ochrous-tinted lakes, and as we swooshed blindly into them we could only pray that the hidden hole wasn't quite big enough to swallow a wheel. Where the road wasn't holes it was a shifting slurry of mud and stones, and passing lorries (very few, fortunately) would first blind the windscreen with their bow-wave, and then rake the whole length of the car with a withering hail of stones from their wheels. When we stopped at a lorrymen's café in Mo i Rana, the car was labouring under a cruel load of muck, and the last wash from a lorry had left me with a rapidly hardening mud pack down one side of my face. My anorak was demonstrating conclusively that there is a great difference between shower-proof and rain-proof, and my bargain sweater was steaming like an old goat. In addition, my overlong toe-nails were beginning to saw their way through my damp socks.

Looking for the loo I opened a door, and there, in front of my mud-splashed glasses, was a gleaming shower with a huge copper tank of hot water just waiting to feed it. I undressed so fast that I almost did myself an injury. I swayed in a voluptuous haze under that steaming rosette until a vision of Dr Arnold forced me to turn it to cold before leaping out, shaving down to the chinbone, savagely pruning my toe-nails and getting into some dry clothes. Then I trotted off, glowing, ready to make a pig of myself with food and beer.

I didn't do too badly on beer, but when I ordered *swine-skotelett*, expecting a pork chop or so, I was faced with an enormous platter containing six meaty three-inch cubes of pigs' ribs, with a haystack of sauerkraut and a huge side-dish of potatoes. Paul was in the same over-sized boat with the fish he'd ordered. We knew we were beaten before we started. Although we trenched away until our jaws were aching, the twin steaming mountains hardly settled an inch. The waitress had obviously never come across such bird-like appetites in her life. The first time we indicated we were beaten, she thought it was some sort of waggishness, and went away with a smile. When we convinced her that we couldn't eat another thing, she looked at us in genuine concern, searching our faces for signs of a wasting disease.

She discussed our symptoms with a couple of the flaneurs, who kept drifting in to make a deliberate tour of the tables before moving on to some other hell-haunt of pleasure in Mo. This was the normal way of referring to the town; it certainly fitted better than Mo i Rana. A rock-and-roll version of 'Danny Boy' was being played thin on the juke-box. Outside in the quiet rain the last tourist straggler from the North pulled up. Like a pilgrim with a scallop shell, he carried the badge of his journey, a spread of reindeer antlers tied on the roof of his car.

A bright morning sun was turning the car into a mud-armoured rhinoceros and making the road steam as we started for the Arctic Circle. Around the bend the road suddenly became loose and broken up, as if some joker had been harrowing it, and we had one nasty skid before realizing that the surface was as treacherous as mud. After a couple of wobbly miles we caught up with a farmer on a tractor, and the dangerous fool *was* harrowing the road. Then I realized that he was part of a road-mending gang.

Their methods are as rugged as the Highway itself. The tractor chugs along at a fast walking pace dragging a couple of scrapers and a rake behind it. This effectively tears up the top layer and roughly redistributes it. Any large stones unearthed are removed by a man riding behind on a bike, and his idea of a large stone is practically in the boulder class. We went ahead of the tractor to do some redistribution of stones on our own account. The steady fusillade of them beneath the car sounded like a speeded-up carillon as various parts came under fire. Overtaking was done in the crouched position, in case a flying stone met the windscreen. The rear lamps, although taped-up, were battered silly; the bulbs hammered into blind scarred sockets. The sun was getting warmer every hour, and by the time we reached the Arctic Circle I had peeled off my anorak, scarf and outer sweater. Paul made a grander gesture, whipping off his shirt to expose his pale, concave torso, and quickly putting it back on when he heard the first mosquito whine. The Circle is marked by a stone pillar holding an ironwork globe and a line of white stones which peters out a few yards beyond the road like a rockery that somebody tired of. On one side of the road impressively wild moorland sweeps up to snow-streaked peaks; on the other is a bright yellow café with the flags of all nations and a Coca-Cola sign. It had closed for the season the day before. An hotel a few kilometres inside the Circle was still open for business. As I was trying, again without success, to buy a bottle of *akvavit*, an Englishman spoke to me in the certainty that I would know the latest Test score. I was a bitter disappointment to him.

Shortly after flushing our first reindeer, we had a second unnerving skid. If the car was allowed to drop below a certain speed on climbs it began to feel its age, and the only way to take them was at a fast lick, even on bends. This particular bend was a blind right-hander which I'm sure turned through more than 180 degrees. About half-way round, still holding on to its precious speed, the car started an eery, waltzing slide that came within a foot of giving me a faceful of very solid rock overhang. We went more sedately after this, if only because some of the climbs were becoming too long to take by surprise, and the water was beginning to hiss and steam around the hare mascot on the radiator cap.

There were four ferries between us and Narvik. Checking the intervening mileages against the time-table, I calculated that we could make Narvik that night—just. At least it was something to drag my mind out of hibernation for a time. We almost fell at the first fence; when we came to drive on board the boat we found that a pin had managed to drop out of the starter motor. The captain, or whatever he was, couldn't be bothered whether we got on board or not, but a gang of excited kids wrestled for the privilege of shoving us up the gang-plank.

There was plenty of time in hand for catching the next ferry, where a couple of English hitch-hikers were philosophically waiting for a lift south. The last four ferries hadn't carried a single car; the tourist season was definitely over. They'd actually had to wait five days in the Lofoten Islands for a ship to the mainland. The temperature dropped rapidly as the light failed, and a thin, mean wind began to whip dust across the road. The only shelter, a primitive hut of a café, had closed two hours before, but, miraculously, it opened again and we dived inside before the owner could change his mind.

Conversation was desultory in the drowsy heat of the shack. The male hitch-hiker discovered that he lived two hundred yards away from me in London. Somebody observed what a small world it was. The rain arrived with the ferry. There was one car on board, and the hitch-hikers raced off for their haversacks. Waiting to go on board, I could see them wrestling into the straps fifty yards up the road, tensing for their last bid at a lift. Even at this distance their screwed-up hopefulness could be sensed. As the car drove ashore, I noted sadly that it was very full.

It was now dark and raining heavily, and we'd have to drive hard to cover twelve miles of bumpy, twisting road in the twenty minutes before the next ferry. The other car on board raced off with the same idea in mind. We tucked in behind, and hoped that the driver was a local who knew the roads. We made the jetty with a couple of minutes in hand. I couldn't help wondering where we'd have stayed if we'd failed. Another sporty drive, not so pressing on time, caught a late ferry over to Narvik.

The place looked as cold as a planet, a cluster of frostily-twinkling lights in the blustering blackness. The side screens were up (it was like wearing blinkers at night), and the wind blasted rain straight from one open side to the other, taking the breath away. A curving string of mercury lamps icily lit the road to town, and then stopped altogether where they were most needed—just where the road and the railway tangled in a subtle knot. The station-master at Narvik must get some peculiar shunting problems. He nearly had a vintage Alvis in his sidings, plus two English-men without platform tickets.

It was nearly midnight when we found the hostel, with a rank of expensive cars outside which certainly didn't belong to poor youths out for exercise and fresh air. There was a light in the upper storey, but my efforts on the door-bell had no effect. I was having a quiet smoke, thinking out the next move, when a police car drew up. This would have been lucky anywhere, but in Norway it was remarkable.

The Norwegian police are something of a joke—never around when they're wanted. But this time they got out and rang the bell. No answer. They zipped off in their Volkswagen to phone the warden. No answer. So they guided us to a place called the Misjonhospitet, which sounded a real bread-and-dripping charity, but wasn't. Hoots, metallic clangs and the sound of shunting floated up bright and clear from the dockside, but when my head touched the pillow they were no louder than a flea's cough.

August 31

Paul hived off early to find a hospitable garage, so I strapped myself into the cameras and strolled into town. Narvik appears a lot warmer by daylight—grass plots and flower beds in the centre, a fountain, a town hall looking self-consciously modern. Two small blonde girls sat on a bench with a pile of shrimps between them which they were demolishing with the neatness of otters. When I tried to get a photograph of their solemn gluttony, they saw me, of course, and practically buried their giggling faces in the pile of pink shells. I found the shrimp stall in the long, echoing fish market, and bought some with the point-and-smile technique. But my big success was that I at last managed to buy a bottle of *akvavit and* a bottle of Norwegian whisky.

There is a severe, official air about a Vinmonopolet which makes customers slink in as if they were visiting a pawn-ship. You go up to the desk (it's a counter really but it feels like a desk), and mutter quietly to the man about your terrible alcoholic desires. He looks at you rather sadly and writes a prescription, which you take to the cashier's desk. Here you get a chit to show you've paid, and you take this to another man who whips the bottles off the shelves with indecent haste, and wraps them up with averted eyes. You then stuff the bottles under your coat, pull your cap well down and sidle out of the door. And presumably go home and get quietly drunk to drown your guilt complex.

Narvik presented a different face again as we left on the ferry, a whole hillside of houses painted in a Mediterranean range of colours—pink, blue, yellow and, a favourite Norwegian colour, madder-red. Even in the rain they managed to look gay. The country became wilder and more scenic than ever. Palely-glowing copses of dwarf silver birch eased the eyes after the endless forests of pine and fir. The long, steady climbs had to be taken in two or three bites to let the car cool off. At one stop we ate the shrimps, simply turning round in our seats and eating off the backboard, sheltered by the hood. As I picked at the coral, shellac-like shells with rapidly numbing fingers, the only sound was the hiss of the drizzle on the radiator. The valley below occasionally made a theatrical appearance through shifting curtains of rain.

As we belted merrily through Olsborg, a mob of tin-hatted soldiers waved and shouted at us in high excitement. Waving back, we raced away along a lovely avenue of tall silver birches. After half an hour's hard driving the road petered out into a cart track, and we realized that the soldiers had been trying to tell us just this. They laughed and applauded ironically as we entered Olsborg again and picked up the right road to Skibotn. This village, 200 miles north of the Arctic Circle, was our turning point. From here we would be travelling south all the way to Tbilisi. To mark the end of a phase we decided to camp here and, with the help of the headlights, found a reasonably flat space among the pines off the road. The short undergrowth, thick with berries, was as springy as a mattress, and soon the pneumatic tent was stirring obscenely as the car engine inflated it.

Cooking in the rain by torchlight has to be kept simple. So, while a pan of beans heated over the blue flame of the butane stove, I lit the wick on one of our cans of self-heating soup. Nothing seemed to be happening, but after a couple of minutes the soup came out scalding. I filled a mammoth hip-flask with the *akvavit*, and retired to the tepee, leaving the rain to do the washing-up. Warm inside my sleeping-bag I took an experimental swig from the flask. Strong but not crude and—yes—quite a pleasing flavour. I passed over the flask to Paul, but had to recover it a minute later to try and clear a catching sensation in my throat. Eventually I realized that this wasn't due to the *akvavit*. Water had penetrated the tent bag and, by some unknown reaction, had started to generate phosgene—or something very like it. Despite the rain, we had to open the flap, and then took another medicinal slug apiece before drifting off to the quiet patter of rain.

SIBELIUS WAS RIGHT

September 1

Horace Walpole, I believe, admitted to doing two things
he disliked every day—going to bed and getting out of it.
I'm right with him on this, especially the last bit. Take this
particular morning. The tent was lurching about in what
sounded like a typhoon. My forehead was throbbing with
bumps from a mosquito banquet. My feet were awash in a
puddle fully three inches deep. But did I get up? I just
moved my feet and settled down for another half-hour of
semi-consciousness. Even so we still struck camp not long
after seven o'clock. The ground sheet (which was integral
with the tent) had proved perfectly waterproof. It hadn't
lost a single drop of the rain which had come in through
the flap, and we had to empty it like a bucket.

There is a Customs arrangement between the Scandinavian countries which, as far as I could see, allows you
to go from country to country without hindrance. Customs
posts are manned, but it seems to be a superfluous gesture.
The Norwegian Customs waved us on without bothering to
come out, and a bored officer at the Finnish post had a
good look at the car on the pretext of examining our
insurance papers.

The landscape became bleaker and more stunted as we
penetrated Finland. A fox, so ginger that it verged on the
garish, trotted across the road, and sat down to watch us
draw almost level before diving into the scrubby forest. A
Lapp woman, shapeless in her bulky clothes, trudged down
the road humping a crude, hod-shaped rucksack made of
hide stretched over a wooden frame. Her weather-beaten,
incredibly lined face looked so tired that I felt it kinder
not to photograph her. There were some Lapp dwellings
a few miles further on, a haphazard complex of huts and
wigwams. A solitary pair of chunky, reindeer-hide slippers

hung above a tangle of reindeer antlers, tourist bait for
some late holiday-maker. A small, almost spherical child
was tethered to a wigwam to stop him straying too far. A
few yards away two reindeer were tethered for the same
reason. They sniffed and moved daintily away as I
approached with the camera. Since I was coming downwind
I thought it might have been my sweater they were nosing,
but when I caught *their* smell I wondered how they had the
nerve to be so disdainful.

Karesuando is marked as a double town on the map, with
one part in Sweden and one in Finland. There were a few
buildings in Sweden just over the river Muonioalu, but the
Finnish town of Karesuando consists of one store with a
petrol pump outside. Without the petrol pump I suppose it
would only class as a village. As we drew up, a couple of
Lapps (I think it was a man and a woman) left the store and
moved off across country. I started to reach for my camera,
and then thought better of it. I was in Lapland, wasn't
I? and I'd see a lot more Lapps before I left, wouldn't I?
The answers were yes and no, respectively. They were
the last Lapps I saw. Later I was told that most of them
were up in the far north-western corner of Finland for
the annual reindeer round-up. Gather ye nomads while ye
may.

For ten solid minutes I browsed through the paper-backs
on sale without coming across a single word which rang the
faintest semantic bell. Considering that Finnish was in an
alphabet I recognized, I can't remember coming across a
more clueless, clotted, umlaut-freckled language in my life.
It belongs, I discovered without surprise, to the Finno-Ugric
family. The familiar face of Donald Duck on a comic book
was re-christened, not unhappily I thought, Aku Ankka. In
Finnish his characteristic spleen came out in phrases such as
'Mitä? Väitätteko, ettette peittäneet hieroa seinäpaperiani
jonninjoutavilla kuvilla?' The familiar Wham! Pow!
Splat! Zowie! were transformed into Räks! Töks! Läts!
Puks! and—a nice one for a blow that missed—Viuh! The
onomatopeia of Loiskis! however, escaped me and, in my
ears, Naps! is a very feeble substitute for Snap! It made the

proprietor's day when we bought a copy of *Aku Ankka*; he was still laughing when we drove off.

We had a similar effect on a woman at Muonio when we tried to discover where we could buy reindeer hides. Verbal communication was out, so I resorted to mime. It was, though I say so myself, a brilliant amalgam of *commedia dell'arte* and Method acting. Spreading my fingers on my head to symbolize antlers, I moved about in an uncannily reindeer-like way. Then I slit myself up the middle (again symbolically) and peeled off my anorak. For the finale I held up the anorak, shrugged up my shoulders and looked slowly around, questioning mutely. The woman laughed solidly throughout the performance, swaying on her heels and holding her face in her hands, only occasionally peeping through her fingers in case it became unbearably funny. Through her giggles she managed to indicate that I'd get what I wanted two kilometres down the road.

It was a sad, deserted kiosk, but an old man came out of a house at a fast clip, surprised and delighted to find tourists who hadn't yet migrated. When he found we weren't after slippers or knives, he took us to a barn where the reindeer skins were being air-cured. We chose three, all subtle grey shading into cream, with the herd owner's initials starkly angular on the rump. I could see by the tentative way he wrote down the price that we were expected to beat him down, but they were only 700 Finmarks the skin (about fourteen shillings), and I hadn't got the heart. Certainly he looked as if a couple of thousand Finmarks was a godsend. He scurried around eagerly, collecting ridiculously small pieces of brown paper and string with which he somehow managed to wrestle the hides into an enormous, strangely light parcel. Business at the local post office was completely disrupted while it was re-wrapped.

Kittila had the wide-open, impermanent air of a town in a Western—wide, dusty street with a thin fringe of clapboard houses, a few lounging figures in denims and bright work-shirts, and the flat sweep of untouched country. As soon as we stopped we were surrounded, blindingly, by the bright shirts. They were thrown into animated discussion when I pointed out, without much hope, the phrase-book sentence, 'Can you recommend a good hotel?' As I'd thought, there wasn't one. But, after a rapid plebiscite, the whole gang conducted us to a house which took boarders. Asked, again without hope, if there was a bath. This hopelessness was equally well founded, so we went out to one of the two cafés, a powerfully depressing place which served as a social centre for everyone from children to old men.

After one beer I'd had enough; the stuff was so weak it was pitiful. Two drunks having an unsteady meal at a nearby table were under the impression that nobody could see them passing a bottle of spirits to and fro under the table to spike their beers. Although the idea didn't appeal to me, I could sympathise with them. Drinking straight Finnish beer you'd drown before you got the faintest glow. Not that getting a glow is the object of the exercise in most cases. When a Finn drinks he drinks to get drunk.

Meanwhile, back at the boarding house, the landlady had made handsome amends for her lack of a bath by stoking up the sauna in the basement. It took a little time for her to get the idea across to us. At first I thought she was trying to tell me that there was a wild Finnish punch-up going on downstairs, and she almost had to drag me down to the boiler-room before the penny dropped.

This sauna was of the simple, country variety. After undressing near the softly-roaring boiler, a silky rug of wood-ash around its log-jammed mouth, I winced my way across a floor thick with splintered chips of wood to the tiny sauna room. The stiff door pulled open suddenly and sent out the hot, dark blast of a tiger's throat. By the light of a single bulb the colour of strong tea, I eventually made out a three-tiered slatted bench supporting a still life of metal scoops, a large block of yellow soap and a switch of birch twigs. Over in a smoke-darkened corner was a crackling stove with a tray of small boulders heating on top of it. A tub of hot water and a cold water tap completed the equipment.

A man who was just having a final swill-down explained the idea. You took a scoop of hot water and a scoop of cold and sat on one of the tiers. Then you threw some of the hot water over the tray of heated stones and sweltered in the steam generated, occasionally dabbling a little cold water over the head to ward off heat exhaustion. After that you washed down in warm water and repeated the process as often as required, finishing off with a cold douche and a light flogging with the birch twigs to produce a healthy glow.

Now this all sounded straightforward, but I was sweating, partly with apprehension, before I started. After getting the prescribed two scoops of water I climbed to the second tier and sat down. I stood up again smartly. I would never have believed that wood could be so hot without actually smouldering. After using most of the cold water to cool the bench down, I made a tentative lob with the hot water towards the heated boulders over in the corner. I'd intended to release no more than an experimental cupful, but the whole lot belly-flopped on to the stones with a terrible hissing roar. Nothing happened as far as I could see. A second later a swirling billow of eye-stinging heat descended on me from the roof like a hammer. This was steam—the genuine, invisible article, not misty vapour.

Breathing became a privilege instead of a right. and the sweat began to roll down fast and free, dropping from my nose, chin, finger-tips with metronomic regularity. Slowly the heat became more bearable, but as soon as I moved, even slightly, it seemed to increase. I felt I had to try the top tier if only because it was there, but I had to inch my way up, the temperature rising steeply with every inch. After two minutes of sitting doubled over and breathing through cupped hands, I thought it better to get to the lower slopes for my health's sake. The heat seemed to have softened Paul's brain, because before I could move he had flung *another* scoop of water on the stones. This second blast started the marrow bubbling in my bones. As I came down the tiers my knees were trying to bend both ways.

Weakly I washed myself and finished with a lukewarm rinse. I'd read that the classic finale to a sauna was a plunge in a cold lake or even a roll in the snow, and I was cravenly grateful that we were miles from a lake, and a month or more from snow. I did give myself one feeble twitch with the birch twigs, but I just wanted reassuring that my nervous system hadn't packed in under the strain.

September 2

A cold wind drove dust spirals before us down the road to the boom town of Rovaniemi. The town was razed by the retreating Germans in 1944, and has since been rebuilt with unrelenting modernity. The biggest copper mine in Western Europe is nearby, and Rovaniemi must be one of its own best customers. Most of the big buildings are clad in huge sheets of copper, and the newest hotel, the 'Polar', looks as if it is carved out of the stuff. The hotel's furniture and fittings were beautifully matched examples of exquisitely expensive taste; only the bill outraged one's sense of proportion.

Don't get the impression we stayed there—we couldn't really afford to walk into the foyer—but we got into conversation with two paying customers, Elmer Cox and his wife, Corinne. They were attached to the American Embassy in Helsinki, and I think it says a lot for American foreign aid that, within ten minutes, we were up in their suite drinking their excellent Scotch. And this was despite the fact that we looked as if we'd just come off the first shift down the copper mines.

They were both intrigued, even slightly piqued, by the blatant prosperity of Rovaniemi. Elmer admitted, with a certain amount of reluctant admiration, that he was being scalped sixty dollars a day for the suite, and his wife asked me, rhetorically, what a town this size wanted with five banks. Their most indignant anecdote concerned an extra pot of coffee which had cost as much as a whole breakfast. The conversation was a lot more varied than this, but these financial trivia invariably crop up when you bump into an American on the Continent. I think it's an understandable reaction to the hallowed European attitude that any American must be incredibly rich.

We stayed talking with the Coxes much longer than we

intended and, after swapping addresses, we decided that we couldn't get any farther than Kemi that night. An eager student of English showed us the best restaurant in town, where we had every intention of stoking the glow started by the Coxes. But it's hard going to feel very gay on meat balls and potatoes washed down with denatured beer. The atmosphere wasn't helped by the customers, a farmers' convention of red-faced men with heavy suits and bovine women who all drank thick, sweet port. They all tipped the doorman as he helped them into their coats, and I pondered how he could earn my *pourboire* with an anorak to deal with. He coped beautifully by dropping it over my head like a lifebelt.

September 3

A great, liver-coloured cloud played cat-and-mouse with us down to Oulu, drenching us and then dropping behind, only to catch us again ten minutes later with our hood down. Stopping and putting it up never seemed *quite* worth it, and after a couple of drenchings it definitely wasn't. My anorak was soaking, and I couldn't get my legs out of the way of the cataract that poured *under* the windscreen. But at least I could look forward to a change of scenery from Oulu to Vaasa since the map showed the road hugging the coastline. Well, the map was against us, too. Occasionally we almost got near enough to smell the Gulf of Bothnia, but the trees stood shoulder to shoulder like hairy guardsmen and blotted out everything except the odd glitter of distant waves.

The day finished on an up-beat. I didn't know at the time that the family of Björn Lundquist (the Finn on the boat who'd invited us to visit him) were living at their summer cottage, and it was pure luck, when I phoned their deserted town flat, that Björn happened to have called in to pick something up. He came racing round in his father's Mercedes, accompanied by his attractive, monoglot girlfriend. She must have loved us when Björn dropped her off so that he could take us to see his family.

The cottage, spacious, white and veranda'd, was the sort

of offspring you'd expect if a Virginian mansion had pupped. It was obvious that Mr Lundquist senior was a man of substance. He was also a powerful charmer, with a vigorous personality which kept his family revolving around him ceaselessly. His wife, teenage daughter and Björn naturally fell into line when he began to chat to us vivaciously in good, idiomatic English, his long-toothed smile almost bisecting his lean, long-chinned face.

The Lundquists, as the name suggests, are of Swedish stock. They are part of a powerful minority, the tenth of the population who speak Swedish as their first language, and run their own newspapers, their own political party and a lot of the country's business. Mainly settled along the coast facing Sweden, they retain—like the Scots in England —strong loyalties towards their country of origin, but have no intention of returning. The native Finnish attitude towards them is understandably ambivalent. This talented but unabsorbable minority must often appear like a large, blond cuckoo in the nest.

Mr Lundquist was certainly a case of non-local boy makes good. Twelve years ago he had changed over from teaching (a more highly-regarded profession there, incidentally) to the timber business, and had built up a flourishing export trade, adding a plastics factory to his interests on the way. He is now one of the town's biggest businessmen, a chartered accountant and chairman of the governors at the school where he once taught. He has travelled widely, is fluent in four languages, and can get by in three more, and he takes a dip in the sea every morning before going to work. A remarkable combination of happily-adjusted provincial and man-about-the-world, with an adoring wife and family, success, health, power, untroubled by mock-modesty or self-questioning. It was only when his wife began to flag that the tireless Mr Lundquist noticed how late it was. He detailed Björn to show us the guest house down the garden, while his wife found blankets. When he bade us good night and went out of the room, it was as if a bright light had been switched off.

September 4

The house gleamed bone-white in the morning air, beautifully sited on a green swell overlooking an arm of the sea. A seaplane droned over by the far shore looking for poachers of wild duck. Björn had been up early to drive his father into town, and wash down the car, and was just finishing ours! Mr Lundquist had left orders of the day— a guided tour of the town, lunch, interview with the *Vasabladet*, the local Swedish newspaper, in the afternoon, back for early dinner, sauna. Björn dutifully showed us the oldest house, a church with a secret passage now blocked up, the harbour, the museum (closed for the day) and so on, but he was subdued, as if he'd done all this too many times before.

We broke the routine by dragging him into a bookshop. I wanted some postcards in the worst taste available. This long-standing habit began in Paris when I found that the bouquinistes often had trays of old postcards of treacly sentimentality, rousing jingoism and period pornography, which were a lot more interesting than glossy shots of the Arc de Triomphe. They were cheaper, too. Björn kept handing over beautiful colour photographs of Finland, but the register was always too good, and he was completely puzzled when I leapt on a batch of smudgy reproductions of Field Marshal Mannerheim signing some document with his spectacles on a slant. It was hard to explain my quirk without offence.

'These are not very good.'

'I think they're splendid.'

'Mannerheim is a hero in England?'

'I wouldn't go so far as to say that.'

'Your friends—they are interested in military history?'

'Well, not exactly. They'll find this—well, it's different, isn't it?'

Mr Lundquist turned up at the newspaper office (where he was very much *persona grata*) to act as translator. I don't know who the interviewer thought we were, but we immediately got bogged down in details of television and whether it was possible to swap films with the BBC. And then—I'm sure this was the translator getting his oar in—there were a lot of penetrating questions about timber and its position in world economy, a subject on which I am spectacularly uninformed.

In need of a little relaxation Björn, Paul and I took it in turns to race the scooter up and down the bumpy lane when we got back to the cottage. Björn's quiet gloom vanished abruptly, and the noise of our fooling around brought the whole family out. I met the youngest members, flaxen-haired girl twins aged seven, and extremely dignified and aloof. Their reserve didn't crack until I was rolling up the tent which had been put up on the lawn to dry out. Then they discovered the marvellous game of pelting me with berries from behind the bushes. I chased them and threw them up in the air a few times. This was a mistake. They thought the new game was a lot better than throwing berries, and couldn't understand why I tired of it so quickly.

I felt rather sorry for Margaretta, the older daughter. At seventeen she was the in-between of the family; too old to romp about with the twins, too young to be able to talk on Björn's adult level. She mooned about the garden taking an occasional swipe at one of the twins. I began to sense a slight constraint in the family circle. Margaretta hardly spoke to anybody. Björn spoke mostly to us, the twins were often solemn and watchful, and Mrs Lundquist's perpetual smile had an air of effort. I noticed this only when Mr Lundquist wasn't there to bolster the silences with his natural ebullience. Later Mrs Lundquist told me that Björn was thinking of emigrating to America rather than following in his father's footsteps.

Mr Lundquist and a business colleague cleared off to the sauna immediately after dinner to discuss a deal. This is quite a common practice among businessmen in Finland, but visiting businessmen would be wise to avoid any tricky negotiations inside these pressure cookers.

September 5

Today the family moved into their town flat for the winter. The flat is elegantly spacious, full of old furniture

43

and modern glass, with an uninterrupted view of a statue of Finland resurgent, I think, in the main square. It would be easy to hibernate here—Mr Lundquist's office is in the same building, and so is one of the town's best restaurants. But winter is the great open-air season—duck-shooting, elk further south, ski-ing, skating, and a visit to the summer house every Sunday, often by car across the frozen sea, an easier route than the snowbound road. We were taking coffee and Vienna bread *en famille* when Björn's girl-friend, conspicuously absent for the last couple of days, returned from exile, obviously relieved that the hairy English were leaving at last (I had recently decided that shaving was dispensable). A pretty farewell speech from Mr Lundquist and good wishes and handshakes all round, except for the twins who were sternly trying to recover their dignity after yesterday's childish outburst. Sitting up on the back of the car, Björn saw us on to the road to Tampere, and then walked back to make his peace with his girl-friend.

Two days of easy living had softened me up. A twenty-kilometre stretch of road under repair rattled my relaxed vertebrae, and the rawly inquisitive wind soon numbed me into a crusader's effigy. Tampere has two galleries of modern Finnish paintings, a museum, a cathedral of renowned frescoes, and a modest café. The café won hands down. The brief warmth barely penetrated my chain-mail and I had turned into church-cold stone again long before we came into Hämeenlinna. Stiffly stalking into a restaurant we dully watched Perry Mason on television as we ate. 625 lines certainly give a sharper picture, but the Finnish sub-titles were distracting.

The youth hostel had been cleverly concealed in a national park, and we did two furious circuits of the one-way road through black tree-lined tunnels before we found it—closed. We were about to move on when the warden appeared, his nightshirt stuffed bulkily into his trousers, and led us, with silent, crushing disapproval, to the dormitory. Unwashed and unshriven, we crept into our frigid beds at the sinful hour of 11.05.

Hämeenlinna is the birthplace of Sibelius, but the town takes the distinction lightly. There is no statue, no street named after him, no busts of the massive, elephantine-eared head in the shops, no souvenir ash-trays. The house where he was born, although there is a plaque to this effect, is not a shrine of glass-cased scores. When I pushed open the door, the place was stacked with shoe-boxes. We bought some thin slices of smoked reindeer and boarded a plane to get some coffee to go with them. This particular plane wasn't going anywhere. It has been permanently grounded in the town centre and converted into a café. Very popular with small boys who can look out of the windows and pretend they're doing some desperately low flying, or take their cherryade up to the cockpit and sit waggling the control column around at face height. We ate our reindeer (dark red and tasting like a robust cross between tongue and ham) overlooking a sports field where the local school children were flinging discuses with manic energy.

After the small towns we'd been used to, Helsinki, although barely a metropolis, was big enough to unsettle us. One-way traffic systems were ultra-sophisticated, and the policemen on point duty had an awe-inspiring repertoire of gestures. Sometimes they would cajole, almost caressing each car as it passed. Then, with epileptic suddenness, the white gloves would flail and tic-tac madly, the white baton would twirl and jab and sweep the traffic past by sheer vehemence. Their best performances are reserved for 4.30, when the short, sharp rush-hour begins.

At 5.30 the traffic stops as if somebody has turned a tap. The policemen shamble off for a rub-down, and the city settles down for a long, quiet evening. The evening had already settled by the time we'd tracked down a repair shop (the exhaust, the wings and the manifold all needed welding) and booked into a cold-water hotel. Thinking that the place might liven up later, we went to see *Ben Hur*. The sound track started in Finnish. When, to my relief, the original soundtrack broke through, it was accompanied by large sub-titles sprouting vigorously up the screen. These were so wordy that I suspected they were projecting whole pages of Lew Wallace instead of the actual dialogue. And each sub-title was repeated below in *Swedish*. If the dialogue was anything wordier than 'Would you care to swap oars?' the accompanying action looked as if it was shot through one of those grocer's windows which has the week's bargains chalked all over it.

Emerging with hot eyeballs a decade or so later, we found the town deader, if possible, than before. After we had walked around a few deserted streets, we retired to our hotel room and depleted the bottle of Norwegian whisky while reading a five-day old copy of *The Times*.

September 7

Finnish design is certainly very good. The sense of line, the feeling for the material—whether it is glass, ceramic, fabric, metal or wood—the standard of artistic discipline, are all remarkable. More remarkable still is the fact that the Finns at all levels seem to appreciate these qualities. Even in the cheaper stores the cutlery has the chaste elegance of scalpels, the lamp shades are bold and tasselless, the tumblers are innocent of gold rims, and, altogether, the amount of rubbish is amazingly small. At the other end of the scale, the small, exclusive shops in the Keskuskatu are full of exquisite stuff, and the Finnish Design Centre makes ours look like a village jumble sale.

But, after wallowing in good taste for several hours, I found myself wanting a change of pace, a little light relief. The cutlery began to look over-austere; the pots harped too constantly on the mud-browns and moss-greens of the Finnish marshes. I wanted to see something downright vulgar, if only to act as a touchstone. Perhaps this standard of perfection is, as Neville Cardus once remarked of *The Manchester Guardian*, too good for ordinary people.

September 8

The Arabia factory just outside Helsinki is the centre of ceramic production and produces everything from utility ware to *objets d'art*, from lavatory pans to rice china. It seems to be a nice balance between business and art. The booming commercial side, with reams of orders from all over the world, brings in the money; and a dozen artists, given a studio apiece, security and a free hand to make exactly what they feel like making, provide pieces which secure an international reputation.

A charming blonde interpreter showed us the mass-production side first. I liked the saucer-making machine. Splat—a fat pastille of clay is slammed on to a spinning form. Down comes the top, a strip of clay makes a writhing scribble in the air as the edge is trimmed, and there's a saucer ready for firing and glazing. Quick-fingered girls attach handles to cups with casual sleight-of-hand. Rows of pink, yellow, blue lavatories make you feel like a plumber dreaming in Technicolor. Tall racks packed solid with plates, cups, jugs and teapots inch their way into the longest firing kiln in Europe. And there is a special breakage machine where biscuit-ware is jogged and jostled in a sandy avalanche along a moving belt.

After the noise of the factory the studios were as quiet as a row of monks' cells. A nuns' cloister might be more apt, since eight of the studios are occupied by women. We moved methodically down the corridor trying to find out who was at home. Each studio, apart from the trailing or climbing plants which seemed to be part of the fittings, had a different atmosphere. One was cluttered with a whole village of house-like pottery with bottle-shaped chimneys and faces peering from unlikely niches. The whole floor space in the next one was taken up with a growing mosaic of hexagonal titles which apparently never repeated. Another was populated with huge standing birds made of beads strung on wire armatures and decked with silvery watches all reading the same time. We found Toini Muona, a small, brightly-eyed woman, building a tapering, branched, rough-fired column as big as herself. She was delighted to talk about her work, and chatted away, as vivacious as a robin, occasionally darting off and reappearing from behind a very jungly palm with a plate or a vase to make a point clearer.

She even asked me which of three platters I thought she ought to submit to a forthcoming exhibition. I believe she was quite serious, but this seemed to be taking artistic humility too far. Before we left she gave us a couple of her signed test-pieces and, with a mischievous look at our guide, told us to keep them hidden. Although these were only beaker-sized, I saw similar pieces of hers selling in Stockmann's, the biggest store, for about five pounds apiece. Lunch at Keski Korvu is something not to be missed in Helsinki. This baronial hall of a restaurant must have felled a forest to provide the timber. Floor, ceiling, walls, galleries and pillars are all of very solid unstained wood. For a fixed price you are let loose on a great table—at least ten yards long—running down the centre of the room, and can take as much as you want of whatever you fancy. Not including sidedishes, I counted forty platters of food. I recognized only two of the ten varieties of fish, but I got a better score on the array of cold meats and salads. If you wanted hot food you could plunge into steaming tureens of meat dumplings, veal goulash and potatoes. And for those with etiolated appetites there were always red caviar and razored slices of the delicious smoked reindeer. I'd had all I could take after two visits to the table, but the way the locals kept galloping up for another tottering plateful made me wonder how the place showed a profit.

When I phoned Elmer Cox to suggest a quiet drink, he immediately took over and said he'd pick up a couple of girls from the office, and we'd go right on to his place and 'hang one on'. While we were waiting for him, a very happy character came up and offered me a drink of milk. Elmer arrived with two blonde sisters at that moment, and told me I'd go blind if I accepted; it was loaded, he said, with canned heat, a domestic alcohol obtainable at most good paraffin shops and very popular with people wanting to shut the world out. They are known as 'park chemists' from their habit of finding a deserted bench to pass out on before mixing their paralysing cocktails.

I was doubly grateful for the advice when I got to Elmer's and found that he and his wife really meant it about 'hanging one on'. After a couple of monster apéritifs, Paul and I stopped patting the two old, spoiled dachshunds and started chatting uninhibitedly with the two young blondes. All evening Elmer shuttled to and from the kitchen, indefatigably forcing steaks on people. His wife complemented his act by keeping the whisky, wine and cognac flowing like a magician.

When we left about four o'clock I suppose a blood-test would have said I was drunk, but the golden sybaritic glow I felt was much rarer than drunkenness. My senses were not dulled; they were selectively distilling the essence of every sensation. I knew the dawn wind was cold, but it didn't chill me. The grey deserted streets were monochrome arrangements of subtle charm. A solitary, whistling cyclist had the haunting fluidity of a flute; the warm odour of fresh-baked bread rising up the well of the hotel ravished my nose.

September 9

I was considerably less receptive in the morning. After yesterday's close approach to Nirvana, a certain withdrawal, almost suspension, of the senses was to be expected, and I husbanded my energies while packing, even to the extent of not speaking.

I believe the run eastwards from Lahti is quite pleasing, but I didn't really surface until I was at a hotel in Lappeenranta, quietly simmering in the modern sauna. (This one had *electrically* heated stones.) Since my stomach was still working overtime on the vast meals I put away yesterday, I ordered *haman mutta vyta*, which the waitress obligingly translated as 'Little but good'. This appetising tit-bit appeared as a breaded veal cutlet, grilled ham and sausages, garnished with cauliflower, tomatoes, lettuce, pineapple and *prunes.*

LENINGRAD BAROQUE

September 10

It took an hour and a half to get into Russia. Half an hour of this was spent at the Finnish frontier, where the customs man had read an article about us and insisted on going through a tall stack of newspapers to find it, without success. The first Russian soldier I saw looked as if he'd modelled for Giles—square Slavic face with monkeyish upper lip and snub nose, grey great-coat belted way up near the armpits and practically smothering his jackboots, automatic gun tucked casually under one arm. He grinned at the car all the time we were filling in a batch of forms on which, among other details, we had to declare that we carried no hashish.

I thought we were being let off lightly until a motor cycle combination roared up. A senior officer stepped out, saluted, took our passports, and roared back down the road again—with us following—to the *main* control. Here our passports disappeared for a long time. We filled in a few more forms, changed some travellers' cheques (the exchange rate had recently been standardized at 2.52 roubles to the pound), and opened up the back of the car while a baggily dressed civilian with a Khruschev trilby (hardly any dent, brim slightly turned up) rummaged around for the hashish we hadn't declared.

The officer at last returned with our passports, and curtly instructed us to report to Intourist at Viborg. He omitted to explain where Intourist was to be found in Viborg, but I had gratifying success with my first Russian phrase—'Gdyeh Inturist?'—straight from the phonetic column in the phrase book. It was understood immediately, but I had difficulty grasping the reply until somebody simply pointed at the railway station. This was a combination of grandiloquent architecture and hopeless services. A broad flight of steps in the hall led up to a large bust of Lenin, which looked across with fierce approval at a heroic group of statuary, a tangle of flags and figures with dedicated faces and outstretched arms. Beneath the steps was a public lavatory which was worse than any cow-shed I've seen; it was also much *too* public. The little brickwork stalls had no doors, and you were obviously expected to chat with your neighbour.

A fat militiaman indicated that the continued presence of the car outside the station entrance might easily cause a mob demonstration. Half-a-dozen onlookers watched mildly as the car was moved under his direction to another part of the desolate square. After collecting two books of tickets (one for camping, one for tours) from Intourist (no town maps, no leaflets in English), we trotted eagerly up the steps to the station restaurant for our first Russian meal. It was a tall, dark room not particularly helped by long green velvet drapes, but there was cut crystal on the tables, and the menu ran to a dozen pages with every item translated into Chinese, German, French and English (in that order) beneath the Russian.

The food was foul in any language. No matter how carefully I lowered my spoon into the soup, orange globules of grease slid over the edge of it like cunning amoeba. The chips which flanked my sturgeon were of two species—one underdone, bloated with grease and pale as a maggot, the other burnt black and corundum-hard. A stab with the fork at one of the latter sent it whining viciously past Paul's nose across the restaurant.

My first twinges of heartburn were aggravated by the fact that my pipe, both lens caps from the cameras and a pair of sun-glasses which clipped on to my own glasses had been stolen from the car. If one ruled out idiots, this could only mean that the thief was a myopic pipe-smoker owning two Japanese cameras, but when I tried to explain this to the fat militiaman who'd moved us on he shrugged as if to say, 'If you *will* go leaving your car in a spot like that . . .'

The camp, some miles this side of Leningrad, had well-appointed tents—duckboards, wooden side-walls, electric lights, beds with sheets—but they were as cold as charity. I sat up, my woollen hat over my ears and an eiderdown around my legs, drinking *akvavit* while waiting for bedtime. I mean you *can't* go to bed at ten, but I had the perfect excuse when Paul remembered that we still had to put our watches on an hour.

September 11

Dutifully reported at Hotel Europe, the Intourist H.Q. in Leningrad. A hare-lipped youth on a bike nearly split himself racing ahead of us to show us the way. He then asked if I had any English money. Since I hadn't, I handed him half a rouble, but this he handed back politely, saying that he merely wanted a souvenir. The Intourist official was schoolmarmish about our unpunctuality. Didn't we know the guided tour had left five minutes ago? Perhaps we had a *car*? Oh, that one with all the people round it! There might just possibly be a guide free.

When we'd cleared the proletariat off the wings, the guide herself, obviously used to decadent limousines with idle extravagances like windows, was scornfully amused. By the time we got back she was full of frozen admiration for our toughness. I had to sit up on the back in the full blast, but I kept smiling rigidly in case she thought I was soft. She was pretty game herself as we went round Leningrad, and kept rattling off her set-pieces about the Peter and Paul fortress, the Church of St Isaac, the equestrian statue of Peter the Great only supported on two back hooves and the tail, the 'Aurora', the ship which signalled the revolution (and gave its name to a popular cigarette), the Winter Palace. By this time I was having to lean forward to catch the mumble coming from the well of her collar. Just before we got to the Nevsky Prospekt, a militiaman stopped us and ordered me to come down. Our guide's head shot out like a tortoise's to explain, but he would allow me to remount only on condition that we went straight back to the hotel.

Here our guide showed real grit. Once out of sight, she insisted that we finish the tour as intended by driving down the 2½ miles of the Nevsky Prospekt to the Metro before making for the hotel. When I asked nervously about the

militiaman, she made a dismissing gesture and a noise like
'Pfrrt!', which indicated that no uniformed twit was going
to mess about with *her* tours. Nobody did either, and the
tour ended as a mildly triumphal procession. As she scuttled
back into the warmth of the Hotel Europe, I wished her a
better car next time.

As we were trying to sort out the restaurants on the
Nevsky Prospekt, a pleasant faced youth, speaking understandable but curious English, stated that if we stood in
need of any assistance he would consider it a privilege to
afford it. He shepherded us into a fairly rough-looking
restaurant, and discussed the charm of Leningrad for about
thirty seconds before leaning forward and saying how much
he admired my shirt. I began to reply that it was just an
old thing I'd thrown on, but he cut in with the suggestion
that we went to the toilet to exchange shirts, and there
would be a cash adjustment my way to the tune of twelve
roubles. Perhaps Leningrad was a hotbed of shirt fetishists?
Or was he kinky about vests? I gave him a hard look. No. I
felt sure he wasn't interested in my *beaux yeux bleus*. And
what the hell was there about a black woollen shirt to bring
out the beast in somebody? I certainly didn't fancy wearing
his shirt—a virulently green, checked job with a collar
which would have been a joke even in a holiday camp. But
twelve roubles was nearly five quid, about three times more
than my shirt was worth. I had to look into this. So, instead
of the double-act strip-tease, I suggested that Paul and I
should go back to the car, pick up a couple of shirts and
meet him later.

A Polynesian hearing of a wrecked trading ship couldn't
have been more excited. Not only shirts, but suits, sweaters,
socks, shoes, anything we liked to bring he would buy. But
we must be very careful not to be seen by police spies, who
were *everywhere*.

I had gathered from his conspiratorial attitude that we
might be bending the law a little, but now it began to look
more serious. He wouldn't go into details of just *how* sternly
such trade with foreigners was regarded, but his expression
put it on a par with plotting against the State.

On the way back along the Nevsky Prospekt he repeated, 'Shoes, shirts, sweaters, socks' like a sibilant litany. Unobtrusively indicating a colonnaded store across the wide street as our rendezvous, he left us quickly without looking back. Some of his nervousness had rubbed off on us, and Paul was for dropping the whole business. Although I didn't agree with him, I must admit to feeling relieved when I saw that the crowd around the car was as big as ever; removing clothes under their noses was out of the question since one of the noses might be police-paid.

There was no sign of the student when we strolled back to the colonnade, and I assumed he'd also had an agonizing reappraisal. But half-way along I was bumped slightly from behind, and he was passing me, whispering 'Follow' out of the side of his mouth. When he stopped by a window ahead, we also showed an unlikely interest in the display of saucepans, and I started to explain the difficulty. We were joined in a few seconds by a man in a rather nasty ginger suit. He wasn't introduced (probably not having the English), and I thought he must be a friend roped in to put some money into the deal. The student complimented us on our caginess, and said that it would be better to meet that evening at the Hall of the First Five-year Plan. This didn't strike me as the wildest way to spend an evening, but when he added that a dance was being held by the Federation of the Soviets' Jazz Band it sounded too good to miss.

At this point the man in the ginger suit walked off without a word. Making conversation rather than wanting the information I asked,

'Is your friend a jazz fan, too?'

'Friend?'

'The one who just left. Brown suit.'

'Yes, yes. I've never seen him before.'

'You've never . . . but he might be a *police* spy!'

'That is quite possible. But I don't think he understood English.'

Such casual aplomb after his previous jitters didn't seem possible. Perhaps it was Slavic fatalism. After tell us how to find the Hall of the Five-year Plan, the student excused him-

54

self to catch a lecture. At the end of the arcade I saw him being buttonholed by the man in the ginger suit and, from the gestures, it looked as if an argument was going on. Paul offered me five to one that we wouldn't see the student again. I didn't take him up.

It was pleasant to get back to being a tourist again. Leningrad is a handsome city, and nobody is more certain of this than a native. He is a tireless boulevardier (and the sheer length of the Vozneseensky Prospekt and the Gorokhovoya Ulitsa demand plenty of stamina), and almost certainly ranks Peter the Great a notch or two above Lenin. After all, Peter founded St Petersburg, and it was merely rechristened after Lenin who was guilty, in 1918, of the tasteless error of moving the capital back to Moscow.

A Leningrad citizen's attitude towards Moscow is similar in many ways to that of the Sevillano towards Madrid. The capital may be larger than his own city, but it doesn't compare in beauty or that indefinable feeling of history. As for the inhabitants of the capital, they're all parochial-minded success-grubbers with little culture and an epicene accent.

But the rivalry between the cities runs a lot deeper than this. Leningrad has always challenged Moscow (and that means the central leadership) as much as it dared, sometimes more. The Great Purge, which possibly claimed ten million victims, was started with the excuse of Kirov's assassination in Leningrad in 1934. One of Khruschev's main accusations against the 'anti-party group' in 1957 was the Leningrad Case—the liquidation of prominent Zhdanovites and all the leading Leningrad officials after the death of Zhdanov in 1948.

This political rift, I may say, was never mentioned to me. Someone did point out smugly that Moscow had never been called 'Hero City', the title Leningrad earned after its two-year siege in the Second World War. Leningrad, or rather St Petersburg, also took a hammering during the Revolution but I must say that I've never seen a building looking so well after a storming as the Winter Palace. It lies at the end of the Nevsky Prospekt, a broad river of traffic and people flowing between high banks of dull modern buildings occasionally accented with a tower or the pale pastel of an old baroque façade, a river of window-shoppers rolling along slowly, kerchiefed girls giggling arm-in-arm, Red Army and Air Force officers with proud, chunky wives and children in bright velvet coats, lottery-ticket sellers, queues for melons from a street stall, pale-faced students with bulging brief-cases, a lone peasant in a padded jacket trudging along warily with frightened eyes. After this thronging current the vast space before the Winter Palace is a desert, and the long trek across the crazed macadam reduces you to a pygmy traversing sun-baked mud. But the Palace is elegant and civilized, the eighteenth century at its most confident, its Wedgwood-green walls and white stucco details gleaming in the pale sun like a sumptuously iced creation by some master confectioner.

I believe that some of this splendid building is partitioned into piddling governmental offices. Fortunately, a very large number of rooms have been left with their grand proportions untouched in order to house the splendid Hermitage Museum. Now I'm very fond of museums; it's museum guides I can't stand. I much prefer going at my own erratic pace, pausing here, speeding up there, and stopping when I've bitten off as much as I can comfortably digest. And if you can only take one bite at a place as vast as the Hermitage, then it has to be a well-chosen one, avoiding rooms mustily deadened with tapestries and going straight for the rumoured batch of Picasso's works which hadn't been seen in the West since the paint dried.

Obviously a case for dispensing with a guide—but, within an hour, I was regretting my decision. Room after gilded room flowed past, absolutely stiff with faded tapestries, lumbered with florid abortions from the china factories of Europe, glittering with regalia and monstrances made by jewellers with more precious stones than taste. Some turgid acreages of discoloured varnish were the only paintings I saw until I blundered into a modern salon.

At least the subjects were modern (and so, quite often, was the handling of the paint), but the atmosphere was didactic in an almost Victorian way. It was almost a case of every-picture-tells-a-story, and the story was always the official one. Some pictures were nothing more than political cartoons in oils, and these were displayed, with a possibly unintentional shock effect, among familiar themes. A bloodied head of Lumumba stared reproachfully at a neighbouring still-life of fruit; a placid, solid nude with the hands of a steel-worker threw into relief the painfully convulsed body of a Negro being tortured with pincers by fat, white, grinning Alabamans; the paratrooper's camouflage of General Massu's uniform had been jazzed up until he looked like Pantaloon. Although there was a conspicuous absence of abstract art, a number of paintings were infinitely superior to the unbelievable exhibits the Russians sent to the Brussels Exhibition, and later to Earl's Court, most of which looked as if they were commissioned for corn-flake packets or magazine covers.

By the time I'd decided that only guides had a key to the Picassos I was past peak receptivity. I was also wearing too many sweaters for comfort, the camera straps were sawing into my shoulder, I had the expected attack of museum feet and I badly needed a cup—no, glass—of tea. Hoping to flush just one Picasso on the way, I started down a vista which obviously led towards the exit. It came to a dead end in the most gloriously gold-leafed, baroque cul-de-sac it has ever been my privilege to curse at. Wheeling sharply, I cut off down another vista, searching for a recognizable land-mark. Two rooms away I caught a glimpse of a huge malachite font I remembered passing on my way in, but when I reached it I was faced with a choice of three ways, none of them looking even faintly familiar.

I've read that a man without a compass in trackless terrain tends to travel in a circle. Where this natural curvature is suppressed, I can now add, he does the next best thing and travels in a square. I proved this by exhaustive tests. Moving off down the right-hand corridor at an easy jog-trot I came back to the same spot along the left-hand corridor in something under the half-hour. Choosing the middle way, I reappeared from the opposite direction having clipped a couple of minutes off the lap time because of the onset of panic. My regular appearances from different doorways aroused the suspicions of an attendant, who froze, almost blending into a tapestry, each time I raced by. When I paused to cool my sweating palms on the polished malachite, he stooped like a falcon from the tapestry and made it very clear that anyone trying to make off with the font would have him to contend with. (At a rough guess the thing easily topped a ton.)

Although I didn't even know the Russian for 'exit' I made it equally clear that all I wanted to do was to get out of the place. He explained, in far too many words, how to go about it, but firmly refused to come with me. Probably he thought I was luring him away while my burly confederates swiped the font. Much later, and by pure chance, I did find a way out, a tiny, revolving door which flung me, close to delirium, on to a windy quayside of the Neva.

I didn't come round properly until I'd downed three or four glasses of hot tea. Paul was sitting opposite me with a jovial, slightly drunk businessman, who was apparently insisting on buying a tankful of petrol for the privilege of riding in the car as far as the Finland Station. Always willing to oblige a fellow enthusiast for a tankful of petrol, Paul bore the man away, while I took a quiet stroll to the Church of the Blood, built on the spot where one of the Tzars had his spilled.

Hanging over a quiet, green canal, this glorious bit of domed nonsense explodes in puffs of vivid tiles like frozen fireworks. After half an hour's soothing contemplation, I returned to a white, shaken story from Paul. Slightly bemused by the volume of chatter from the businessman, he'd shot through a confusion of traffic lights when the relevant one was at red and amber, which was not a good thing to do. A militiaman had shrilled him to a halt with the intention of fining him on the spot. The businessman had started to argue truculently. A crowd had collected. The militiaman had become excited, and only the calm authority of a passing Intourist official (who leaped off a bus to weigh in) had got affairs sorted out without roubles changing

58

hands. Seeing the symptoms of delayed shock, I took Paul into the Hotel Europe and forced some tea between his teeth.

Here we recognized a pleasant Swiss couple from the camp, who were using the hotel as a base for light skirmishes into the city between the serious business of writing postcards to Thun. They were intrigued by the Soviets' Jazz invitation when I mentioned it, without the commercial details, and I had to say, 'Why don't you come along, too?' although I knew from experience that people always hold you responsible for anything unpleasant that happens.

Something did, of course. As soon as they took the floor, the wife was ordered to the side-lines for the unnatural crime of wearing slacks. That ruined her evening. Mine was ruined by the band which was simply too good. And too imitative. It was a very loud 18-piecer, with the stand-up oo-wah routines that Glen Miller used to perpetrate. I had pictured something in a stream all of its own, a group perhaps in high-necked silk shirts and knee-boots adding a Slavic dimension of tragedy to a blues, or pounding out a Collective Farm Rag with a hot balalaika solo.

The dancers, too, although they were mostly young, were just as staid and old-fashioned, especially in the matter of clothes. The women's boxy shoulders and clumpy shoes had an air of the forties, and the men wore sober suits with wide lapels and even wider trousers. Apart from the odd gopak, it could easily have passed for a blacked-out dance during the early part of the war in Britain. With one significant difference—the women were enfranchized in the matter of picking partners. If they wanted to dance with a man, they simply asked him, and Paul was adopted by a big blonde as soon as he arrived.

I had noticed the student cautiously stalking us from downwind, and he waited until we had grown to a sizeable crowd before he approached, his face pleading not to be greeted like a long-lost brother. At the interval, the crowd of us moved outside to find a drink (the Hall of the Five-year Plan was strictly teetotal), and the student whispered to me that the blonde with Paul was a loose woman. I didn't tell

Paul in case he got over-excited before we'd managed the complicated business of getting our drink.

There were no bistros, pubs or anything like that, and we had to fight our way into a food store, which also sold liquor and was still doing frantic business although it was long after ten. The counter selling the drink was besieged by a mob who, to judge from the inflammability of the atmosphere, were simply back for a refill. There was no beer left, so we bought a bottle of vodka, which we took across to a dark little park. (Drinking in the streets is not allowed.) A number of people had had the same idea and bench space was at a premium, but we found an unoccupied corner and did some rapid bottle passing.

The student was urgently trying to organize a trade delegation. He wanted me to collect some clothes from the car and slip down a quiet alley where he and some friends would be waiting. Even after a few healthy slugs of vodka this sounded distinctly sinister. I had no desire to be coshed and stripped by clothes-hungry spivs. Instead, I arranged to meet him at the Metro on the Nevsky Prospekt in the morning. He made a firm offer of twenty roubles each for shirts (£8) and—here he looked carefully over his shoulder —*if* I had any pounds sterling he would give four roubles each, almost twice the official rate.

The dance had warmed up when we got back, or I had, and I tried to teach a girl to jive. The gentlemen in the band blasted away at me encouragingly, but the girl was obviously trying to decide if she ought to loosen my collar and put something between my teeth. I failed equally dismally in trying to pose the simple problem of who was taking her home. Surely this wasn't another decadent Western custom which hadn't penetrated?

I was pondering these questions on the ride back to the camp when there was the most damnable wailing shriek which raised every hair on my body. At the same time a powerful searchlight came tearing towards us high off the ground, and Paul slammed on the brakes. I tried to go over rather than through the windscreen, but I had to settle for a compromise and, inelegantly draped, watched a monstrous black train thunder over an unguarded level crossing ten yards away, blasting off another hellish scream. The Swiss, following in their Volkswagen, were just as shaken as we were, and gladly shared our heel-tap of vodka back in the camp. The wife was most upset: 'Free love and State abortions—and they don't allow slacks!'

September 12

The Swiss still hadn't got Leningrad taped, and they meekly followed us into the city through the morning drizzle. They were going to the Hermitage, but they *were* smart enough to go on a guided tour. It took a little time getting them settled, so that when I stepped carefully out of the car by the Metro, two shirts insecurely stuffed under my plastic mac, I was late for the rendezvous. I hung around in the booking hall expecting the student to bump into me in the approved style, but after twenty minutes the only excitement was that the shirts were beginning to slip dangerously low. I also had a suspicion that I hadn't stuffed the two pound notes deep enough in my hip pocket. To check this I had to do a cautious exploration under the mac with one hand, while clutching the shirts to my belly with the other. To a casual observer it must have looked as if I was suffering from lumbago and an unsupported hernia simultaneously —but I wasn't convinced that the militiaman standing by a pillar *was* a casual observer. When I thought I glimpsed a shirt-sleeve dangling below my mac I thought it was time to go. I only hoped Old Ginger hadn't swooped on the student.

When I called in at the post office to send off some exposed films I discovered how subtle official discouragement could be. I think it was a feast day because everybody else in the queue seemed to be sending bulging, ill-packed parcels of sweets. The dear old thing in front of me had to take out a handful to conform with the weight limit, and the clerk obligingly re-packed it to give it a better chance of survival. My parcel was neat enough, but when I explained the contents I was told that, while letters and books could be sent abroad safely, all films were examined in the Customs

61

by the drastic process of unrolling them in broad daylight. This was said with a broad smile, which invited me to agree what wags the Customs men were. 'But I could take exposed film out of the country?' 'Of course.' 'Then why can't I *send* it out?' 'The Customs insist on . . .' 'All right, all right. I'll buy a box of sweets and send them in that.' 'I do not think that would be allowed.'

Leningrad still looked handsome even in the rain. The Moskva Prospekt running wide and straight for ten kilometres out of the city gleamed like a bolt of grey silk. The cool, diffused light gave a pearly sheen to the puddles, and the huge cobbles between the tram-lines gleamed like caviar from some monster sturgeon. The steppe-like width of the road shrunk pedestrians to black, spry insects as they crossed in three or four stages, hobbling or skipping out of the way of trams, cars and trolley-buses.

The only traffic on the road to Novgorod consisted of lorries, but there were plenty of them. We had to overtake a monotonous procession of these drab-olive siblings which could be told apart only by the unlikely-looking registration numbers painted large on their tail-boards. A powerful reason for overtaking the lorries was that we couldn't stand their nauseating exhaust, which smells as if they're running on turnip oil. It's actually a low-octane petrol, and Paul, the mad scientist in him coming out, thought he'd try a tank of it. One had grown to accept a fair amount of exhaust leaking through the floorboards, but the putrid fumes that came seeping through now were outside the conventions of war. I was soon leaning out at a dangerous angle to catch some unpolluted air, and even Paul had his head round the windscreen. We were very glad when the last evil-smelling drop gurgled out of the tank and we coasted to a halt.

We *should* have been alarmed. Petrol stations are like oases on this road, often with half a day's drive or more between them. We had more luck than we could have hoped for. There was an unmarked oasis tucked away off the road only two hundred yards further on. It also had high octane petrol which smelt as sweet as a pine forest after the other muck.

Novgorod in the rain was bleakly unwelcoming. A few huddled citizens loitered damply around the garishly painted entrance to the Park of Rest and Culture. The camp, on the outskirts of town, was even less inviting. It was closed when we arrived, and what I could see of it through the gates as we sat waiting in the drumming rain looked pretty soggy. (This proved a laughable underestimate.) When the female commandant splashed over to open the gates to the mob—consisting of us and a Russian couple with a small child—it was obvious that we were unexpected, unwanted, end-of-the-season visitors, and she raced through the formalities before retiring to her disturbed winter sleep, indicating that our choice of tent was wide-open.

After paddling around for a time, we found one which had a duckboard which wasn't actually afloat. Hoping for a good, hot *borscht* we waded back to the buffet. This had a welcoming sign in three languages, and was closed. After a cramped rummage in the car, we found some instant coffee, a damp bag of sugar and a battered tin of spaghetti, a supper which lacked roughage, among other things. At the risk of completely rupturing our relationship with the commandant, we went to try and buy some bread from her. By this time the office was closed, too, and we sloshed round to the back of the building where a light was coming from an outhouse.

Knocking at an outhouse in the pouring rain, feeling your feet slowly settling into the bog and knowing that whoever is inside is probably asleep—this is absolutely unbeatable for making you feel like a mental defective. Then an old woman materialized out of the bushes carrying a basket of wet, leathery fungi which looked anything but edible. Shouldering open the door, she invited us in out of the rain. Peeling apart the damp pages of the phrase-book, I found the Russian word for bread, and she nodded and went off, shouting for the commandant—something I'd hoped she could avoid. She came back with a melon-sized loaf and the commandant, who looked as if she didn't believe that anybody was witless enough to travel without bread. The old woman wouldn't take any money. Who would be grasping enough to take kopecks from an idiot?

There was only one electric plate for cooking in the communal kitchen and the Russian family already had a stew bubbling away on it. While we waited our turn, we pretended to busy ourselves cutting up bread and opening the can, but the smell of stew was painfully delicious, and I was strongly tempted to take a cold, wormy spoonful of spaghetti to give my juices something to work on. Then the wife placed the steaming pot on the table and, in German, graciously invited us to share it. I don't know how many refusals Russian etiquette demands, but we couldn't summon up more than one, and we had our faces in the stew with indecent haste. When I was offered the jar of butter I committed another solecism by using it on my bread instead of in the stew as they did. But their friendliness was so open and warm that I was given no chance to be embarrassed.

The husband, who had a few words of English, explained that he was an engineer from Leningrad. He laughed continually, showing four gold front teeth. The wife, in between urging us to eat more, explained in halting German that they were returning from a holiday in the Crimea where the weather had been *wunderbar*. Here she smiled gratefully at her husband, and he flashed back, but the centre of their existence was obviously Andrey, their small son. He was shy at first, and insisted on eating his share of the stew out of our sight, being fed on the run by his father or mother. Later he started to act up a little for our benefit, and when his mother gave him some grapes he began throwing them around, watching the effect on us out of the corner of his eye.

When we got to coffee (we insisted on providing this much), he spilled most of it by waggling the table vigorously. Then he was given a gentle talking-to, but he never looked in danger of being slapped, and he knew it. When the father understood where we were going, he went out to his car and returned with a road atlas of Russia which he insisted he had no further use for. It's difficult to see how one can compete with this sort of generosity.

The Arctic Circle, Norway—marked with white stones

Peasants at Vishny Volochek. Secret police pounced just afterwards

The Winter Palace, Leningrad. Crazed macadam and baroque

A PUBLIC BRUSH WITH THE SECRET POLICE

September 13

The Russians had breakfasted and left long before I got out of bed. Shaking the water of the camp off our feet, we drove through country which increased in dullness with every kilometre. The landscape became flatter, the road straighter, a perfect combination for producing boredom. A bend in the road was an event to be looked forward to, literally, for miles. The car was kept at fifty or more all the time, but there was no impression of travelling. I started to sing, but it sounded too much like a pathetic attempt to keep up my spirits.

A bloated mosquito splattered against the windscreen in front of me. I studied the frail tendril of blood which had appeared at the same moment as the impact; it was a clotted question mark . . . a nobbly beckoning finger . . . a sea-horse . . . and then it blurred and trickled rosily in a quick flurry of rain. I took bets with myself on the raindrops zig-zagging down the glass until they dried up. Then there was a long blank period until we passed some brightly-painted, six-foot high toadstools with seats around the stem. Trying to guess their function kept me pointlessly busy. A shelter from the rain? Hardly—you'd have to stand on the seat bolt-upright against the stem, and even then you'd get your legs wet. A ju-ju erected by the local collective fungus farm? A meeting place for a coven of witches? Were children brought here to be told fairy tales?

Too difficult. I turned my attention to the small, wedge-shaped kilometre posts showing the distance to Moscow. 351 . . . let's see, that's not all that far. Not much over two hundred miles. 350 . . . at this rate five hours would see us in Moscow. Maybe less—no, have to stop to eat. Say five and a half hours at the outside. 349 . . . yes, it was definitely Moscow tonight.

But it wasn't. Just short of the 333 kilometre-post the

engine suddenly gave out an appalling clatter. We pulled up so fast that boiling water lurched against the radiator cap and went up in a fizzing plume, and then the only sound was the ticking of the cooling engine. Paul sat quite still, as white-faced as if he'd heard a death-rattle. When he finally got out and lifted the bonnet, it all looked surprisingly normal. But a check showed that one piston had seized, which probably meant a broken con-rod and God knows what frightful internal injuries.

Paul began to drag out tools, muttering madly about settling down for a three-day repair session. Camping by the roadside didn't appeal to me, so I walked to the crest of the next rise and stared, with fairly mild surmise, at Kuzenkino, a village whose natural squalor was unspoilt by anything resembling a garage. The houses looked like well-weathered fretwork, with small, paper-stuffed windows obscured by boxes of plants, but one of them did have a telephone wire running to it. When I got back, Paul had had another desperate idea, and was revving up the scooter ready to race off and despatch an S.O.S. to Intourist in Moscow. 333 kilometres is a long way to send help, even in Russia, and I countered with the suggestion that we might cadge a tow to Vishny Volochek, the next largish place *en route* where there might be a mechanic. (The nearest *official* service station was Kalinin, but this was over a hundred miles away.)

Here our differing attitudes towards the car met head-on. I don't think it's too strong to say that Paul was emotionally involved with the car. In the first overwrought minutes, my comparative cold-bloodedness must have appeared brutal to him. But this empathy with a car is like faith—you either have it or you don't—and our argument was as bitterly unyielding as a debate between a Jesuit and an agnostic, if a lot less polite. It was cut short by a lorry which stopped and offered us a tow to Vishny Volochek.

We were untied at the bus station with the assurance that the breakdown lorry from Kalinin would be phoned for immediately. Black knots of peasants—flat-capped, jack-booted men, kerchiefed women with bundles—waited cheerfully although there wasn't a bus in sight. I had just taken a couple of photographs of them when a bony-faced man in a dark-blue cap and dark-blue mackintosh came up to point out, with passion, that photography of peasants was forbidden. A crowd collected while I looked up the Russian for 'Why?' and said it. His rapid reply meant nothing to me, but it incensed an onlooker who began to argue fiercely for my rights as a tourist. My champion was winning, to judge by the grunts of the crowd as he demolished objection after objection, until blue-mac took him aside and showed a card from his wallet. This quietened my man down considerably.

Paul and I had taken advantage of the diversion to slip off to the station café for a pint of *braga*—a dark draught beer with a sweet thick taste. A new barrel was being broached by the barman. Since *braga* continues to ferment in the barrel, this is always a dramatic operation, and all the customers gathered round. At the first tap of the mallet a gusher shot six feet in the air, spattering everyone with beige froth. Roars of applause.

Bony-faced was waiting for us outside, accompanied by a fat-faced man dressed exactly the same. They started to question us, in Russian, of course, passing the ball between them rapidly. One question seemed to be: "How much Russian do you speak?' I trotted out 'Please, thank you, one, two, three, four'—and indicated that was my lot. Fat-face added, with grim emphasis, 'Dazvidanya!' I think I had said this on leaving the café, but I hadn't noticed him around when I said it. It seemed better to make a clean breast of also knowing the Russian for 'See you around' and he nodded his head ponderously as he made a note in his book, and went away for a conference with his colleague.

The crowd took us up again, and a couple of jokers got some easy laughs with a few heavy cracks about our beards and how they must frighten the pretty girls. To show they meant no offence they dragged us off for another *braga*, and the whole crowd followed and jammed inside, elbow to elbow, to talk to us or, at least, to make noises in our direction. One man produced a pencil and said proudly,

'Painseel!' I clapped him on the back in congratulation but I must have overdone it. Each time his satisfied glow wore off—and this took less than a minute on average—he reappeared with the same act, and I developed a Pavlovian twitch in my congratulating hand as soon as he thrust the pencil under my nose.

But this wasn't the only thing being thrust under our noses. Everybody was rummaging in pockets and thrusting gifts forward—a bottle of vodka from one man (before handing it back I took a swig which lit up the inside of my skull), sausage and bread from another. A stiff, smoked fish was smartly handed over like a baton, and a small wizened fellow with clown's eyes pressed a garlic clove on me as a little something to remember him by.

The noisy air was heavy with matiness and a brutal load of smells when someone spied the blue-macs approaching along with two militiamen. Suddenly we were lepers. Most of the crowd melted through the door; the rest got as far away from us as possible. Officialdom must do a lot more than merely frown on association with foreigners to make such generous-hearted people act like this. I didn't blame them in the slightest, but we could show them that the bogeymen weren't frightening us, at least not much.

We finished our *braga* with a frothy flourish before going out to meet the delegation. The militiamen looked even nastier than their plain-clothes companions, probably because they didn't have to be secret about it. The younger one, who looked about twenty, was working hard to develop the hard eyes and rat-trap mouth of his superior. We tried to explain that our stay in their unlovely town was enforced, and that as soon as the breakdown lorry appeared we should be as delighted to leave as they would be to see us go. After we showed them the jammed piston they had another huddled conference, which ended in us being escorted to a small room in the station. (Some of our erstwhile drinking companions watched expressionlessly through the steamy café windows as we were led off.) The militiamen then left us with the blue-macs for an uninterrupted *tête-à-tête*.

For the first half-hour the conversation dragged a little.

They simply sat, slowly leafing through my phrase-book and dictionary, looking for inflammatory stuff. How anything as simple as the Cyrillic alphabet could suffer such a change in translation clearly worried them. Eventually Bony-face pointed at the wind-on handle on my camera and pointed to a word in the dictionary. It said cinematography, but I got the point. No, it wasn't a ciné-camera. Then he pointed at another word—light. This wasn't so easy until he made the action of exposing a film. Nothing doing, no, niet. I put the last one in for the benefit of Fat-face, who was still convinced I spoke fluent Russian. He stiffened like a pointer suspiciously, and waited quiveringly for me to carry on and condemn myself.

Bony-face persisted. He got up excitedly, pointed at the peasants through the window, then at my camera, and, with a great slashing gesture, severed one from the other categorically as he repeated, 'Niet! Niet! Niet!' Then he made a move for my camera. I stood up quickly and said I would like to speak with his senior officer, the British Consul, Intourist in Moscow or any combination of these, and that until there was some consensus of higher opinion I was certainly not going to submit my film to a blue-coated fart like him. To my surprise he sat down and sulked, as if I wasn't playing the game properly. Ten minutes later the militiamen appeared in a motor-cycle combination leading a large lorry they had commandeered.

Our playmates went out for yet another conference with another blue-mac who jumped out of the lorry. He wore a lighter cap, probably signifying a higher grade of secretiveness. The conference became heated when the militiamen joined in to thrash out some point of protocol. It may have been about the order of the procession which was led, in the end, by the militiamen. Two blue-macs travelled in the cab of the lorry, and the third watched from the back to see that we didn't slyly cut the cable that jerked the car along behind. Turning off the main road, we bumped and swayed along a cobbled road with quarry-sized pot-holes into a busier part of the town, collecting an increasing crowd of people who trotted along beside the car. I hadn't a clue whether we were going to a garage or a cell. When we stopped outside the militia headquarters the cell became an odds-on favourite.

Our escorts hurried off inside, and we sat tight waiting for our summons, while the crowd swarmed about us. A beefy type in jackboots came out with an amplified hand-megaphone and started blasting a hole in the crowd, telling them to clear off. But their curiosity was stronger than their fear of burst ear-drums; they simply parted before the frontal assault of the speaker, and flowed back again behind it. I hoped they wouldn't tire of us too quickly. Their presence was clearly embarrassing the police and possibly inhibiting their natural nastiness—at least outside.

The expected summons never came. The boys emerged looking grim. Either all the cells were full or some superior had given them a collective rocket for making a fuss over two innocuous tourists and an old car. The procession bumped on to a garage on the outskirts of the town. A towing bar was produced, but the bolt was too big, and someone was sent off to turn another one. Everybody now appeared anxious to see the back of us. Although I didn't believe it, I gathered we were going to be towed all the way to Kalinin, getting on for a hundred miles, and all without charge. The lorry driver didn't seem at all put out at being commandeered for this job. He was on the Leningrad-Moscow run, and by the time the bolt appeared he must have been at least three hours adrift, but he boasted away cheerily to our escort about the speed and power of his lorry. It was a Skoda imported from Czechoslovakia, and he was willing to fight anyone who said it wasn't the fastest for its weight on the run.

A very drunken peasant lurched towards us, and was angrily about-turned by a militiaman. Five minutes later the peasant reappeared, having fallen somewhere, his face streaming with blood. The militiaman frog-marched him to the side-car and rammed him in viciously. Then he slapped a tarpaulin over the bleeding face and roared off to H.Q. But not before the senior blue-mac had cadged a lift on the pillion. The remainder of the group—two blue-macs and

70

one militiaman—obviously wished they'd thought of it first. I don't know whether it was knocking-off time or whether they were getting worried at leaving the irresponsible Vishny Volochekians unpoliced for so long, but they were all becoming very edgy. Shortly afterwards, the militiaman moved off muttering something about going home before his *borscht* burned, and then there were two.

When we finally attached the towing bar, it was dusk and the air was sharpening. Paul and I climbed into the car, but the driver insisted on some company, so I took the mate's seat in the cab. As we pulled out on to the road, I leaned from my perch to see how Paul was managing from his end. Bony-face and Fat-face stood watching us in their long blue macs like cheated vultures. I had only known them a few hours, but in that short time I had come to dislike them very much. And they waved at us, they actually waved.

The lorry driver set off to show that his lovely Skoda was, despite its bulk, a greyhound, and soon we were nudging seventy on the straight. I had to stop him a couple of times in the first ten miles to assure myself that the car and Paul were still with us. Weighing in at a mere ton, the Alvis exerted about as much drag as a celluloid duck trailing behind a galloping rhinoceros. Paul had never travelled so fast in the car before, and he seemed to be enjoying the experience. The lorry driver certainly was. It was obvious that he rarely got the chance of having company in tow, and he didn't hesitate to let the slower Russian lorries he overtook know he had it. He'd start blasting his klaxon and flashing his incredible gamut of lights when he spotted a lorry a mile off, working away with feet and hands like a mad organist. If he thought he was impressing me he was right, but I couldn't help wishing he'd spare more hands for the wheel when he cut dashingly in front of some lumbering lorry to show that he was not only passing at speed but with a car tacked on behind as well. Then he would shrug at me to indicate how far out of his league such pitiful opposition was.

His shrugs were highly articulate, but actual conversation was limited. From time to time he'd given the engine-housing

71

between us a great slap and bellow 'Harosh!' This can mean anything from 'fabulous' to 'pretty fair', all according to how you say it. There was never any doubt about his meaning and I would pat the housing and shout back, 'Harosh! Dead harosh, mate!' It was his postscript I didn't like. Taking both hands off the wheel he would slowly turn to me and stick up both thumbs vehemently as a sort of triple underlining of 'harosh'. I have a childish fear of unattended steering-wheels, and my thumbs-up reply always came back at the speed of light. I even tried initiating the 'harosh' routine myself in the hope that he'd forget the hands-off-the-wheel, but he never did.

When we stopped at a pull-up for upper bracket lorry-drivers, we found that the back wheels of the lorry had been machine-gunning the car, driving stones into the radiator grille like a mosaic and putting one sidelight out of action. I felt I had to ask our driver to have a drink, but I was relieved when he chose *kvass*, a drink that neither cheers nor inebriates.

Weirdly isolated discs of mist rushed out of the dark at us on the run into Kalinin. Hovering at chest-height, they looked as solid as soup-plates in the headlights, but the driver knew all about them and barrelled through, shouting out the make of any vehicle which passed. 'Moskvich . . . Zil . . . Volga.' I thought the last one was a car I hadn't seen pass (there *is* a make of this name), but he was actually pointing out the river itself. And right on it, Kalinin. I can only say that the Committee for the Preservation of Romantic Associations of the Volga ought to have Kalinin moved right off it. Kalinin only drags the Volga down.

The service station was locked for the night when we found it, and the old biddy acting as caretaker wasn't going to take the responsibility of letting us in. While our driver reasoned with her, I watched the big jets whining past low overhead, picked out in winking lights, to the nearby airport. They came along every five minutes like a good bus service, and I counted six before our driver gave up the struggle. I felt it was about time we got off his uncomplaining back, but when I told him to unhitch and get weaving for Moscow

72

he brushed the idea aside and towed us off to the Intourist hotel. It was full, of course. At least that's what the manageress said, and our tireless driver was off on an even longer argument. He was joined by a policeman who'd seen us arrive and could vouch for our immobility. They made a good team and took it in turns to attack the manageress.

An Australian group was sitting about silently, furious with everything. Their car had broken down, and first one and then another came over to tell us what stupid sods they were travelling with. We were also asked how we'd managed to get hold of a translator in this bloody town to argue with that stubborn cow of a manageress, and if we could put in a word . . .? We didn't have to. When the manageress cracked under the pronged attack of the driver and the policeman, she cracked wide open, and the Australians were in with us on the first wave.

Even then, with two more hours' driving to Moscow and at least five hours behind schedule, the driver fussed about to make sure we were settled. And I'm certain he meant it when he offered to tow us on to Moscow if we liked! That man had a heart as big as his beloved lorry. Before he finally went on his way, he scribbled out his address in Leningrad, but we both knew it would never be used. As he moved off I gave him the thumbs-up sign and shouted a last 'Harosh!' And this time I didn't mean the lorry.

September 14
Neither the hotel nor Kalinin improved on acquaintance.
When I picked up the phone I was put on to the Intourist interpreter who was now on duty. 'Could some breakfast be sent up?' No, she didn't think there was any room service at this time. 'We had to go to the restaurant then?' No, it didn't open until eleven. 'Well, where *can* we get breakfast?' If we *had* to have breakfast (she made it sound like a wilful extravagance), there was a café in the town. Directions would be supplied if we came to her office.

I was glad of an excuse to get out of the room. Although it was really a small suite with a bathroom and a sitting-room, the cluttered, claustrophobic décor hardly left enough space to turn around in. If you were foolish enough to fling open a door it bounced right back off some massive piece of furniture, and huge pictures of woodland scenes jutted from the walls, looming above your head like threatening draw-bridges.

The Intourist office was right next door to us, and the girl interpreter turned out to be much more willing to help than I'd expected. She agreed to have the car picked up and then go along to interpret at the service station after we had had breakfast at the café.

Her directions for finding the café were clear, but she forgot to explain the system of ordering. It was a serve-yourself place with the innovation of having the cashier at the beginning. Before you even got within smelling range of the food you had to have a clear idea of what you wanted, express it concisely and pay for several coloured tickets. Only then were you let through. Probably a very good system in its way, but a complete wash-out from my point of view. Although I had a very clear idea of what I wanted, I couldn't express it at all, let alone concisely. I tried to explain to the cashier that if I could make my choice *first* I would come back and pay in full, but both she and the system were inflexible. She waved me aside impatiently, the embodiment of intolerance for the odd man out, and turned her attention to the queue of people behind me.

I'd decided to buy one ticket of each colour and take my chances when the manager appeared and led us to a corner table, where he immediately had us cordoned off with screens. But not before I'd noticed that the standard breakfast was cabbage soup, a wedge of black bread, and black coffee. Our breakfast, brought by a counter-hand press-ganged into service as a waitress, was not standard. It was the foreigner's special—eggs boiled for fifteen seconds, cold ham, chicken and fried potatoes—but which nationality they were catering for I couldn't guess. The screens were presumably to prevent the peasants from becoming discontented with their meat-less lot. An unnecessary precaution. I could have calmed any insurrection by showing the stunning bill.

Paul went off with a spare con-rod to explain about the

complications attendant on a seized piston. I went off to capture the soul of Kalinin in stirring photographs. I wished I'd gone to the garage. The liveliest incident I saw was some women washing their rather large smalls in the Volga, and I was about to photograph them when one of the Australians came up and said he wouldn't do that, matey. He explained that the police were supposed to be touchy about this sort of thing. He also pointed out that my photograph couldn't help taking in part of a bridge, and that I'd be nabbed for photographing objects of military significance by the joker who was watching me from across the street.

Sure enough, when I turned round—slowly of course— there *was* a man pretending to read a newspaper in the drizzle. A man wearing a blue mac. I felt I owed the Australian something, but the best I could offer him was a drink of *fruktovaya voda* from a nearby machine. This is a sort of do-it-yourself pop. You rinse the cup over a fountain, put in three kopecks, then get a squirt of red syrup from one nozzle, followed by a squirt of soda from another. Guaranteed not to be stimulating or habit-forming, but what do you expect for three kopecks?

The grey nullity of Kalinin eventually drove me back to the hotel. Suspecting that Kalinin might be hiding its charms, Paul and I sought out the Intourist girl, and we had a conversation that had the clean lines of an exercise in classic logic.

'Do you have a map of Kalinin?'

'I have no map. Why do you want a map?'

'I'd like to see the sights of the city.'

'There is nothing to see in Kalinin. You do not need a map.'

I felt numb at the prospect of days in the hotel, dragging from room to *restoran* and back again. Brightly the girl suggested playing gramophone records. Paul, looking as if he'd like to return to the garage, joined me in a feeble huzza. In the grey fag-end of the afternoon we sprawled in over-stuffed Victorian armchairs, hopeless and carless in a sight-less city. I chain-smoked through the music, lighting up one *papirosa* from the smouldering cardboard tube of another, sinking deeper into the chair as the paralysis of depression crept higher. By the time the girl had descended to playing a scratchy side of the Don Cossack Choir singing 'Monotonously rings the little bell' I was wallowing in Russian despondency like a native. At last I could appreciate Chekov's line, 'We must go to Moscow,' as a heart-cry of almost unbearable poignancy.

When the phone jangled, it was like an intrusion into private grief. But the call was from the service station. The car was repaired and ready to go. There was a full second's pause until the fuse caught, and I came rushing out of my deep well of gloom like a rocket. 'Free, I'm free I tell you. We *must* go to Moscow—but tonight, Paul, tonight. Goodbye, little mother.'

The girl took it all calmly. I think she must have seen a lot of these mercurial outbursts. She came down to see us off and, in a touching little speech, wished us a good journey with happy memories of Kalinin. She added the hope that we would visit her city again, so sincerely that I hadn't the heart to ask what for. The Kalinin gasworks gave us a stinking farewell that seemed more fitting as we pelted out of town like kids out of school.

Out in the country we were steadily eating up the straight road when an old peasant woman shambled into our path like a deaf zombie. There was no chance of braking in time, and our swerve—luckily there was nothing coming the other way—nearly took us off the road at the other side. When we stopped and looked back she had returned to the verge, and was making no attempt to cross although the road was clear. I had the chilling feeling that she wanted to be killed.

The bright lights of Moscow were still many miles away when we hit the hollow-eyed shells of half-finished blocks of flats, the ghost town of a new suburb that only existed on a map as yet, the savaged landscape of a sprawling building site which at night looked more like a bombed city. The dumps of bricks could have been rubble, the foundations gaped like black craters, the incomplete concrete piles looked as if they had been sheared by blast, a rusty fringe of reinforcing wires sticking out of each one.

The thumbnail maps provided by Intourist showing the hotels and camps in the main cities are helpful in getting you to the right latitude and longitude, but from there you're on your own. We might have spent half the night trying to track down the camp in the unpleasant-sounding district of Ostankino if an obliging taxi-driver hadn't driven a couple of miles out of his way to show us. A taxi-driver who hadn't got a fare, who was in a rush to get home—and who refused to take any money. Then I knew I was really abroad.

MOSCOW, TU N'AS PAS CHANGÉ, WORSE LUCK

September 15-19

Despite the hardness of the ground, I woke up smiling. Lying in the yellow half-light of the tent I luxuriously toyed with the thought that Kalinin was a hundred miles behind and Moscow, a Garbo-eyed mistress in furs, awaited my pleasure. It was the last time I smiled for days.

The first impression was exhilarating. Your eyes don't quite believe the rainbow assault of the Cathedral of the Blessed St Basil, a glittering folly which seems to be by Fabergé out of Hieronymus Bosch. It would be completely in keeping if, whirring with giant clockwork, the jewelled domes levered open to disclose unbelievable birds and beasts, and the whole fantastic edifice began to twirl to a thunderous bronze carillon. Surrounded by the cobbled sea of Red Square, and with the long, sullen, earthen-red wall of the Kremlin as background, this gayest of all churches could hardly have a more incongruous setting. But it's hard to suggest who could have designed a congruous one. The sixteenth-century frivolity of St Basil's certainly doesn't chime with the austerity of the squat granite block of the mausoleum outside the Kremlin walls. This simple tomb, like a galantine made by a cubist, has a perpetual queue of pilgrims trailing to it across Red Square. St Basil's is closed.

It is a short step from here to the hub of Intourist at 1 Gorky Street, but it is like walking out of a sunlit clearing into a shadowy jungle of officialdom. It was days before we managed to machete our way through the wrist-thick lianas of red tape, days which are now welded into an amorphous mass of frustration. Hence the inclusive date-line.

Our needs were simple—a few books of tickets (already ordered and paid for) to complete our journey through Russia—but there were plenty of tragic cases ahead of us with much more complex problems. Eventually a tough, capable-looking blonde appeared with our dossier, and sat down in a cosy *troika* with us. 'First let me tell you the bad news,' she smiled. 'There is no boat from Sochi to Istanbul.' Actually this wasn't news at all. An hour before I left London the agent had phoned and told me that there now didn't appear to be a boat, although the booking had been accepted weeks before.

I was hoping to be able to use this blunder as a lever for getting permission to cross the Turkish frontier, our original plan. So I registered a nice balance of surprise and indignation. 'But there is a boat,' she comforted, 'to Odessa—and we have booked you on that.' 'Odessa?' suspiciously. 'Yes you should be able to get a boat from there to Istanbul about ten days later.'

My indignation was not feigned this time. 'Ten days in Odessa?' 'It is a lovely city. You will like it.' 'Not after ten days I wouldn't—and what if there *isn't* a boat to Istanbul?' 'Then you go home through the Ukraine.' That settled it. Odessa might be the loveliest thing this side of Welwyn Garden City, but I was not going to swap Istanbul for the Ukraine.

'What about crossing the Turkish border?' 'There are no roads.' 'No *roads*?' 'Not for tourists.' 'Look, we'll settle for a two-lane goat track if we can get across the border.' 'The border is closed.' 'Trains?' 'The border is closed.' 'Oh—well, isn't there a boat which could drop us on the Black Sea coast of Turkey?' 'No boats do this.' 'Could we fly over the border?' 'But there is your car.' 'Planes have been known to take cars.' 'Don't be silly!' Back to square one. 'Where can we get permission to cross the Turkish border?' 'The Ministry of External Affairs.' 'Right. We'll be back.'

At the Ministry nobody spoke anything but Russian (External Affairs with whom?) and it took two hours for someone to write down the address of the Visa Office for us. This was nothing to do with the Ministry, of course, and was very cunningly tucked away in a little-known street at the other side of the city. Here, after a decent interval, we were told that a visa would be granted if our camp commandant

79

wrote a letter to the Visa Office. The camp commandant had never heard such nonsense. This was definitely a job for the head office at Intourist at 1 Gorky Street. Did we know where it was?

Aged beyond our years we returned to Intourist, where the blonde began to explain that Intourist could not possibly write such a letter because there were no roads . . . I wasn't getting into that cross-talk act again, so I tried a different tack. 'The border with Iran wasn't closed, was it?' 'No-o-o.' (She was suspicious now.) 'So we can cross the border?' She smiled, back on familiar territory, 'There are no roads.' 'Of course there are roads, damn it. Look!' I stabbed at my map. 'But they are not tourist roads.' 'Oh God.' 'Tourists can drive as far as here,' she pointed at Tbilisi. 'But no further.' 'But you allow tourists in Erevan.' 'They come by plane.' 'And train?' '*Ye-e-es.*' 'Then we can go by train and take the car with us to Erevan and over the border.' 'You could —if there were any platforms.' '*Platforms?*' It turned out she meant flatcars. When I pressed her about getting us a platform ticket she said, naturally, that it was impossible. They were all booked for months ahead. But would she try? Yes.

She said yes. She actually said yes. This was the first grudging inch she had given, but it was a sweet victory. It wasn't the right moment to follow it up—she might harden in desperation—but I felt that if we kept coming back at her we'd escape Odessa yet. I brought up a minor issue—a visa for Albania. At the Embassy they could, or would, only speak Albanian or Russian. So could we have an interpreter? 'Intourist interpreters are only for tours. They cannot go to Embassies.'

We left, promising to call again, and dropped in at the Hotel National, where we were given an interpreter without a quibble. He was embarrassed by the fact that I had to sit perched on the back, and averted his eyes from any policeman. We only got one whistle, which we ignored. (The whistler caught us on the way back, but we'd dropped the interpreter by this time. I was sitting in the normal place, and a stolid determination not to understand him saved us from a fine.)

At the Albanian Embassy everything was ridiculously easy. Much too easy. Two bored, tieless men needing about four shaves between them simply took our names and promised faithfully to send visas on to Tbilisi, or perhaps Istanbul. I think they just wanted to get back to picking their teeth.

In between major assaults on Intourist we had made a couple of trips to the local journalists' union to see if they could arrange some non-Intourist visits. Although they were very keen to help, they didn't seem to have any pull on the Fleet Street level. Our border-crossing was altogether outside their scope and, although they tried, they couldn't get us a back-stage visit to the Bolshoi. They did put us on to the right man in the cinematographic operators' union to fix a visit to a film studio. When we tracked him down he said, 'Sure, whenever you like.' 'Tomorrow?' 'Tomorrow no—but any other time.' 'The day after?' 'Well, that would also be difficult.' '*Dasvidanya.*'

When Paul and I bounced out of our corner for another round with the blonde, pretending to an energy we didn't have, she looked as if she'd made a remarkable recovery. Before we could lay a glove on her she said that the only way we could get the car to the Iranian border was to let an Intourist man drive it there from Tbilisi. Our fists hit the table together as we chorused, 'No, by George!' I could see that our firmly united front shook her, and I bored in. 'Is there a platform available?' 'It is possible.' 'Good. Book it.' 'But you will have to travel on a separate train.' 'Never mind, darling. How long does it take?' 'A day or so. I don't know.' 'Are there beds on the train?' 'Of course.' 'I still think it would be a good idea to stop a day in Erevan, don't you?' 'This can be arranged in Tbilisi.' 'Our exit point from Russia will have to be changed on our visas, yes?' 'Er—yes. We can arrange this.' 'And we'll need a visa for Iran, shan't we?' 'I don't know. I really don't know.' That was it. She was beaten.

But there was still the visa to get, and we had to husband our strength. I phoned the Iranian Embassy to find out precisely what would be needed. A letter from the British Embassy. 'I see. And photographs?' Photographs would not be required, definitely. It wasn't the first time we'd been to the British Embassy; Ken and Honey Millar, a delightful couple from Dundee, had made us very welcome, and now Ken rushed along to the right man for the letter. We made it to the Iranian Embassy with very little time in hand.

Breathing noisily, we presented our credentials to a sallow little man sitting underneath a violently-coloured photograph of the Shah and his new, fertile wife. Not to be out-done he presented his compliments, along with a huge form asking for antecedents, distinguishing marks, kith and kin in Iran, etc., to be completed in triplicate, and, a very civil touch, strong coffee to refresh us as we scribbled away furiously. Then he asked for three photographs.

The fact that we had brought some with us shows the state of disbelief we had reached about authoritative statements.

By the time we'd mopped up this last pocket of resistance it was four o'clock on our fourth day in Moscow. But this sort of delay is a flea-bite. I was told of visiting businessmen who'd hung about for weeks waiting for a single signature on an agreed contract. The free world has absolutely nothing to teach Russia about bureaucratic evasion. As soon as you enter an office or a ministry with the simplest request you are jarred to a halt by a massive inertia, and slowly smothered in timelessness.

To study Slavic timelessness at its purest you must go to a restaurant. A Russian waiter's concept of time is almost medieval. You have to order everything at once, from soup to coffee, but this is merely to initiate the paperwork in the tangled hierarchy of the kitchen. It certainly doesn't mean that the courses will appear at regular, predictable intervals. Two courses may appear together—with an aren't-you-lucky smile—or with a full hour's interval between.

I remember my first meal in Moscow vividly. It was at the Metropol, which has a cathedral of a dining-room lined with rows of huge malachite pillars and dimly lit by a huge stained glass roof-light. The waiters strengthened the religious impression by gliding about with the solemnity of acolytes. Here, I thought, is a temple of good food and discreetly efficient service. It was not. A simple but expensive meal (2½ roubles) of crab salad, roast duck and coffee took two hours and twenty-five minutes to serve. And the roast duck was, without question, the toughest thing I've ever tackled with a table knife. I nearly had it on the floor twice. Five days later, I still had two parallel scars on my right index finger from the *blunt* side of the knife.

Nor is there much point in moving around among Moscow restaurants. Menus and prices are identical (they're all from the same printer), and atmosphere and cooking vary only between narrow limits. The National is perhaps the best. It is less like a railway-station hall than most, and the cook seems to have fewer off-days. It was here that we discovered how to speed up service. At four o'clock on our fourth day we went for a celebratory lunch, and we'd disposed of three courses and a bottle of Georgian wine in a mere hour! This was when I learned that resturants are also identical in that they all close from five to seven. So, if you can manage to postpone your lunch until four o'clock, the waiters really move to get you out by five. But fine timing is essential. If you walk in at ten past four you will be turned away; no waiter is going to shorten his life by trying to serve a lunch in fifty minutes.

If you want to buy your own food you must go to a *Gastronom*, one of the large shops stocking everything from vodka to tanks of live fish. The system has been carefully designed to take as much of the shopper's time as possible. Each commodity has its own section in the *Gastronom*, and you're supposed to go to, say, the cheese counter, decide what and how much cheese you want, then buy a ticket for this amount from the cashier of that section (one section, one cashier), return to present your ticket at the counter and, finally, get your cheese. You queue for each of these operations (*Gastronoms* are always milling with people) and when you move on to the next commodity you have to repeat the whole sequence.

I tried it once, but the treadmill pace had my nerve-ends curling by the time I'd collected a piddling little packet of tea. The next time, fighting down my native urge to queue,

I walked up to the cheese counter, said in ringing English, 'I'd like a piece of that about so big, please,' and handed over a five-rouble note. Not only did it work, but the queue never even looked like lynching me. The aura of foreign ignorance was too strong.

It was actually Intourist who put me on to queue-jumping. I was sobbing on a sympathetic Intourist girl's shoulder in the bureau of the National, telling her how I'd been in Moscow three whole days and all I'd seen was waiting-rooms and offices. Wiping my eyes, she said that she'd get a guide right away who would take me to the Mausoleum, and wouldn't that be nice? I thought of the five-hour queue that wound out of Red Square and through the gardens alongside the Kremlin, and said that I'd rather be tucked up in bed. But when the guide led me off we didn't go to the end of the queue but practically to the head of it—just where it enters Red Square. This was queue-jumping on a galactic scale, but it was official, and nobody made a murmur.

In fifteen minutes we had shuffled across Red Square and wheeled right to enter the door flanked by two colossal, ribboned bouquets and two rigid guards with fixed bayonets, who stood on tiny mats to ward off the chill of the granite. Surprisingly nobody asked me for my camera, but several keen-eyed soldiers kept moving about the chamber like suspicious shop-walkers. The only sound was the susurrus of feet, as the column of people shuffled up the steps at the side of the plate-glass catafalque. Lenin's head comes into view as you rise. It seems to glow in the strong, hard light; the grey bristle at the side of the head glints metallically.

As you round the guard at the corner, the face comes into full view. It is a neat, compact face—fine eyebrows, lean nose and the suggestion of a sardonic smile above the crisp jut of the beard. It is not difficult to imagine him looking almost as fiercely dedicated as his idealized portraits. The cloth of the coat is stretched smoothly over his chest with the tension of a tailor's dummy, and I had the feeling that the head and hands had merely been attached to it. Stalin, lying a yard away, looked stupid in comparison. The closed eyes lay too near to the ruthless hook of his nose. The moustache almost camouflaged a mouth which suggested little, certainly not amusement. His grey hair surprised me; I had always pictured him with a luxuriant dark Georgian poll. He seemed less content, much deader than Lenin, and his thick, insensitive hands pressed at the cloth as if he had suffered a seizure. But, at least, it looked as if there was a body inside his plain uniform.

Inside the Kremlin museum are relics of two other men who ruled Russia with absolute power, but there are no queues to see the staff with which Ivan the Terrible impaled the feet of courtiers who displeased him, or the immensely long, narrow-shouldered robe of Peter the Great. Their thrones are there, too, one ivory, one carbuncled with gems, but they have degenerated from symbols of terrifying potency to atrociously expensive chairs. Some idea of the cruel splendour of those courts does come through from the sheer proliferation of fur-trimmed crowns, rich sweeping robes and barbaric jewels; the sycophantic presents from a score of ambassadors—tapestries from Bukhara, turquoised daggers from Persia, Indian ivories and filigree silver, subtle Chinese carpets, and huge flagons and pewter plates from England's Elizabeth; the gold dinner service Catherine presented to Count Razumov, and the coach with which Razumov wisely repaid the compliment.

After this robustness, the belongings of the latter-day Romanovs seem epicene and lacking in vitality. A waterfall of lustres and spiralled glass which revolved prettily to the tinkle of a hidden music-box; scores of watches of feminine delicacy, one made entirely from boxwood—except for the spring—by some painstaking carver; a silver frigate in a crystal ball hung with drop pearls; a working model in gold of the first train to travel on the Trans-Siberian Railway; the mechanically fascinating, aesthetically terrible jewelled eggs laid, regardless of cost, by Fabergé to be fondly swapped over the imperial breakfast table every Easter. The knots of tourists moved softly in grotesque cloth slippers (provided to protect the parquet), from case to case, straining to filter out their guide's voice from the polyglottal babble of other leather-throated guides.

The buildings of the Kremlin are a museum in themselves. The forbidding sweep of the saw-edged wall is prison-like, and one expects the buildings inside to be stamped with the same bleak geometry. Instead, the place is a teeming warren of palaces, churches, offices, a spired, domed, bell-towered welter of styles and centuries which has produced such vigorous architectural mongrels as Russianized Byzantine and Muscovite Baroque. Breathing space is at a premium. The Cathedral of the Dormition, under whose gold-blazoned domes Tzars were once crowned and wed, is overshadowed by the Great Kremlin Palace, the nineteenth-century Russo-Byzantine hulk where the Supreme Soviet holds its sessions. The severely classical rotunda of the Senate House cold-shoulders a brutally modern glass-and-concrete parallelopiped of offices. The bell-tower completed by Boris Godunov, not to mention the huge broken bell apparently left where it fell, fights for attention against the crisp play of light and shade on the fifteenth-century Palace of the Facets. The overcrowding is emphasized, as you leave, by the sight of St Basil's—or, more properly, the Cathedral of the Intercession on the Moat—splendid and unchallenged on its own island.

But this is all more or less tourist country. Although Russians do visit their own museums, even when it isn't raining, the Kremlin is no more a regular haunt of Muscovites than the Tower of London is of Londoners. The place to study the people is across Red Square in the huge store of GUM. Although this is the Harrod's, Selfridge's and Gamage's of Moscow all rolled into one, it has an atmosphere more of a museum than of a multiple store. The lay-out is based on an old market. The main lanes, lined with shops and open stalls, look as if they were designed to allow two carriages to trot past abreast, and are connected with alley-ways. This pattern is repeated in the galleries above, with wrought-iron bridges spanning the lanes. From one of these I watched the throngs moving at little more than the pace of the queue outside the mausoleum. Few people seemed to buy anything; most were content to stare at the goods and saunter past.

Everything had a curiously archaic look. I was reminded of some coloured French postcards I had had at school to improve my vocabulary—La Plage, La Salle de Bain and so on, starring a golden-haired little prig called Armand. Le Magasin, with its wide-trousered assistants, potted palms, and unlikely-looking bolts of material, had a strong resemblance to GUM—except that the articles in GUM had a more strictly standardized mediocrity. There was literally nothing I felt the slightest urge to buy.

The off-the-peg suits, for example, were an expensive joke. I saw one—indifferent material, ludicrously wide lapels and 22-inch turn-ups—marked at 150 roubles. For £60, the equivalent, I would expect Savile Row to make me a masterpiece.

One thing which you *can* get at GUM is a quick meal. It's cheap and fairly nasty, but it is fast. In fact, you are hustled off the stand-up tables before you've finished by fat, cheeky sparrows who swoop from the rafters to clear up. If you have fifty kopecks to spare, you can descend to the champagne counter and finish off with a glass of almost palatable Georgian fizz. The dated atmosphere of GUM is preserved by banishing all modernisms like radios, electric samovars and television sets to an annexe known as Malenky GUM—the little GUM. Here people do buy things, and there is a perpetual scrum around the record counter. Although you can have your choice played if you don't mind hearing five others at the same time, most people grab their discs and run. New pressings of artists such as David Oistrakh and Sviatoslav Richter playing anything at all are sold out before they've cooled properly. After all, there are few things a Muscovite can buy which will set him off in any way from his neighbours. A record or two may therefore become symbols of individuality—and, besides, they're cheap.

I found an example of this unquenchable urge to be different when I met a *stilyaga*. The word stems from the Russian for style, and this boy had a very sharp coiffure, executive-type horn rims, dangerously narrow trousers and —even more dangerous—a strong American twang to his English. He had visited the United States, and was rapturous about Los Angeles. This immediately placed him in the upper classes since such trips are not for everybody. This is where *stilyagi* differ from their English equivalents. In the main they do come from the upper classes in the Soviet or from the semi-intellectuals; an intellectual who was seriously opposed to the party wouldn't make such an easy mark of himself. The *stilyagi* are against, or merely bored with, existing conditions, but they are not politically minded and are content to make their protest stylistically.

The *stilyaga* came to the point with American directness. 'You wanna do business? Clothes, shoes, the works—I buy.' He and his large, quiet companion arranged to come out to the camp at ten, and I described our easily-distinguished tent. I should have recognized it as an omen when the exhaust pipe fell off with a coppery clang as we drove across Red Square. Naturally it didn't fall off completely—that would have been too easy—but hung by one corroded bolt. Immediately, a militiaman was on our necks like a shot albatross, and before we managed to wrestle the bolt free there was a bigger crowd round us than round Lenin's tomb.

The boys appeared at the tent punctually, having slipped in through the side-gate unnoticed. (The main gate was always locked and guarded by a crone, apparently on duty twenty-four hours a day, who examined your camp pass whenever you entered or left.) The bespectacled spokesman told his large companion to flash their wad of roubles to show they meant business, and then started examining the goods. I'd put out all I was willing to part with, but he seemed convinced I was hiding the real treasures like transistor radios ('I give real big money for these'), and went rummaging in my bag like a ferret. 'What's this? How much?' punctuated his reiterations about the badness of Communism.

Paul was outside keeping watch, so I let the *stilyaga* exhaust himself, and merely put ridiculously high prices on everything I didn't want to sell. When he actually wanted to buy my spare pair of glasses just for the frames I thought he was going too far. Again my dark woollen shirts were coveted, and after a little coy hesitation about stating a price, he offered me nine roubles each. I asked for forty, and he went into a terrific act, flinging himself about and swearing I was trying to ruin him, until his companion shut him up by pointing out that the commandant's office was only ten yards away. He then whispered his absolutely final offer of forty roubles for the two. I insisted that I was selling only one shirt, and he eventually bought it for thirty-five roubles —a thirty-shilling shirt for £14—plus half-a-dozen ballpoint pens (they don't seem to be made in the Soviet) at a rouble apiece. The large man counted out the money, whipped his coat off, put on the shirt—it looked a bit tight on him—and resumed his coat, slipped the ball-points into his socks and was ready to go. He looked as if he'd done this sort of thing before.

The *stilyagi* insisted that we should all walk together towards the gate 'like friends'. So we strolled across with them, but, as we did, the crone emerged with deliberation from her hut, and also started to make for the gate. There was no speeding up on either side, but the atmosphere was suddenly as tight as a drum-skin. The fast talker began to talk very loudly in a twanging travesty of American, intended to impress the crone with his utter foreignness. She wasn't a bit impressed, and there was an evil little smile on her face as she demanded our passes. I produced ours, and she looked at it for a long half-minute under the lamp. The big fellow behind me began breathing heavily. When she said, in Russian, of course, that the pass was only for two, the little man started pulling at the gate.

The crone leaned on the gate and glittered up at him with horrible relish. She *knew* he was Russian. I could sense the naked fear forking like lightning between the *stilyagi*, and I felt that the big man was within an inch of bashing the old woman and making a run for it. I grabbed both men and steered them back to the tent with the suggestion that we ought to find the other pass. The little one was actually trembling under my hand. I told him fiercely to take it easy, but before we'd gone three yards he broke like a hare for the thin scrub which bordered the camp, closely followed by his big companion. They crashed off into waist-high weeds, panic-stricken, without caring if the crone was still watching. She was, and she shuffled into the office, where I heard her piping away excitedly.

The commandant called us in to ask a few questions about our Russian guests, as it was politely put. We played everything with a dead bat, and were soon released. Back in the tent I found that my sheath-knife had vanished. I had told the *stilyagi* it could not be bought, and they had taken me at my word. I could hardly begrudge it. They had obviously taken risks which didn't apply to us. But some of their fear still stayed with me, and when an acorn dropped on the tent I jumped in my sleeping-bag.

Other contacts with Muscovites were more pleasant—such as the hilarious lunch we had with a Red Air Force pilot and his simpering fiancée. We had to share their table in the crowded restaurant of the National one day, and it was plain they were having a blow-out, including everything from caviar to champagne and a carafe of cognac. It wasn't their first bottle by any means, and the horse-toothed girl with a coiffure like a black mop was by this time looking like a luscious temptress to the pilot. We ordered a couple of bottles of beer with lunch, but the pilot, waving the beer away imperiously, insisted on our joining them in their drink. (The only language link was German, and a fairly tenuous one at that.)

He sloshed out two large glasses of champagne, spiked them heavily with cognac, and pushed them across. We couldn't elicit what the Russian for 'Cheers' was, so we settled for 'Prosit', and took an experimental swig only to find the pilot glaring at us indignantly, his glass drained. Apparently it isn't only vodka which must be downed in one, and he insisted that we finish what was left and do the right thing by the next glass. This drained the bottle and the carafe, so he ordered more champagne and cognac and, not to be churlish, so did we. On their own, Georgian champagne and Armenian cognac are no more than fair, but together they certainly become more than the sum of their parts and make a pleasing and potent drink. Despite the fact that we were still waiting for our grilled pike, the pilot persisted in thrusting apples and chocolates across the table until we had a small wall in front of us. It seemed childish, but he was really being madly generous. I found out later that dessert apples cost about four shillings each.

We were to meet an interviewer from Radio Moscow here, but when he appeared he seemed more interested in the girl, who by now was giggling continually and no longer bothering to keep her thin ringlets out of her drink. The interviewer was Armenian, and his liquid, slightly crossed eyes raked her with a smouldering look which must have mown down the girls of Erevan like corn. The pilot was engrossed in trying to write down the address of his brother in Rostov for me. Giving it up as too difficult, he looked up in time to see his girl being ruthlessly undressed by a pair of eyes he didn't recognize and didn't like. When he stood up and reached slowly for a bottle it wasn't to pour another drink and we quickly took the Armenian away before massive retaliation began. I heard the bottle drop as we left.

The interview, through an interpreter, ran through the usual questions. Realizing that the tape would be edited, Paul and I had decided to sandwich our sharper digs in complimentary phrases. The Armenian didn't pick us up on any of them, and finished with a proud speech about Armenia, a country which he could say, without bias, was the superior of England or America in anything you'd care to mention. Remembering his ogling in the restaurant, I felt I could safely exclude women from his claim. In fact, when I came to think about it, I couldn't recall seeing a beautiful woman since entering Russia. It had been too early in Leningrad to remark on this paucity. South from there it had been peasants all the way, and they had success-fully laid the myth of the pretty peasant girl. In Moscow I'd expected better things. But the place was full of frumps. You can go for days without seeing anything worth a second glance. There may be nothing basically wrong with Soviet women but they have little idea about make-up or doing their hair, and they all seem to wear mail-order frocks.

There are reasons for this lack of femininity. In a young

State—and the Soviet Union *is* young—power-plants must come before powder puffs. Again, when men and women start standing shoulder to shoulder as comrades, there is often an over-belligerent attempt on the part of women to establish equality. And Soviet women have been only too ready to take on men's jobs—tough, physically tiring jobs which make nail-varnish a joke. They did it during the war, and, because of the man-power shortage, they are still doing it. I saw women on the railways and labouring on building sites, and there seemed to be one or two in every road-mending gang. With hair scraped under a cap, cosmeticless faces and baggy overalls, they were practically unsexed. Turning back into a woman just for an evening must hardly seem worth while.

Russian architecture is even harder to love. Moscow is not built to the scale of man; it is built to an Idea of Man. And Man, as opposed to man, is ten metres tall. In 1934, the newly-created Union of Soviet Architects decreed that buildings had to be 'national in form and socialist in content'. The resultant buildings are Frankensteinian monsters which got out of control of their creators and grew into sprawling mountains, plastered with egregious detail and lacking any sense of style. The positioning of the so-called 'tall buildings', including the tower of the university, was a post-war attempt to give point and scale to the landscape of Moscow, but they look so much alike that they are simply confusing.

Groups of statuary, and there are so many, are inflated to ridiculous proportions. Any sense of intimacy has been destroyed, but there is no grandeur in its place. The wide, long streets favour neither motorist nor pedestrian. You can drive half a mile before finding a U-turn which lets you take the direction you really want. Trying to cross from one pavement to another, where it isn't forbidden, means braving a tarmac waste which would frighten an explorer. Usually you have to cross by subways which are a *verst* or so apart. But perhaps the best example of what happens when architecture has such a dogma imposed on it is the Metro in Moscow.

Several architects were given a Metro station and a theme

apiece. In this case the themes were 'The Struggle for Freedom', 'Agriculture', 'Mother', and so on. Plenty of scope you'd think, but every design was identical in calling for hundreds of chandeliers, quarry-loads of marble, acres of mosaics, yards of ceiling paintings and lots of big bronze groups. The selection committee was congratulated on its amazing insight, and everybody was as pleased as anything. People still are. When I crassly inquired how much this little frolic had cost, I was told that cost was immaterial. This was built for the people, the most precious possession the Soviet had, and nothing was too good for them. Including passports? I asked, but this was declared irrelevant. Still, the Metro trains did run to schedule.

It came as a pleasant surprise, not to say a revelation, to find that Moscow had an English pub. Standing at the bar drinking English pale ales, hearing English voices telling English jokes I'd heard before, watching the varied throwing styles and computer-quick arithmetic of a darts game, I should have said I could be nowhere but England. And yet a good man with a cricket ball could throw it over the Kremlin wall without moving from the bar. Because this pub, just across the narrow Moskva river from the Kremlin, is in the attic of the British Embassy. It was built, almost in desperation, by the staff of the Embassy as an answer to the lack of unofficial social life in Moscow. There are subtle hints of beleaguerment. The draught beer ran out last week, and there are only cans left (for which you pay in roubles). The place is open only a couple of nights a week. The camaraderie is more intimate, the laughter heartier, the conversation slightly out of touch.

The edginess of the atmosphere, along with the unaccustomed strength of the beer, made 'Time, gentlemen, please!' sound more than usually morbid to me.

September 20

The last day in Moscow has an aureole which separates it from the other days in my memory. For one thing it was the coldest day. I could feel the chill from the ground in my hip-bones, numbed as they were by hard lying, and I wasn't sorry that tomorrow we were starting south for the vineyards of Georgia. Also it was the best day. We had all the visas and things buttoned up, and there wasn't a single hour spent in a waiting-room. Before, it had not been possible to plan anything, but now there was a chance of a ticket for the Bolshoi (it was an opera night, not ballet, but I wanted to have a look at the theatre) and the man from the cinematograph operators' union had at last laid on a visit to Mosfilm studios.

None of the films I saw being shot there looked as if they were designed for the international market. Films intended for home consumption are like *vins du pays*. Most of them don't travel very well, but they give you an insight into popular taste which you don't get from more ambitious products. The Russian film-goers' adulation of children keeps an army of child-actors fully booked up.

It's easy to sympathise with the Russian attitude. Their children *are* delightful. Although outrageously spoilt, they preserve a natural politeness and a most unchildlike generosity. I had often been completely charmed, if slightly embarrassed, by their habit of greeting me as 'Uncle', and pressing a badge or a bunch of flowers on me. But I thought things had got out of hand at Mosfilm. All three films I saw in production there had a child as the central character.

'Alyonka' was being filmed from a story by Sergei Antonev, the novelist, about the trials, tribulations and eventual success of pioneers opening up the virgin territories of Khazakhstan. The title role, however, is not played by some well-muscled shock worker, but by an eight-year-old girl who hugged a white rabbit and was too shy to speak to me when she was introduced. Boris Barnet, the director, had been in films for forty years but still possessed terrifying energy. Brushing aside the interpreter, he told me that the film—a feature-length one—would be completed from start to finish in six months. This included two months on location and six weeks in the studio.

The second film, 'Nakalonik' (Naughty Boy), was based on a Sholokhov story about the Civil War—and set near the Don, of course. The undaunted hero is an incredibly resourceful six-year-old boy who makes an epic ride to save a village from the Whites. The shock-haired star came in, carried by a studio nanny. He looked a little tired under the orange-brow make-up but, aware of a star's duty to his public, he smiled warmly as he shook my hand and announced his name, Vorva. Before he left I gave him one of the badges *I'd* been given. The interpreter translated his grave thanks and his regret that he had nothing to give me in exchange. He was uncomfortably like the infant Macaulay in his dealing with adults.

While we were waiting for Karilov (who looks in his early twenties) to finish directing a scene, word came that the Chief Engineer was free to see us. I wasn't exactly agog at this, but the size of Mr Konoplev's office suite dispensed the idea that he was concerned only with sparks and carpentry. He is, in fact, responsible only to the general director, and often sits in on creative group meetings. There are six of these groups, each one more or less autonomous, with its own creative chief, staff and workshops.

Mr Konoplev then gave a practised run-through of Mosfilm's history. Founded in 1918 from a small private studio, it is the oldest film studio in the Soviet Union, and covers 125 acres and employs 3,000 people. Up to twenty films can be under way at one time, and the annual output is something like thirty films. Of these, twenty-five will be feature-length, the rest shorts on artistic or scientific subjects. Salaries are modest; writers are paid by the scenario (2,000-8,000 roubles) and established stars by the month (2,000-4,000 roubles). (2·52 roubles = £1.)

The third film was being shot in a gale of good humour. 'Vzroslie Deti' ('Grown-up Children') is a modern domestic comedy, and everybody on the set, including our interpreter, laughed a lot. Azarov, the young director, raced over between takes to explain the plot to me in gleeful instalments, almost as if he'd just thought them up. A young married couple have to share the flat of the girl's parents (not unusual in Moscow), and there is the expected conflict between the generations. The conflict sharpens and acquires a pivot with the arrival of a child. The delighted grandparents dandle it, croon songs to it, speak in Russian baby talk: the parents think this treatment is certain to turn the child into a *stilyaga*.

I presume it all ends happily but I never found out, because Azarov eagerly began to talk about English football teams. The actor he had just been directing (People's Artist Gribov, an actor with a great following both in films and in the theatre) broke up the discussion with a single dry comment. 'That's what we really appreciate in your culture—Tottenham Hotspur.'

I did manage to get a seat for the opera at the Bolshoi. Unfortunately. Paul opted for the circus and, although I don't particularly like circuses, I'd have swapped with him at any given moment of the four hours of rubbish I sat through in an expensive orchestra stall. Actually I sat in the orchestra stall for only the last two or three acts, because I arrived late, having had to walk miles out of my way to find a subway to cross the road. Usher passed me to usher, to usherette, until I was somehow spirited into an over-crowded balcony about four floors up, where a cluster of eager heads mercifully hid the first act from me.

At the interval I saw that I could have been put even higher. Altogether there are six balconies all glittering with gold paint and scores of small chandeliers. Conditioned by English theatres, I tore off to find a bar, prepared to battle for a hasty drink. But here the Russians are as far ahead of us as they are on rocket fuels. A spacious buffet welcomes you, bottles of beer and champagne already set out on tables. You help yourself from a counter of tasty canapés (and Russians certainly take caviar for granted), sit at a table, have a waitress open whichever tipple you prefer, and pay her without stirring from your seat. All this makes for a genuine interval of calm, with plenty of time for appraising what you have just seen. In my case that wasn't a great deal, but after the interval I found my rightful seat where I was exposed to the full blast of mediocre singing and appalling acting going on all over the vast stage.

The opera, composed by Tchaikovsky on an off-day, was called, I think, 'The Sorceress'. She is a fatally attractive

St Basil's, the Alvis and me

The road to
Orel. Very
straight

The Georgian
Military
Highway.
Very muddy

peasant girl, and when I saw that the other principals were a lecherous boyar, his jealous wife and his handsome son, I knew that the story could be written in a couple of quite short sentences. However, it was dragged through four very long acts by an indifferent cast, with an understandable lack of conviction. Although any ideological subtleties were lost on me, I did get the idea that the peasants' chorus was regarded as the hero of the opera. The audience perked up every time they tramped in, shaking the real tree on stage, to bellow out one of their wordy petitions.

The fairest summing-up I could make was that the Bolshoi should stick to ballet.

VERY FLAT, THE UKRAINE

September 21

When Théophile Gautier wrote, 'Il faut visiter les pays dans leurs saisons violentes, l'Espagne en été, la Russe en hiver,' he was thinking of the comfortable nineteenth-century traveller who never stirred without several trunks full of suitable clothes. His thesis doesn't apply when you're travelling light, you've sold your only other warm shirt and you feel the first bite of a Moscow winter. It is time then to seek a gentler season further south.

I had at last found the camp's hot shower working, but it unmanned me for the sharp-edged wind, which was cutting flocks of dead leaves adrift and making the oaks rain acorns. But I still felt guilty about leaving Moscow. Out of the city's thirty-four theatres I had visited only two. (The other one was the Puppet Theatre, which I enjoyed a lot more than the Bolshoi.) I had completely ignored the Agricultural Academy, the Railway Transport Institute, the Exhibition of Economic Achievement, and out of 116 museums I had visited only one.

In a last-minute attempt to improve this score, we made a quick dart into Lenin's Museum, where Paul wished to pay homage to the demagogue's car. An official held us back in the hall along with a crowd of Muscovites, already wearing their winter coats and fur hats, until a bell announced that the museum was open. Ignoring the rest of the exhibits, we made straight for Lenin's car. This gave me a moment of pure, jingoistic pleasure. The car is a Rolls-Royce. Roped off from the other exhibits in a regal enclosure, it emanates an impregnable superiority of breeding.

A last fond look at St Basil's, then through the suburbs followed by the non-man's-land of building sites and on to the Steppes of the Central Russian Highlands. The Highlands are flat, very flat—like the Ukraine which follows, and the Rostov Plain which follows that. And this presents a lot of flatness—a thousand miles of it, in fact, before the foothills of the Caucasian mountains give your tired eyes something to focus on. There was nothing for me to do but smoke and think. I didn't do too much thinking, but my cigarette consumption rose steeply.

At Serpukhov a little unpleasantness broke the monotony. A petrol station is marked here, but we had to turn off into the side-streets and bump around for some time before we tracked it down. Facing the pumps across a stretch of waste-land was a spectacularly ruined church, the ribs of its dome standing out against the sky like an onion's skeleton. I wanted a shot of this, but I knew that a militiaman would be skulking somewhere, and any photographer-like motions would be certain to upset him. It would all have to be casual, unobtrusive, sneaky. My theory was that they couldn't nab me just for carrying a camera, and that if I waved a cigarette in the air with one hand and actually looked the wrong way nobody would notice my other hand squeezing the release.

I needed a figure in the middle distance to give the scene some scale, and I waited until an old woman hobbled across with a bag of cabbages. Smoking with great panache and looking almost over my shoulder, I pressed the button. She couldn't have heard anything—she was too far away—but for some reason she stared across at me as I was taking the photograph and saw the camera. She stopped, retraced her steps. I knew without any doubt what the old bitch was going to do. She reappeared shortly with a militiaman, pointed a knobbly finger at me and settled back to watch the fun. The militiaman came across without haste, greeted me with the now-familiar 'Tovarich' and a steely salute. He buttoned up my camera for me and led me back to the car, where he looked through every single document we possessed. When he finally indicated that we could go, the old woman seemed disappointed. I think she expected her citizen-like action to have earned me the bastinado at least. As I climbed back into the car, I favoured her with a smile that turned her cabbages rotten.

Clearly I should have to be even sneakier. Understandably, Paul was getting restive at my camera-happy state which attracted the time-wasting attentions of the police even when it didn't get us within smelling distance of a cell. I wanted a breathing space myself, and I acquiesced in the mood to the extent of not stopping the car at Yasnaya Polyana to hunt for the house of Tolstoy.

But the weakness passed and I thought, 'No, damn it. If I bring out my camera only when there is something with the Intourist seal of approval on it, I'll be the sort of house-trained, blinkered tourist they're trying to produce.' So I started sniping shots over the car door, sometimes at speed. The results were rarely successful, but they bolstered my self-respect.

At a roadside eating-house in Mtensk we were invited to join a very convivial table. The invitation came from three artists, on their way to fulfil some commission in Sevastopol, and two lorry drivers relaxing after driving from Kharkov. Their relaxation was drinking a raw-edged rum, which took an effort to get down in the orthodox single gulp. But there was melon to cool your mouth afterwards—huge wedges of black-pipped, red-fleshed, green-rinded honeydew melon which covered the table in a gaudy still-life. Our relaxation must have become quite noisy, and the table behind told us to belt up. Instead of upsetting the lorry drivers, these hard words seemed to please them. They rose, smiled beatifically, their evening about to be consummated in a lovely punch-up. The artists hauled them down before the other men, just as tough and much more sober, could hammer them into complete insensibility. We bought a bottle of vodka and offered the drivers a peace-making drink, but they were inconsolable.

The camp at Orel was just far enough away to let the cold establish itself, and we were grateful to be offered a warm hut, instead of a tent, at no extra charge.

September 22

The water runs out of the taps here as white as milk, and doesn't look drinkable until it's been allowed to settle. This domestic phenomenon started a conversation with a middle-aged couple on holiday from Tallinn in Estonia. He apologized for his English by saying that having to learn Russian had driven it out of his head.

Although almost any fact taken at random about Estonia would have been news to me, I was surprised, almost shocked to learn that it was only in 1940 that Russia took the country over, along with Latvia and Lithuania. The man's tone left me in no doubt that he considered the Russians the worst kind of liberty-takers. But he sounded pathetically unconvincing when he said, 'Estonia will always be Estonia.' His wife shushed him as if he'd gone too far.

Droning on along the arrow-straight road, I tried various ways of defeating the deadly predictability of the landscape. I started to read, allowing myself to look up only after every chapter—but each time there was no visible change, no sign that we had moved at all. The road bored Paul almost as much, because there was no real driving involved. We tried to get a game of poker dice going, but he couldn't leave the wheel long enough to play properly; an automatic pilot would have been useful on these long stretches. So I lay back, closed my eyes and sang any songs that came into my head, like a man in solitary confinement trying to keep up his morale.

There was something to look forward to between Oboyan and Belgorod. I'd read that the flotsam of the Orel-Kursk battle of 1943 had been left untouched, and that knocked-out tanks, guns and trenches littered the country like an open-air museum of war. No longer true. The place is now as tidy as a civil servant's desk, swept and scoured by neat-minded peasants of every last tank track, every single shell-case. The sole survivor is a Soviet tank on a plinth at the roadside.

We met the artists again on the road. A highly gregarious lot, this time they were travelling in convoy with two engineers and two women who were making for the Caucasus. Everybody was hugely impressed with our car, crowding round and taking photographs and saying how 'harosh' (first tone) it was. Shortly afterwards a mudguard fell off.

But this is nothing to what can happen on this road. We were just about to overtake a lorry when its wobbly back tyre detached itself and went bowling ahead. The lorry slewed sharply as the hub dug in, and the load was neatly deposited across the road. Whatever these lorries carry, it seems to be accepted that they will shed a fair percentage along the route. Great lumps of scrap iron and bricks bounce off just ahead of you; sand or gravel pours out as if trails were being deliberately laid. The only items they never seemed to lose were peasants, a very common cargo, who huddled together for warmth as they were transported from one county-sized field to another. Still I suppose the other peasants make a row when one of their number does fall off, and the driver has to stop and pick them up again.

They certainly don't stop to retrieve food. The road, especially where there was a slight bump, was often strewn with maize cobs or cabbages, sometimes an odd melon. You could quite easily live off the road if you augmented the day's taking of vegetables by running over a goose when nobody was looking. It's a great country for geese. The verges are snowy with them, and they cross and recross the road like nursery friezes, dignified and haughtily unflappable.

The scarcity of hotels on this road means that you're bound to keep meeting the people travelling in the same direction. Even if you are charmed by a village, an unlikely event, you can't stop there because there's nowhere to stay. You have to get to a sizeable town before you find an hotel, and, since sizeable towns are at least half a day's drive from each other, travellers usually end up at the same place, often at the same hotel. This, I discovered later, could be a nuisance, but it was quite pleasing to find the artists and the engineers at the same watering hole in Kharkov.

September 23

I'd always had the idea that the black-earth belt of the Ukraine was a lush, golden granary with big-hipped, laughing girls in embroidered skirts romping in the wheat or

102

dancing gaily around combine harvesters. Well, the earth is black—but the rest is for the tourist brochures. Maybe the harvest was finished, but the laughing girls had gone to ground and the only women I saw were a few dehydrated hags in black, scratching a very gnarled root-crop out of the dark soil.

The cumulative monotony of the country produced a strange mental state in which my mind retreated so far that I began to experience total recall of my childhood. Incidents surfaced which had been buried deep for over a quarter of a century; forgotten places appeared in photographic detail. Without effort I recalled children who had been in my class at school when I was five. Their faces, their names, even their smells rolled by as easily as calling an attendance register.

How far back I'd have reached I shall never know because a militiaman broke the train of thought sharply. He dragged us back ten miles to a telephone post in order to check our credentials with someone in Kharkov. By the time we were pointing in the direction of Rostov again, the door which had begun to open in my memory was firmly shut and I began to consider Communism instead.

Politics of any kind bore me, and I am usually roused out of my torpidity only when they impinge directly on me. And Russian Communism impinged on my liberties to an extent which I resented. To begin with, you do not decide where you would like to go; you are told where you *can* go. You are checked and cross-checked at every point on your rigid itinerary by the omniscient Intourist organization, harried along the route by suspicious militiamen (today we had to show our documents three times), discouraged from making contact with the people (who are, I'm convinced, discouraged even more strongly) and forbidden to take photographs of almost everything of real interest. Not absolutely everything. I once got out of the car in completely open country, and militiamen immediately materialized on a motor bike to tell me that the camera round my neck was not to be used. I pointed at a self-congratulatory poster about maize production at the roadside and said I only wanted to shoot that.

Oh, that was different. 'Please be my guest. There we are. Sure you don't want the sun moving a little?'

If you exhibit a normal curiosity, you are treated as a potential enemy. But if you meekly accept the pabulum offered, then officialdom smiles on you—and your trip becomes as uselessly insulated as a Royal tour. What are they afraid of? Materially they have made, and are still making, tremendous progress. But to try and assert to visitors that the entire face of Russia doesn't have a single wart is childish. To try it on Russians is even more childish.

I can see that a reasonable case can be made out for telling a dense peasant only as much as is good for him. As long as he gets enough to eat he won't grumble overmuch. Which is all very well for the peasant but what about the poet?

As I have said, I am a political innocent, but it seems to me that it should be possible to fill all bellies without policing all minds.

The first hint that we were in the south—a lunch of *shashlik* (roast meat on a skewer) and raw onion salad. It was also the first place we'd called at that definitely wasn't for tourists, an asbestos shack next to a petrol station. The proprietress made it plain that her food, not to mention the décor, was not for the likes of us, but she gave in after a time and allowed us in. I think she may have been right about the food. The *shashlik* tasted good, but I had the trots all next day.

Saturday night in Rostov, and the pavements full of Don-basin Albert Finneys just released from a hard week on the capstan lathes and ready for a bit of a romp. The car provided it. As soon as we pulled up outside the hotel we were hemmed in by a joking mob so thick that I couldn't open the door. Four militiamen started to shove the crowd around, and for once the crowd retaliated and shoved back. There was a scuffle around the bonnet which bent the hare's ears, and the militiamen had an undignified, sweaty five minutes—one of them lost his cap—before things began to go their way.

In the foyer of the hotel Paul and I were stopped by the

Ancient Mariner. He was a tall, bald, pear-shaped American, and he was standing so still that you noticed him immediately. It almost seemed as if he was waiting for us. He approached and began talking at once in an urgent yet strange monotonous voice, reeling off personal details with the precision and disinterest of filling in a form. Profession—doctor; route—the Caucasus followed by the Near, and possibly the Middle East; transport—scooter.

He was a difficult man to leave. Not that he was interesting. His grey voice took the juice out of his anecdotes, and his lustreless eyes slid across your face, constantly looking over your shoulder for something. But there was a feeling that you were needed, not particularly as a person but as a catalyst.

Most of the big spenders of Rostov seemed to be in the dining-room when we went in for dinner. Champagne corks were popping in a ragged volley and the dance band was thumping vigorously. We were squeezed in beside a long table of remarkably handsome Russians. The women were huge-eyed and opulent, but it was a well-distributed opulence. The men were lean and olive and wore striped blankets over their shoulders.

They turned out to be folk-dancers from Chile, and were the undoubted success of the evening. They started off quietly enough by standing up and chanting some message of goodwill in Russian, at which the whole dining-room stood up and applauded. Some bouncy Armenians replied with a national dance which resembled the *bouzoukia* of Greece. No further encouragement was needed. A Chilean couple did a courting dance, all smiles and coquetting with handkerchiefs, to a sung accompaniment from the rest of the troupe. An energetic *gopak* followed as the Russian contribution—the man squatting, his legs pumping, the woman tripping on surprisingly light feet despite being built like a Rubens' model.

Then the Armenians did an encore, nearly knocking themselves out this time, and the Chileans quickly replied. Russians leaped in to join the Chilean dance and, without pausing, the Chileans carried on to dance the *gopak*. The quality of the dancing deteriorated, since everybody was trying to do some other country's dance but the whole place was alight with vigorous bonhomie.

A woman looking like Benny Hill in a wig dragged me on to the floor although I tried to tell her that my doctor had forbidden *gopaks*. Afterwards she carted me back to her table like a hunting trophy to show me to her husband, her sister and her brother-in-law, who all forced champagne on me at once. After drinking several bumpers with them, I thought what a nice lot the Rostovians were. The glow produced by the *gopak*, the champagne and my mad social success dimmed ever so slightly when they seemed to be asking me which part of Chile I came from.

A rude map of South America was drawn in spilt champagne, and questioning fingers began stabbing all over it. They were so keen for me to be any sort of Latin American that I considered a brief adoption of Brazil. It was less likely that someone would speak Portuguese. But in the end I told them.

They didn't actually ask for their money back, but they looked hard at my beard. I suppose it was the Castro cut of it which had started them off on the wrong foot. But I must say that they rallied well. Instead of moving the bottle out of my reach, they insisted that I finished it—a sort of consolation prize for being only English.

September 25

Although it didn't seem possible, the Plain of Rostov was flatter than anything which had gone before. It was, without doubt, the plainest plain I've seen. A dung-heap was a landmark visible for miles. We had to tie struts of string across the side-screens to prevent them bending too far under the steady thrust of the cross-wind. Born in the bitter marshes of Siberia, this wind had only to rush the chilly barrier of the Urals before streaming, unimpeded, over the vast flatness of Russia. Our share of it was scarcely bothered by a single hillock on its sweep across Kazakhstan and the basin of the Volga all the way to the Sea of Azov and the Crimea.

But the soft south began to establish itself. The first vines appeared, and small boys stood at the roadside holding up bunches of grapes to tempt us to stop and haggle. (One boy nearly hit us with a bunch as we swept past.) And at long last, hills began to thrust out of the monotonous flatness near Armavir—the foot-hills of the Caucasus. I couldn't take my tired eyes off them. The wind lost its cutting edge, and the sun began to blaze. Villages took on a warmer, more colourful squalor, which was half-Mediterranean, half-Eastern. People sat gossiping outside lime-washed cottages, their eyes flashing at us from the shade. Crimson chains of peppers and heavy swags of bronze and yellow corn-cobs hung on the walls. The fatly smiling pigs basking in the road never opened an eye as we drove round them.

Pyatigorsk, however, sits purse-lipped, aloof from these happy-go-lucky villages, a tidy-minded spinster in tailored tweeds. For Pyatigorsk is a spa town, and the atmosphere of a spa must be a genteel compound of meticulously raked gravel walks, well-pruned shrubs and long, unsensational days of sipping the waters or lying in them. An ultra-genteel touch at the hotel: the pillows were neatly pyramided on the bed under a lace veil like a dumpy bride.

LIMPING THROUGH GEORGIA

A QUIETLY weeping day of drizzle, which almost made me envy the people who had nothing to do but stay in the warm lounges and take the waters. The clouds to the south were a towering, sulphurous wall, and a man who had just driven in from Tbilisi assured us that the road over the mountains would by this time be impossible. Mist, sleet and freezing rain—apparently the whole lot was up there. But we could certainly get as far as Ordzhonokidze, the administrative, economic and cultural centre of the North Ossetian Autonomous Republic (North Caucasus). I hoped so. Then I'd have at least a couple of lines to write in my log under a date that promised little else.

Actually, the weather was a minor worry. For a long time the car had been receiving first aid rather than the overhaul it badly needed, and now its condition was deteriorating almost hourly. The noise from the almost useless exhaust system was shattering. The plates in the silencer had corroded wafer-thin and were breaking up rapidly and the exhaust pipe had cracked off near the engine, making quite an effective blow-torch. This fracture had been roughly bound up with an asbestos bandage secured with copper wire, which didn't really hold the thing together or cut out any of the noise but slightly lengthened the odds on the engine changing over to external combustion. (The odds always shortened at night, when shreds of glowing asbestos came shooting through gaps in the floor like fire-flies.) There was also a back spring which had cracked a leaf or two, the con-rod repair sounded like a botch-up, both mudguards had the palsy, and an undiscoverable oil-leak was worsening all the time. It was a toss-up as to which of these conditions would cause the inevitable breakdown.

Paul was deeply morose about the car's ailments, and even

I felt a stirring of compassion. In fact, I found myself making a sort of religious vow that if the car managed to get to Tbilisi I would see that it was given the finest treatment money could buy. But between us and Tbilisi were the great mountains of the Caucasus.

On reaching Ordzhonokidze we automatically sought out the Intourist hotel for lunch. It jolted me when I suddenly realized that this was a conditioned reflex. Intourist, that huge mother-figure, kerchiefed, square-faced, stupid-cunning, already had me tied to her apron-strings. Not that the girl at the hotel was a bit like this. Easy to look at, she chatted in understandable German as she led us to the garden restaurant and ordered a local speciality for us—a plate-sized pie of minced mutton which finished me about half-way through. When we returned to the car, the silver hare on the bonnet had a delicate posy of flowers between its paws. The girl was watching shyly from a window, and she laughed in confusion when I thanked her. Her little-girl charm obliterated, for a short time, the smothering mother-figure looming behind her.

The clouds had retreated, and the late afternoon sun was shining strongly as we took the Georgian Military Highway which leads to Tbilisi. We were fairly blasé about distances by this time, and started off at four o'clock to cover 120 miles over a mountain range. What we didn't know was that the trip took eight or nine hours under perfect conditions. As we wound upwards towards the Dzerakhovskaya valley, the Valley of the Sun, the water began to bubble and hiss out of the radiator cap, and the posy was soon wilting, parboiled in the steam.

Squeezing through the rose-grey granite walls of the Daryal gorge, we followed the rocky stream of the Terek, already in cold shadow, the road becoming rougher and steeper at every writhing bend. Long stretches had to be taken in second gear, and even first, and the radiator began to erupt with the frequency of a geyser. The engine seemed to be having trouble with its breathing, and the banging from our so-called silencer thundered like a cannonade through the gorge. At this crawling progress I didn't dare to think about the time we'd take to reach Tbilisi—if we reached it at all.

Just before Kazbegi, the engineers, Lev and Stefan, whom we'd met before Kharkov, came racing out of a house at the roadside, waving their arms at us, their mouths full of food. They obviously had something important to tell us, but communication was difficult even when they'd got rid of the food. English and French meant little to them; Russian nothing to me. (I realized that we couldn't have addressed a word to each other when we'd met before, but must have merely smiled.) Finally we settled on German as our only possible link. My grasp of the language dates from a few crammed lectures of technical German when I was reading engineering. But they managed to tell me that the locals had said it was dangerous to try and cross the pass to Tbilisi because of heavy mist.

So where were they staying?

At a *lager* for tourists along the road.

Intourist?

No. It was for Russians—but they'd be able to get us in.

That decided it for me, but Paul took a little convincing. He wanted to press on for Tbilisi, insisting that we could always camp if the weather became too bad. I suggested that setting up a tent on shifting scree in a freezing mountain mist lacked consumer appeal. While we were bandying words, the two women joined us and were introduced as Stefan's wife and his mother. This was a late holiday to Tbilisi and then the Black Sea, a trip across Russia and back for a week at the seaside! They had bought some large, flat cakes of Georgian bread, which they shared with us, smiling but wordless. Their unforced friendliness came down solidly on my side of the argument.

The *lager* was at the foot of the 5,000-metre peak of Kazbek, where legend says the Tent of Abraham rests. The tents at the *lager* were more modest affairs, but there were camp-beds, blankets and sheets. The single stone building housed a cafeteria and a dormitory for women. The camp commandant wasn't at all happy about letting two English-men stay the night, and it required an impassioned argument from Lev to convince him that we were too young to die on the inhospitable pass. The snow-covered Kazbek still glowed in a sun we couldn't see, but the valley was blue with cold. Lev and Stefan grabbed a ball from the car, and soon we were all warming up at volley-ball. Girls in track-suits raced across from the dormitory and punched the ball with unfeminine vigour.

When we went in to supper we started to queue at the counter with everybody else, but a hawk-faced woman cut us out of the crowd and firmly led us to a table set for two. Then, while the other campers had to collect their own food, we were waited on by the woman. I tried to explain that we preferred to sit with our friends, but she clearly had her orders, and I felt that she'd have kept us separated by brute force if necessary. I looked across at Lev and Stefan inquiringly. They shook their heads, almost imperceptibly, so I let it go. The ridiculous thing about this segregation was that all four of us were sharing a tent.

Afterwards we stood around the car by the light of a torch while Paul attended to its minor ailments—the major ones couldn't be touched—and I tried to answer posers such as 'How many kilometres per litre?' I passed round our flask of vodka to warm up both us and the conversation. We moved on to sport. They were both keen footballers and knew more about the English teams than I did. Hearing a Russian enthusing about Wolves and Spurs in German has a dream-like quality—especially with three huge Georgian shepherds in ankle-length cloaks of black sheep-skin as the rest of the audience.

They had materialized out of the night, followed by deep-chested hounds, to stand, silent as pyramids, looking at the car. Everything about them was black—eyes, moustaches, cloaks, goatskin hats which straggled over lean, Ivan-the-Terrible profiles. The powerful silence they brought with them slowly suffocated the conversation. Once we stopped talking the night was so quiet that it seemed heresy to begin again. Then, without a word, they turned and melted back into the darkness like three black sails. The pale shapes of their loping hounds could be seen long after the shepherds had been swallowed up.

Even Lev, who was friendly with every stranger, hadn't spoken with the shepherds. He explained that they would speak Georgian and nothing else. He also told me that their hounds were not used for herding sheep but for killing the wolves and jackals which attacked the flocks. Conversation then thawed rapidly in a spate of stories about Georgia, the land of the Golden Fleece, whose history is a continuous battle against a score of invaders—Scythians, Macedonians, Romans, Arabs, Mongols, Turks and, merely the latest of a long line, the Russians.

When we got round to literature, I was puzzled by the Western authors they had read. It was a weird list—Dickens, Mark Twain, Jack London, John Galsworthy (a name which looks tremendously exotic in Cyrillic characters), Jerome K. Jerome, John Wain, Iris Murdoch. The clue to this selection came when I discovered that the Jack London work they'd read had not been *White Fang* but a forgotten tract of social criticism. And every single author in their list, in fact, has at some time, in some book, criticized Western society. Such a biased reading list must produce a strange picture of Western civilization, a picture so incurably rotten that there is a faint chance that some readers will wonder how it still manages to survive.

Then I made the chastening discovery that my own list of Russian authors was equally patchy. After mentioning the obvious ones, I found a gap between Gorky and Sholokov and then an even bigger gap until Dudintsev and Pasternak. The last two caused a wise, I-thought-as-much shaking of the head. And, of course, it was justified. They both *did* cause literary scandals—and where was the rest of my modern Russian reading? After adding Ehrenburg, with slender justification, I was stumped.

Humbly, I asked for the modern authors I ought to have read. I was given a stack. I hadn't heard of one of them. I asked which of these were critics of the system in some way. I knew the question sounded bad—as if I wanted to bolster up my partial view—but the answer was very illuminating. 'But you asked for writers, didn't you, not critics?'

I began to see light. The party, with massive logic, makes certain that the orthodox view of the Soviet is presented by the simple system of not publishing anything else. If you don't toe the party line, you don't get published—and if you don't get published, you don't eat.

The women went off to sleep in the car (the dormitory was full), and we retired to the tent to finish the vodka. I was teaching Lev and Stefan how to play poker dice when the lights went out, and we were forced early to beds as cold as chain-mail. Glowing cigarettes trembled in icy hands as we talked on.

The last remark I remember was sad. I asked them if they'd like to travel abroad. 'Of course, America, Germany —England, too,' they added politely. 'But it is expensive.' There was a pause before Lev finished, 'And the Iron Curtain is thicker from this side.'

But my last thought was pure delight. Intourist didn't know where I was.

September 26

The cold, crystal morning air brought every ridge on the snow-covered peak of the Kazbek into pin-sharp detail. The frost-thickened hood of the car made it look its age, and the hoary grass crackled underfoot as I went across to collect our passports and settle for the lodgings. But there was nothing to pay. Lev and Stefan were playing volley-ball, and when I tried to find out if they had included us on their bill they pretended that the game was too absorbing for them to answer such an unimportant question.

As we said goodbye, I presented ball-point pens all round with a bow. Lev immediately pinned a badge on me. It was a tinny miniature of the poet Lermontov, but he made it seem like a decoration. For once I thought we'd come out of the exchange on the credit side but, as we were driving off, Stefan's wife raced after us with two large wooden dolls she'd hurriedly grabbed out of the car. You can't win, you just can't win.

Winding with the Terek into the Baidary Gorge, the road

becomes cosseted with buttresses and tunnels to protect it from avalanches. But after this it is out on its own in a mountainscape of splendid savagery. The frozen cataract of a mineral spring encased a hillside in a strange, nutmeg-coloured armour. On a hump which gleamed like a rich silk cushion a great hawk was tearing at a vole. As I got out of the car and approached slowly with my camera, the hawk unhurriedly raised its head and regarded me with cool arrogance. I was within twenty feet when it glided away in a bored fashion, the vole dangling like an elegantly held glove.

At a lonely check-point on the approach to the Krestovy Pass a guard indicated (on a Chinese watch!) that time was advanced an hour in Georgia. It would have been believable if we'd been asked to put our watches back two centuries. Shepherds with the cruel faces of pillagers beneath huge fur hats of Mongolian dishevelment stood brooding on some smouldering memory, intensely still and black in a drifting scum of sheep. On a rocky bend designed for ambushes, a gang of fierce-eyed, moustachioed brigands shook their fists with a hoarse, exultant shout. It took me a second or two to realize they were road workers waving at us.

It's a place where you feel you have to wave. The vast stillness makes you feel a noisy intruder. The mountains dwarf you, and you need to make reassuring contact with any other dwarfs you meet. Two of them came running out of a hut at the top of the pass, waving at us with the energy of castaways. We'd met them before—an Englishman travelling for an educational publishing house and a Canadian fellow-traveller—as far back as Kharkov and at several places since. Hugh and Frank lived in an enviable state of excited appreciation. Each time they had had an adventure more breathtaking than the last. This time they had spent the night in the hut—it was a meteorological station of sorts—and they had just had a tremendous breakfast of barbecued sheep, and all for a couple of cigarettes! I was dragged inside to meet the old man who was cook and general dogsbody.

The place was a shambles, but it was certainly open house; it was accepted without question that passers-by would drop in and take pot-luck. The old boy warmed up some hunks of sheep on the stove, and carefully wiped a fork on his trousers before handing it to me. The sheep-ribs were good, but I wasn't sure how to tackle the second course of a freshly boiled lamb's head. Did I pick it up and gnaw it or split it open for the brains? The traditional tit-bit of travellers was fortunately an impossibility. The eyes had already gone. With the old man watching me expectantly I had to do something, so, putting on a knowing gourmet's look, I prised open the jaws, tore out the tongue and ate it as quickly as possible. Then I went outside into the fresh air.

On the doorstep there was a mountain dog with a ghastly wound in the leg. When a little ramble in the mountains was suggested, I was more than willing. I felt better after an hour of clean, cold air, snowy peaks and tiny, vivid flowers. While Hugh and Frank went on with boyish zest to climb a ten-thousand footer (the pass lies at over seven thousand feet) we turned back and began the descent to Tbilisi and the waiting arms of Mother Intourist.

The road twists down from the pass like a snake in its death throes. The villages of Mleti and Gudauri are five kilometres apart as the crow flies but fifteen as the road winds. We probably hold the speed record for at least a part of this descent. It was an unintentional attempt triggered off when three mountain dogs came racing for us in a very unplayful way. Despite their size they moved at a tremendous speed, and they plainly intended to leap smartly into the open car and crack our thigh-bones for the marrow. With their encouragement we went swinging into the bends like a rocket-assisted bobsleigh. I was grateful that we were going downhill. If the dogs had caught us on our painful climb at the other side of the pass, we should have been easy meat. The thought kept us going hard long after the baying had died away.

It was some time before I noticed that the landscape had already changed from winter to spring. The hard ice-filled ruts in the road had become dusty pot-holes, and the gentler slopes of the country were flaming with bright shrubs. The shepherds looked kindlier and more approachable, the sheep plumper. After Passakauri, where the Chornaya and the Belaya—the Black and the White—Aragvis become one river, the road paddles refreshingly through countless fords, the land gives up the pretence of being related to the fierce mountains, and relaxes in to a warm valley of vineyards, orchards and tobacco fields. It makes a soft berth for Mtskheta, once the capital of Georgia until Tbilisi took over in the sixth century, and now dreaming away its retirement like a veteran general among his roses, a little shrunken inside comfortable old clothes.

The only photograph I'd seen of Tbilisi was a beautiful shot of weathered, big-eaved houses cliff-hanging over the Kura river, and I was expecting the first glimpse to be just as stunning. Well it isn't. From the Zemo-Avchaly hydro-electric power station, you get an uninterrupted view of factories and suburbs. The impression does improve as you run in along tree-lined avenues of hotly glaring buildings blackly scalloped with arches and colonnades of shade. Then the people explode on you. The men, short, swarthy and invariably moustached, shout their conversations and thump each other to get home their points; and the women, with eyes wet-black as olives beneath bruise-dark lids, midnight hair and hips like mobile melons, the women are a sight for deprived eyes.

But, with Intourist waiting, this was no time for being a flaneur. The car had to be rushed off for vital repairs before it disintegrated; the flat-car had to be arranged; tickets had to be picked up; a hotel booked in Erevan. Three days would not be a second too long for us to get this into the thick skull of Intourist. Georgi, the man we had to deal with most of the time, spoke excellent German loudly and rapidly. It was better than nothing but only just, and half an hour's conversation with him used to leave my brain shaking with fatigue. After a lecture on the dangers of staying outside the Intourist fold, he said that the car would have to be driven to the border by one of their drivers. I stamped on this old chestnut firmly. The apprenticeship in Moscow was paying off. He was unbudging, however, about not letting us stay in either of the Intourist hotels in Tbilisi.

There was a delegation at each one. When this happens the hotel is, in effect, sealed off whether there are rooms to spare or not.

So it had to be the camp outside the town. Here the only hut was put at our disposal, since the whole place was completely empty. So, apparently, was the larder. When we went to the buffet, we had to cajole the women into serving us some sausage, and when I asked for tea she went through a hand-wringing paroxysm that suggested I wanted the blood of her only child. The camp commandant, who spoke French for a pleasant change, came in and sorted it out. He told her to belt up and put the kettle on. It sounded good in Georgian.

While I was sipping a vilely weak glass of tea, the light from the doorway was cut off by a familiar pear-shaped cloud which said, 'My scooter nearly stopped in one of those fords.' Sinking to nebulous rest at my table, the Ancient Mariner began his compulsive catalogue of experiences, beginning with the place where I had last seen him. The arrival of Hugh and Frank, tired but happy and full of tales of strange butterflies and mountain sickness, made the Mariner's needle jump back to the first groove, and I slipped away to the hut to do some writing. He followed in ten minutes with a request to share the hut, since a tent might aggravate his slight chill.

I had put him down as lonely at first, but there was something deeper than mere loneliness. He kept pouring out reminiscences as if to prove his existence by sheer weight of circumstantial evidence. As soon as he stopped, the identity he had created for himself began to dissolve, and the only way to stop the frightening drift into faceless limbo was to start talking again about something, anything, it didn't matter what as long as it proved he had lived and was still living.

September 27

After the car was handed over for rehabilitation we collected an Intourist car and a guide and toured the city. The old part, which looked interesting, was curtly dismissed after one panoramic view from a hill overlooking the Kura (the cliff-hanging houses are close by), and the rest of the trip was devoted to the new town—a succession of stolid, over-large institutions of this and that which rolled easily off the surface of my mind.

Afterwards I went back on foot for an unguided nose-around in the old quarter. At least I intended it to be unguided, but a student tagged himself on, introduced himself as Georgi (a highly popular Georgian name), and led me to a Greek Orthodox church, so Greek that it might have been lifted bodily from a stark-white village on the Aegean. When I went inside, the candle-tongued dimness was swooning with incense, and the resonant baritone of the luxuriantly bearded papas dropped like slow golden retsina from the dome on the humble heads of black-shawled women. This was the first religious ceremony I had seen in the Soviet, but Georgi said that there were several practising churches in Tbilisi, although no young people attended. He was a tolerant atheist, and remarked, 'Religion is for old women.'

I began to think, with rising hope, that Georgi was a Tbilisian proud to show off his city without any desire to buy the shirt off my back. Not so. He simply took longer than usual to come to the point. Wearily I explained that I was wearing almost everything I possessed, but he insisted that the dark blue cotton shirt I had on was dispensable. Naturally he promised enough roubles to distort my pockets, and this started me thinking about our emaciated wad of travellers' cheques. I also remembered the catalogue of repairs for the car—the estimate was forty roubles—and that clinched it. I agreed to meet him outside the camp after dark with whatever Western fol-de-rols I could rake together.

'Don't deceive me,' he kept repeating. 'I not boy.'

I said I not boy either by a long chalk, and fixed a rendezvous for 7.30. At 7.28 I put on my baggy sweater and stuffed underneath it my blue shirt, a nylon shirt Paul said he thought he could spare and a pair of sandals he definitely could. At 7.29 I walked quickly towards the gates, hoping the camp commandant wouldn't be strolling about. Looking

like a precocious case of middle-age spread, I walked slowly
down the dark road, my hands deep in my pockets to support
the bulge. At 7.31 a hiss came out of some shadows, and
Georgi puffed on a cigarette to indicate his position.

He went off to get a taxi, while I waited in the same patch
of shadow, wondering if I could pass myself off as a harmless
English eccentric to any patrolling militiaman. Georgi was
away a long ten minutes, and by the time the taxi came I
was ready to believe he'd nipped off to inform. I humped
myself inside clumsily, and Georgi said, 'How do you do?',
loud and English, and shook my hand. When I started to
reply he put a finger to his lips and pointed at the back of
the taxi-driver's head. It didn't make sense. Why did he speak
in English, or even at all? He certainly worried the driver
who kept glancing round, suspicious of our now heavy
silence.

Georgi paid him off in an ill-lit suburb, and led me quickly
to some half-finished blocks of flats and through an archway.
Here he left me while he walked back to the entrance to
check if we were being followed. Then we stumbled around
the muddy ground between the blocks (a few flats were
occupied, but must have been lacking in some services to
judge by the number of trenches we had to leap), while I
passed the articles across one by one, with a brief sales talk
on each, and he stuffed them into his briefcase. After haggling about prices for some time, he decided that he didn't
really want the nylon shirt or the sandals. I told him that
I was damned if I was going to traipse back to the camp
with them, that it was a strict package deal or nothing.
Eventually we settled for fifty roubles the lot. Hardly a
fortune but it should cover the repairs. As we came out of
the archway, our feet heavily brogued with mud, he handed
the briefcase to me, and said that if anyone stopped us it was
mine!

He wouldn't hear of it when I suggested that we parted on
the spot. He was very firm about getting a taxi before I
returned the briefcase. As we waited, I asked him what the
penalties were for this sort of thing. He told me he'd certainly be thrown out of the university, where he was study-

ing engineering, and probably imprisoned as well. My tactless question didn't help his nerves at all. He savaged a cigarette with quick, hard drags and his bone-dry mouth put feathers round his words.

'Fool, fool,' he muttered, hitting his head savagely with his hand. 'I have to stop. After tonight—finish.' I had also decided to sign the pledge. It wasn't worth being deported, or worse, for a few grimy roubles. Anyway I had nothing left to sell.

He warned me again not to speak in the taxi, but when I dropped off to catch a trolley-bus into town his nerves had returned, and he replied to my 'Dasvidanya' with a smiling 'Good-bye'. I got the impression that he was intending to wear both shirts and the sandals at the next student hop.

These clandestine transactions burn up a lot of nervous energy and I was in bed long before midnight. Two hours later I was wakened by a blaze of light in the hut. Filling the doorway, the Ancient Mariner began to drone out the latest instalment of his saga.

September 28

Our guide—a pleasant if rather bovine girl—had a tough day today. It started when I bought a copy of *Krokodil*, and winsomely asked her to read to me. *Krokodil* has been called, by some loose thinker, the Soviet *Punch*. Certainly these magazines are of approximately the same size but there the resemblance ends. *Krokodil* has no advertisements, and might easily have been set up by enthusiastic children using a rubber printing kit. It is not really a humorous magazine at all, but an organ for inculcating right thinking, and every cartoon, every story, every filler has a moral sting. The serious cartoons I saw were mainly concerned with foreign affairs—racial segregation in America, the attitude of West Berlin to East. The 'funny' ones were about turpitude at home—work-shirkers, drunkards, unimaginative scientists, corruption down on the collective farm.

An oafish worker lies in bed smoking a huge cigarette. Through the window can be seen factory chimneys.

Caption: 'If he goes on smoking the chimneys will stop.'

A *kolkhoz* manager is shown signing the card all collective workers must have. A woman stands waiting for it, knitting furiously. He is wearing his bribe, a large woollen hat, as he says, 'Of course you are a worker.' (Apparently this is quite a racket. With their false credentials, these women don't work but knit all the time, selling the finished goods and giving the manager a kick-back out of the profits.)

The girl was making heavy weather of translating the captions. As she struggled to the end of each one she looked up waiting for me to roll about with laughter, but all I could do was to repeat dully, 'I see,' although this was often a flat lie. She gave up eventually, and called in a sharp-looking youth who had a non-Soviet shirt and a strong American accent. His English was excellent and idiomatic, and he galloped through *Krokodil*, even managing to explain the puns, and went on to tell a couple of dirty non-Russian jokes in a racy slang.

Our girl guide was put out by this stag session. Not by the jokes (it was her turn not to see the point), but because she couldn't take part in this enviable ease of communication. Petulantly she threw the copy of *Krokodil* on the table, and said that swapping jokes was not a very good way of spending a day in Tbilisi. When we weakly agreed, she said that now she would take us to the shops to buy our presents.

This wasn't a success either. The things I wanted weren't available, and the things which were available I didn't want. At the record shop there wasn't a single disc of classical music, and the only Georgian folk-music was an album of a complete opera. Paul wanted an abacus. All through Russia we had seen the abacus used slavishly for the simplest addition, and he particularly fancied the tiny version waitresses often had swinging in front of their apron.

While he was trying one of these for ease of bead movement, he was tapped by a confident youth who wanted to swap an ikon for a shirt. This character wasn't at all put off by the freezing attitude of our guide, and he followed us out of the shop for some way before giving up. The girl then told us that he was a person of low morals who sold imitation ikons to tourists. She seemed to put ikon-faking on a par with white slavery, and said that we must go to the museum to see real ikons, but first the funicular, yes?

The city was flashing toothily in the sun, and everybody on the plateau was excitedly pointing out landmarks, everybody except a sad huddle of dark-polled, tireless Georgians who were under the mass hypnosis of the Ancient Mariner. He caught sight of us and came across, leaving the Georgians to wander off in a daze, shaking their heads. Before he could get into his stride we told him—quite truthfully—that we'd had to stop some youths playing about with his scooter at the bottom of the funicular, and he departed at a lumbering canter.

On the return trip in the small, yellow cabin we were hemmed in by a singing quartet, their arms tightly wound round each other's necks as they bellowed slowly at the nearest face, oblivious, drunk with the lugubrious harmony of the song. Our morning treat wound up with a schoolboyish lunch of *hadji-puri*—a large bun of hot bread scooped out in the centre and filled with egg and cheese— and a big jug of *fruktovaya voda*, glowing with the clear innocence of a wine-gum. Seeing bull-necked Georgians, who obviously shaved with an axe, drinking this sweet cherryade had a certain piquancy.

The girl had had a quiet lie-down after lunch, and came back, rested and composed, with the intention of continuing our treat with a visit to the museum of ikons. Mumbling that he had to go and say something comforting to the car, Paul slid off rapidly. The compression of the girl's mouth indicated that she thought he was up to no good, but she was calmly determined to show one of the English the sort of ikons which weren't on the market for shirts. Her calm was shattered before we reached the museum.

I ought to explain that there is a modern version of the stocks in Russia. This is a notice-board carrying photographs of offenders with a list of their misdemeanours beneath. I had seen one on show in GUM, but, as with everything else, there had been a queue in front of it. As the guide and I walked through a tree-shaded square, I noticed one of these photo-dotted boards, and asked if it showed the bad lads of the town. She said that they were not real criminals, and changed the subject. I pressed her to translate some of the exotic Georgian script but, remembering her struggle with *Krokodil*, she shrugged and said that they were petty crimes —wife-beating, drunkenness, absenteeism from work.

I started to focus my camera. A shoulder appeared in the reflex viewfinder, and I stepped to one side. The shoulder followed, and I moved back. This time the whole viewfinder was blocked, and I looked up straight into the belligerent face of a small man in a snowy-white flat cap standing squarely in front of the lens. Each movement I made he mirrored faithfully. He wasn't trying to get himself photographed but making quite certain that I didn't photograph the notice-board. I indicated that he'd oblige me enormously by moving, and then the row started.

His face flushed patchily like a slice of salami, and his moustache shot about like a caterpillar in convulsions as he began to bombard me with angry words from point-blank range. I'd never realized how juicy the Georgian language was. Every word came out in a heavy spray that soon turned the lenses of my specs into a sort of pebble glass. I had a chance to wipe down when my brave guide interposed to ask the little fellow what he was complaining about. It seemed that he didn't know much about photography, but he knew what he liked, and this notice-board didn't come into that category.

When asked to define the proper sphere of photography, he flung out his arm at a statue of Lenin, which was throwing a sharp blue shadow over the square with an uncannily similar gesture to the little man's. I asked the guide to explain that I hadn't brought enough film to shoot all the statues of Lenin, and that I'd prefer to choose my own subjects anyway. This brought an absolute cloudburst of passionate rhetoric from the Lenin-lover, which boiled down to the statement that he didn't agree with my choice and would fight to the death to stop me exercising it.

By this time there were several violent arguments going on in the crowd which had gathered, and the rights of the photographer were being thrashed about with religious frenzy. It looked as if we were only seconds away from picking sides for a punch-up, and I thought it was time to seek sanctuary in the museum. The notice-board, now ignored, could hardly be seen for people, but I promised myself I'd return and photograph it—at a fast sprint if necessary.

There was a cloistered peace about the museum of ikons which soothed me immediately, but the girl was still muttering under her breath when the guide came to collect us. (It wasn't an open museum, and one had to sit in a waiting-room until a guide was free.) I followed obediently, expecting to be quickly bored by an endless repetition of one theme.

It was one theme certainly, but a theme with variations. Within the canon of religious art, even Byzantine art, there was scope for different schools. The early ikons are faceless, a gem-studded robe and a golden halo enclosing nothing; but in the artist's eye the dark wood must have writhed with images, and it is difficult not to sketch in features and a beard. In the sixth century, just about the time when Mtskheta began its long sleep, it became no longer idolatrous to paint the face of Christ, and the space beneath the halo was filled with many different interpretations—lean El Greco ascetics, pudgy landlords, dark-eyed visionaries, men-about-town with stylishly curled beards.

The ikons mirror not only the fashions but also the economy of the time. Simple blocks of wood flowered into fretted triptychs, the amount of gold used varying with the standard of living, the number of precious stones diminishing from a rash of carbuncles through a wraith of seed-pearls to nothing but a coat of varnish. The later faces become standardized, almost like oleographs with their uncertain shadows and undecided draughtsmanship. The early ones are much the best. One I remember was painted in obsessive detail, the pale lips taut beneath the moustache, the crisply-eyelashed eyes set at different levels as if the Messiah had suffered a stroke.

The guides didn't believe in Christianity, they simply explained. Although they didn't know the Stations of the

Cross, they knew the exact tally of the turquoises in any given ikon, but their uninvolved tone made their ecclesiastical treasures as remote as flint arrow-heads.

There was a stronger flicker of religion at a mosque in the old quarter. We knocked up the guardian who emerged like a tortoise in a fez. He raised no objection to the girl entering the body of the mosque, the male's preserve, didn't object to photographs and didn't even ask us to remove our shoes. But the overlapping carpets were unfaded, and his pruney eyes glittered when he said that Islam was alive on holy days.

I discovered Paul behind the Tbilisi Hotel in quietly ecstatic reunion with the car. Amazingly he had found it waiting, welded and re-sprung, at a bill well below the estimate. There were several small jobs still to be done—topping up the battery and fixing the back doors, which had almost shaken themselves free. Paul had made an unlikely ally in the imposing chief of the kitchen staff, who was sending his minions off in all directions for bottles of distilled water, drills and screws.

The front of the Tbilisi Hotel was as pillared and pompous as a bank, with a massive, gilded Stalin seated in the foyer to underline its respectability. (He is probably gathering dust in the basement now.) But the back, which nobody saw, had no need to keep up the pretence, and it relaxed into a cosy, untidy, self-contained village which vibrated with the noise and exuberant life of a Neapolitan tenement. The staff quarters ran round two sides of the square, the communal balconies cluttered with bird-cages, tubs and window-boxes of flowers. Lines of washing were everywhere —damply partitioning the galleries, hanging like capes from the hand-rails, dipping in idly flapping arcs overhead. Knots of women, their arms folded like a twist of flat sausages over their bosoms, stood gossiping outside the doors. Off-duty waiters strolled about in their vests, singing, flexing their muscles, lathering their chins for the second shave of the day. Brown, thin-legged children wrestled and squealed in the dust. The hotel kitchen was open to the square, sending out the clangorous pulsing heat of a stoke-hole, and occasionally a cook would be silhouetted in the doorway as he gulped down some cooler air.

The car was soon teeming with men holding funnels, pouring water, drilling holes or offering loud advice. Anybody who strolled over out of curiosity, which meant almost everybody, was immediately enrolled and fitted into the scheme of things by the kitchen boss, who stood back from the mêlée, hands on hips, like a general watching the progress of a battle. There were a lot too many cooks, but before the broth was spoiled I grabbed a handful of ball-point pens and paid them all off.

After we'd finished, the kitchen boss shook our hands and led us to a table in the open-air restaurant, insisting that we leave the ordering to him. This restaurant, which had never been suggested by Intourist, closed off the square in a shady, vine-tangled warren of alcoves and arbours. There were no menus in sight, and no tourists. As the customers drifted in, they embraced their favourite waiter before making their way to their favourite table, shouting their orders over their shoulders as they went. And waiters with laden trays trotted—actually trotted—in and out of the kitchen, where they had terrible arguments with cooks, arguments which changed into shouted pleasantries to their clients as they emerged at the double.

Friend greeted friend with violent affection. A hand-shake begins at shoulder height. The hands are brought sweeping down to meet with a ringing slap, and gripped fiercely while the free hand jerks the friend's head forward into a hard, unshaven kiss. A group sang wildly ululating dirges in a fervour of closed eyes and wobbling, bristly Adam's apples and applauded themselves with high yips and a thunderous drumming on the tables with bottles. The meal had the same bold, simple vigour as the atmosphere—a salad of roughly chopped onions and tomatoes (with a small, glossy-green pepper which had the eye-watering attack of Madras curry), a smoking *shashlik* on spits the size of sabres, and a bottle apiece of cool, dry, amber wine. Soothing my tongue with the last misted glass of a wine I didn't know, and listening to a song I couldn't understand but which made

126

the warm dusk throb, I found myself liking Tbilisi very much.

I don't know if the camp commandant sensed this, but as soon as we arrived back in camp he ordered up a bottle of champagne and began to teach us Georgian. A group from Rostov joined in, and we ordered more champagne and caviar. Everything—the lesssons, the caviar, the champagne —went down with roars of laughter. When we finally split up, the camp rang and echoed like a canyon with bellows of 'Dasvidanya!'

September 29

Not a good day at all. . . . Lots of hanging about waiting for things to happen. Not improved by having a skull filled with an unlikely mixture of kapok wadding and egg-shaped stones which shifted around as I walked. Drove into town and dumped a couple of bags in the hotel foyer, where Georgi, the German speaker, tried a last-minute coup by asserting that everything movable had to be taken out of or off the car. To carry out this bland request would have needed enough porters to man a couple of safaris. Moving my jaws as little as possible, I told him, in my pidgin German, to stop messing us about and start the palaver with the stationmaster. It seemed to get across and Georgi went away.

I moved off to get a drink of something, anything, to soften the piece of biltong in my mouth. I hadn't managed to catch the waiter's eye before a bouncy character detached himself from his friends and came over with a bottle of wine under his arm. He matily poured me a glass of wine, which I drank like a dune absorbing a raindrop. He chatted away in what he obviously thought was German as he refilled my glass. Even to my ears it was a mangled travesty of the language, and I didn't have the faintest idea what he was getting at until he reached over and fingered the collar of my shirt appreciatively.

I was not amused. It was my only remaining warm shirt, the shirt which would have to see me back to England, and he wanted to whip it off my back. I pushed the second glass of wine away but he wouldn't take no, niet or nein for an answer. He thrust the glass back at me and produced a handful of roubles like a grubby posy. I pushed the glass and the fist away; he pushed them back again. This went on for a ridiculous length of time, the wine slopping out over the table, the stones rolling villainously inside my head, with him getting angrier, me getting wearier.

When I half-rose to go he pulled me back with a bump that lanced my eyeballs. I decided I'd have to hit him as soon as I could open my eyes again. When I did open them, the Ancient Mariner was descending in a cool grey cloud like a full-blown *deus ex machina*. My enthusiastic welcome startled him slightly, but he was immediately interested when I explained about the shirt bandit, and his eyes were almost animated as he asked, 'Do you think he'd like to buy this suit? It's a dacron mixture.' I couldn't see a ready sale for a very long, pear-shaped suit in any mixture, but I said that it was worth a try. And he did try, rounding with awesome dignity on the now apprehensive Georgian, and pinning him to the chair with slow rivets of Russian. When I quietly excused myself, the poor lad made a desperate attempt to come with me—and it wasn't simply the thought of my shirt slipping through his fingers. He wanted to escape before it was too late, but he was eased down with firm authority.

My hangover began to lift as I walked out thinking of the neat poetry of justice. The Ancient Mariner had, for once, rescued me from boredom. In return, he might possibly sell a suit and, at the very least, would have another anecdote to keep his identity afloat. It was the last time I saw him.

When Georgi returned from the station three hours later, I assumed that every detail had been settled. But he had merely been going through the preliminaries. Now we all had to go to the siding and stand by a flat-car to witness the car being tethered with cables, chocks hammered on both sides of the wheels, and every eyelet on the tonneau cover being wired and secured with a lead seal. We also had to take off every removable mirror and lamp, and stow them in the back, and then check off an exhaustive list of contents. It was all very impressive, but after three hours of this I began to get levitation hallucinations, since my system had had nothing to work on but last night's champagne and the morning's wine.

When Paul and I finally ate in a deserted and echoing dining-room at the hotel it was 4.45, and we put away a meal with all the trimmings which cost us ten roubles. They even cooked us some *blinchikis*. This is one item in the Russian cuisine which I ordered with unswerving gluttony. These delectable little pancakes—made of maize flour, I think—are served with sour cream, and are often stuffed with curd, too. Since they have to be made to order there is always a show of reluctance or even blatant lying when you ask for them, but persistence is well worth it. When they are piping hot—another difficulty incidentally—and lightly sprinkled with sugar, they can rescue the most appalling meals and quieten your fears that all Russian cooks are conscripted from forced labour gangs.

After mopping up the last of the *blinchikis* we had just time to have a shoe-shine outside the hotel while the car waited to whip us to the station for the Erevan train. And the shoe-black tried to buy my *socks*. Tbilisians simply don't know when they're beaten. I'm no longer surprised that the city has risen thirteen times from smoking ashes.

On the ride to the station Georgi brought the Intourist car's tyres months nearer to a re-tread. There was no panic —we arrived with five minutes in hand—but he loved making the tyres squeal on corners, and the car was government property, so who was worrying? A small man, who came along for the ride, told me very gravely that the first thing I must do on returning to England was to protest against the training of German troops in Wales. He said that the Soviet regarded this as a serious abuse of the rights of a country with its own customs and its own language. There wasn't time to ask him about his views on the rights of Georgia, but his fervour for Wales was commendable.

After a soprano shriek, the train began to roll slowly through the warm, purple dusk. I was watching the bumpy carpet of the lamps of Tbilisi swinging past, and had just identified the funicular, sticking up like an illuminated derrick, when a stone splintered on the carriage a yard from my head. We were passing through the shanty quarter of the town, and I couldn't make out where the stone had come from until the embankment suddenly dipped and a gang of kids jerked sharp and active across the skyline like Lotte Reiniger cutouts, flinging stones as they ran. I suppose they had to take their sport when it came. There were only two passenger trains a day, and stoning goods trains is no fun.

When darkness fell there was nothing to do but go to bed. The beds were already made up and a speaker beneath the table was sending out an Eastern-flavoured music like sweet-sour pickle. I wasn't wild about the music, but there was no way of switching it off. There was a control knob, but this merely switched the volume from loud to not quite so loud and then back again. Still, with a blanket over the ear, I heard only the crescendos.

Tomorrow I would wake up in a different country with different people speaking a different language (even with a different alphabet) and eating, I hoped, different food. There was another more practical reason why I welcomed being unconscious *en route*. Erevan is less than two hundred miles away but the train takes a full eleven hours to reach it.

IDOLATRY IN EREVAN

September 30

The first surprise came when I looked out of the window and found myself staring at Turkey. I wasn't on the wrong train. The piece of Turkey I was looking at was Mount Ararat. It must have been over twenty miles away across the Araxes River, but its venerable white thatch dominated the country with the easy command of a patriarch. The early, unheated air provided the clearest view of the mountain I was to have until I reached Turkey. Then the train was curving away past truckloads of soldiers with rolled-up sleeves and floppy, tropical hats as we trundled into the suburbs of Erevan. The second surprise was that Intourist in Tbilisi hadn't warned Intourist in Erevan of our arrival.

Georgi had sworn that he had booked our rooms. He had certainly deducted in advance the villainous sum of sixty roubles (there is no cheap tourist rate in Erevan) for our one day's stay at the Hotel Armenia. Intourist could be inefficient about most things, but when it came to the business of keeping tabs on their tourists I had never known them slip up before. The Hotel Armenia had a reputation to maintain as the best hotel in Erevan, and therefore in Armenia, and the manager made certain that we realized just how lucky we were that he had a couple of rooms free on the top floor. I began to see what he meant when our breakfast was completed by a pardonably proud waiter sweeping in with a plate of toast.

It wasn't very good toast—the bread isn't designed for it —but toast of any sort means that pioneers of unwavering Anglo-Saxon tastes have brought enlightenment along with their pots of marmalade. Even the site of the hotel seemed to have been chosen to suit members of the international set. From the back you could look straight across at Ararat, by now a faint, smoke-grey cone in the heat haze. At the front the tall, elegant arches and carved frieze of the façade, all in warm-coloured tufa, faced the main square which was dominated by a twenty-foot statue of Lenin. For once he had been excused his overcoat, but he still looked over-dressed in his lumpy, bronze suit, and his pate gleamed sweatily in the hard sunlight.

But our *de luxe* time was a-wasting. At our twenty-odd pounds a day level we had a car, a driver, and a guide awaiting our pleasure, and the miser in me was frantic at the idea of their eating their heads off for nothing. We were assigned to Nora, a shy, dark girl with a not unattractive moustache, who reeled off all the places worth visiting. We reduced this to a short list with the intention of trying to combine two of them but, perversely, every place was at a different point of the compass, and eventually we settled for a ride to Lake Sevan, the largest lake in the Caucasus. On the way out of town we stopped while I bought a couple of records of Armenian folk-music. Foolishly I put these on the ledge behind the seat where the sun could get at them. When I picked them up later they were as pliable as Pontefract cakes. I've tried to get the buckle out of them since, but every attempt to play 'Help me across the stream' ends with the needle being unhorsed.

Still looking like an inland sea, Lake Sevan must have been even larger before they started tapping off water for a hydro-electric scheme whose pylons go striding off in all directions over the naked hills. What was once an island out in the lake is now a peninsula, an over-large head on the end of a thin, chalky neck of land, which sent the sun bouncing into our eyes as we walked across. Two cosy little churches of the ninth century squatted comfortably at the turfy summit of the former island. The steep path leading to them passed a clump of intricately carved tombstones, as ancient and withdrawn as a group of geriatric patients. The carving was blurred by strata of lichens, which overlapped like stained, corroded, paper-thin medals. The churches, too, showed a crazed instead of a comfortable old age. Clumps of grass dotted the roofs, and weeds whiskered out of cracks in the walls like patches missed while shaving. Inside, there was the neglected air of a condemned house, except for a couple of candles and a few jars of flowers standing in front of a patchwork of crude ikons and coloured magazine pages stuck on the smoky walls. The guardian of the churches was a death's head of a man, who shuffled around with his cramped, horny hand held like a permanent begging cup.

Razdan, the river flowing out of Sevan, gives its name to a pebbly white wine as dry as the hills. We tried some at a pleasant little restaurant called 'Minutka' (which freely translates as 'Just a minute') along with some excellent mountain trout of sweet, pinkish flesh. 'Minutka' is not taken too literally. When we arrived half a dozen people were having a wild party, drinking straight out of the bottles and singing and dancing to an accordion with an abandon that shook the floor. They were still going at it when we took the road back to Erevan.

The Armenian interviewer in Moscow had been, I discovered, a comparatively mild jingoist. Every Armenian is intensely and uncritically proud of Armenia, especially when it comes to the language and literature of the country. Unless you have a medical certificate saying that you have a rare allergy to the Armenian alphabet, you cannot escape the Matenadaran, the museum of manuscripts and incunabuli. Actually an allergy would be easy to develop. The Georgian alphabet looks weird enough with its trailing fronds, but the Armenian one looks permanently disoriented. Although there is a disturbing hint of familiarity about it, whichever angle you try it from it *still* looks upside down. Apparently the same monkish genius was responsible for inventing both alphabets.

The alphabet must have looked even stranger to the third member of our party—a plump little Buddhist, crisp in saffron robe and crew-cut. He was tailed by a man from the local newspaper with a flash camera, which he used every time the saffron robe bent over a case. In trying to get a candid close-up of the exotic visitor, the photographer let a bulb off about six inches from my face, and I saw the rest of the incunabuli through a swarm of phosphorescent amoeba.

I became more appreciative when we left the incunabuli and moved on to the manuscripts. Some of the pages had the same pure, disciplined penmanship, the same enamelled glowing colours as the Book of Kells—but these pages were much older than Kells. Just in passing, why is it that the secret of preparing these colours—the piercing blues and rich undimmed reds—why is it *invariably* lost?

My hopes about Armenian food took a knock when I saw the same old Intourist menu at the hotel. *Shashlik* was simply rechristened *kebab*. From an alcove high up on one wall the music of all nations was being mangled by a four-piece band looking like an overcrowded cageful of birds. Walking off another bottle of *Razdan* around the warm, dusky streets, we bumped into a very happy trio of lecturers from the Oriental School of Languages. Between them they could have communicated with almost anybody within a radius of a thousand miles. Except us. Although they could muster a dozen languages, English wasn't one of them. They tried us in everything from Armenian to Arabic before one man reluctantly decided he would have to use the jejune English he had. He happened to be the drunkest and he took his frequent failures to communicate very much to his professional heart. His face twisted with painful effort, and when he had to grope for a word he would beat his chest and comically howl with frustration.

After ten minutes of histrionics, he finally made his point. It was a good point. Whatever happened, we mustn't go to war. Handshakes and heavy back-slapping all round.

They must have been drunker than I thought, because they wound up by inviting us to attend a forum along with several visiting foreign professors (including one from Cambridge) to discuss the Kurdish problem tomorrow. I didn't even know what the problem was. I still don't.

October 1

Nora had bigger fish to fry today, but before she left she introduced us to another guide, a shy youth who looked like her brother. Before our train went there was time for a brief flip around town—a couple of main streets, the covered market, the Victory Park. Erevan is a city of sunlight, but the buildings are not eye-slitting glares of salt-white blobbed with inky shadow. This is because everything is built of tufa, a soft volcanic rock which seems to bask in the sun. It is a beautiful building material—simple to quarry, simple to carve, light, strong, an excellent insulator—and, in this climate, it weathers perfectly. Also it has a natural variety of warm shades from a ripe peach bloom through cloudy amber and tawny yellow to a clear, rich gold. As the light changes so do the colours. In the morning Erevan glows like a pale honeycomb. In the hours before dusk you could believe that the city is built of gold.

Victory Park, laid out to commemorate the glorious Soviet victory over the forces of Fascism, has a curious ambivalence. It is like a park—there are trees, shrub-lined paths, places for kids to play—and yet it feels more like a place of worship, a secular open-air church with the State as the godhead. Posters proclaim parts of the creed as you enter, and a likeness of the prophet Lenin himself accompanies a number of photographs of the faithful who are working to fulfil his prophecies. As you stroll along the path, your footsteps hushed in thick, white dust, oil-paintings of Soviet leaders, four times life-size, loom at you suddenly from the shrubbery. Khruschev at that time shone like a benevolent, pink moon from the branches of a tree. A leafy shadow shifted across the clever face of Mikoyan, the local boy who made it to the Kremlin, animating his knowing eyes and foxy smile.

The path led past these overpowering ikons to a symbol of the godhead made flesh—a sixty-foot bronze of Stalin towering on a hundred-foot pedestal above you, above Erevan, above Russia. Those terrible eyes the size of meteorites must have saved many Armenian souls from the mortal sin of national deviation, a sin endemic to the country according to Party theologians. It was certainly no accident to put the largest statue of Stalin in the Soviet Union overshadowing the main avenue and looking into the heart of Erevan. Now that the symbol has been toppled and melted into ash-trays or door-knobs, some of the implacable hell-fire of the creed must have gone, too, and Victory Park must have diminished to a pantheon of mere demi-gods.

The last call was to the covered market to buy some food for the train journey. Ambivalence again—this time of old and new, of apathy and ebullience. A colossal bronze screen, fretted and pierced like a giant doily, fills the arch of the portico. The fifteen-foot door cut through this looks like a mouse-hole; you scuttle through and find yourself in a high, spaciously echoing vault, more like a hygienic hangar than a market. The traders seem cowed by this space, and cling unhappily to the walls like people who've come to a dance too early. Old men squat on their hunkers among green-marbled hills of melons thinking nostalgically of the dirty, bustling life of the old street markets. They no longer shout to attract custom; the echo is too intimidating. Besides, all the prices are regulated, and there's no competition.

In contrast with this apathy, the customers chirrup away like cicadas as they handle the fruit and vegetables with a rough proprietary air. It is definitely the customers' show; the stall-holders stand by like mute extras, and dully watch their aubergines being juggled, their melons prodded by a flow of exhibitionists who yell advice and pull each other from stall to stall, occasionally embracing when they make a good buy. One man went too far, and bit his friend on the neck as he kissed him. This started a row, the injured party showing the teeth-marks to passers-by while the other man protested that it was only a little bite. Finally they made up and kissed, of course—and the man bit him again and raced away, laughing his head off, with the twice-bitten man in pursuit.

Not only here but throughout Russia it is quite common for men to link arms or hold hands, but it is done in a way which doesn't suggest effeminacy at all. Sexual deviations, in fact, seem to be as rare as political ones—or, at least, as well-concealed. An Intourist girl in Moscow had told me: 'Prostitution and homosexuality have been wiped out in Russia.' She made this *ex cathedra* pronouncement as if she were announcing the extermination of wheat rust throughout the Union. Although I couldn't believe her, neither could I argue with her since I'd never seen an obvious tart or pederast. While I wouldn't say that a Soviet *News of the World* is an impossibility, it would need longer prongs on its muck-rake.

One racket which ought to be exposed is the official price-fixing of Intourist meals at a level which bears no relation to the cost of the raw materials. We bought a loaf, a large piece of goat cheese, butter, tomatoes and peaches—enough for four people altogether—for well under a rouble. Any restaurant meal always costs about three roubles. Another racket is the price of spirits. This was deliberately bumped up to discourage the few hardened sinners, who were un-moved by Khruschev's example in giving up the drink. The amount of brandy produced in Armenia should make it a cheap booze, but it isn't, and I'd been advised to buy the three-star, never the five-star. Having tried both, I was certain there wasn't any justification in making the five-star almost twice as expensive. Of course, five-star was the only brandy available in the market, and the discouragement policy worked on me quite successfully.

The brandy, or rather the lack of it, gave me an attack of tourist's conscience as I rode to the station in a hot car. There must have been a chance to see a brandy factory —and I'd missed it. Worse still, here I was about to quit the Soviet, and I hadn't visited a collective farm. As a matter of fact I had asked about both of these at the hotel (where, incidentally, the floor-maids had hung about for tips —first time ever), although I guessed that these visits would take a week or so to arrange. My estimate was on the short side.

Lingering in the corridor of the train, not knowing how to say goodbye, the shy youth opened up a little and told us that his father was a languages professor who translated English books. I gave him Muriel Spark's *Memento Mori*, and then he asked, with tense off-handedness, if there were any English newspapers I'd finished with. All I could find was a tattered copy of *The Guardian* which I'd bought an age ago in Helsinki. It was wrapped round some shoes in my bag, and was dirty as well as torn, but he folded it carefully and put it in his inside pocket. There was now no difficulty about saying goodbye. He smiled warmly, shook hands and loped away for a quiet, illicit read.

The train swings southwards from Erevan on a long curve that shifts the hard, hot square of sunlight from one side of the carriage to the other. The country shrinks to a narrow strip of arable land between two ranges of bleached and thirsty hills, which approach threateningly as if to squeeze the green juices out of the crops. After a while the pressure wins, and the fields degenerate into miserable patches before dying away altogether. Only then do the hills retreat, leaving behind a desiccated landscape where only odd clumps of thorny scrub can survive the whipping of the dust devils. A cow which had been too adventurous lay with legs sticking out stiffly from its distended barrel of a body.

The railway begins to hug the border, and soon it is Iran, not Turkey, on the other side of the Araxes River. Here the river is the border, but the point is triple-underlined with a barbed-wire fence, a raked stretch of ground (which just might be a minefield) and another barbed wire fence on the other bank. In case any deluded fool has ideas about trying out his wire-clippers, soldiers with automatic rifles leap from points along the whole length of the train at every stop. It is all done with a practised, casual air, and the soldiers joke easily with each other as they line both sides of the train, holding their rifles loosely—but you feel that the safety catch is off. Some of them patrol the crowd on the platform to make certain that nobody tries to stay behind with the vendors of melons, grapes and bread.

Although the stops are frequent—the train is *scheduled* to take seven hours for the 300-kilometre journey—mingling with the crowd is not the best escape plan. You would then have to get off the station, and, as I found out later, this is controlled too.

We were, of course, travelling soft class again. Soft class provides individual compartment service, and we rang for the attendant with confidence. There were the usual radio (this version fortunately had an off-position on the switch), adjustable ventilation, double-glazed windows and reading lamps. A slight drawback is that all compartments are sleeping compartments, and this means that the upper bunks stick out above your head in an intimidating way. I detected the heavy hand of Intourist in the fact that we never had any travelling companions.

There was a restaurant car on the train, and the attendant was visibly shocked that two people in soft class—two foreigners at that—should be making a picnic meal. We merely wanted a couple of glasses to finish off a bottle of *Tsinandalis* we had had since Tbilisi, but we largely ordered a couple of bottles of spring water as well. When the attendant brought them, I unthinkingly slid a few kopecks across the table to him. He spurned them vigorously, almost angrily, and I remembered that you don't tip anybody— barbers, taxi-drivers, lavatory-attendants, the lot. This doesn't mean that they never *accept* tips, but the excellent theory is that nobody requires them because nobody is being exploited in the matter of wages. And, as I say, some people get offended if you forget this.

Not so railway porters; you *have* to tip them at a fixed rate of thirty kopecks for every piece of luggage. Strictly speaking, this isn't tipping because the charge is mandatory, which means that most Russians carry their own luggage. If you let a porter take a hold-all, a brief-case and a camera—as I did— he is then entitled to ninety kopecks, and unless you're pre- pared to hang on grimly while he fishes out ten kopecks change for your rouble note—which I wasn't—he finishes up with the equivalent of eight shillings, a princely tip.

But it's difficult to avoid having a porter. It seems to be a rule that all people going soft class must employ a porter, even if he can only carry your hat. And if you're foreign you have to go soft class. This is a must, too. I had inquired, not too seriously, about hard class, and the Intourist refusal was adamant. It had been explained that hard class compart- ments were bedless and full of peasants carrying buckets of fruit and eggs to market. Definitely not for the likes of sir.

The uniformed woman in charge of our carriage was a motherly old body who was convinced that the bearded foreigners in number twelve were quite incapable of looking after themselves because they didn't speak Russian. Paul and

I were taking a breather in the corridor when a shrivelled Kurdish woman who had sneaked in from the hard class began begging from us. I only caught 'Pozholsta . . . babushka' (Please . . . grandmother), but her hand like the claw of a dead bird and her face, brown and shrunken inside the frame of her white head-dress, were eloquent enough, and I was reaching into my pocket willingly when the motherly body came bustling along and drove the crone off angrily. Then she came back and herded us into our compartment like a hen with foolish chicks.

I had been begged from before by a Kurdish woman—a young one this time, with a baby in her arms—while walking through a park in Tbilisi. And the reaction of the guide then had been the same sort of upbraiding. Are the Kurds natural beggars, or is their poverty something the citizen is ashamed of and therefore covers up with anger? Perhaps this was the Kurdish problem.

After this incident our mother hen kept popping her head in to see that we weren't being solicited through the window by Kurds hanging off the roof or sprinting alongside the train. She brought glasses of tea without being asked, and was amazed and delighted when she was thanked in Russian. (Russians are so childishly pleased and grateful when a foreigner speaks even a word of Russian that they open up like flowers. I'm really ashamed that I learned so little of the language.) In the last half-hour she warned us about five times of the approach of Djulfa, our stop, and eventually handed us carefully on to the platform.

A reception committee from Intourist awaited us—a man in a pearl-grey, Khruschev-type trilby and a tousle-headed interpreter who immediately put his cards on the table by saying that he spoke 'little-little' English (and he wasn't being modest). Djulfa looked like a whistle stop. I couldn't see any lights beyond the station, and when I asked where the town was the interpreter made a gesture up and down the platform. At the time I thought he hadn't understood the question. Later—much later—his answer made sense.

All the services we needed certainly seemed to be remarkably handy. No messing about with hotels and restaurants.

Everything was on the station. A room had been prepared for us off the Customs office and, when we wanted to eat, the station buffet would be delighted to serve us. Grey Trilby then cleared off, but our interpreter never left us for a second during the whole evening, although conversation died after a harrowing ten minutes. Eyes narrowed, forehead like a relief map with concentration, he would listen to Paul and me with painful attention but, no matter how much we pared our questions to the grammatical bone, he would end up shrugging, 'No onnerstan'. Little—little English.'

When we had washed at a tiny tap which eked out a tepid thread of water from a cistern at the back of the wash-stand, we were conducted to the buffet. The proprietor, a huge, bald djinn with gold teeth and a moustache like a spread of buffalo horns, gave us the VIP treatment, bowing us deeply into an inner room curtained off from the masses. (The masses consisted of two unshaven men in very wide flat caps who were drinking tea with the moodiness of drunks.) Menus were handed out with a flourish, but it was an empty gesture. Everything was off except chicken and *shashlik*. The chicken was ruinously expensive—nearly a pound—but it seemed worth lashing out on our last dinner in the Soviet. Also I was getting very tired of *shashlik*; in the last week or so I'd had enough to provide a barbecue for a Cossack troop. The chicken arrived cleavered down the middle and symmetrically spread-eagled. Even then it barely covered the plate, and I assumed it was a tender young thing which had barely lost its down. It turned out to be a wizened dwarf which had died of a fierce cramp. The tendons twanged like tennis-gut as I sawed at them, and the knotty little muscles were as hard and juiceless as crab-apples.

Our interpreter—I retain it purely as a courtesy title—watched in silent indifference as I wrestled with the dwarf. It was barely disarranged when I gave up for fear of spraining a wrist. The interpreter smiled slyly as he rose and led us back to our quarters. I noticed the bars on the window for the first time, and our translator's true function became clear when I went out to clean my teeth at the trickle. He had already settled down for the night on a couch just outside our door. He sat up quickly, then grinned shamefacedly when he saw that I held only a toothbrush. Obviously it was in standing orders that all lodgers at Djulfa were potential escapers and must therefore be guarded.

Our interpreter-guard was in for an uncomfortable night. Shunting went on desultorily outside the window for most of the time, the huge locomotives chuffing out steam with a peculiar whip-crack and occasionally screaming hysterically as they bumped into one another. I promised to take myself away from all this in the morning, to Iran.

THERE'S A LITTLE RAILWAY STATION
TO THE SOUTH OF AZERBAIJAN

PAUL and I hurried through breakfast, eager to be on our way, and came back to find three Customs officers waiting for us. They did a very thorough job on our hand baggage, opening everything which would open and prodding anything that wouldn't, and finally went off with our gramophone records and every scrap of paper with words on it, whether printed or written.

Their haul included my notebook, and I felt I'd made a large-calibre blunder in not secreting it about my person. It contained full details of my illegal deals not to mention some harsh comments on the system, militiamen and so on. I could only hope that their translator was the man with 'little-little' English. But everything was returned within the hour, all except a couple of newspapers—one in Georgian, one in Armenian—which had been bought for the weirdness of their typography rather than anything else. When we asked why these had been kept, we were told that taking newspapers out of the country was forbidden. They wouldn't, or couldn't, explain why.

Then we asked brightly where we could find the car. Was it already in Iranian Djulfa, or was it waiting in a siding in Soviet Djulfa? The demolishing answer was: 'Neither.' It hadn't arrived yet, but might possibly turn up tomorrow, or the day after. When we protested that it had been on the way for three days already, a spruce *Gauleiter* of an Army officer (he was in overall command of the station) told us curtly, in fairly good English, that we had no legal complaint until six days had passed. Six days to travel three hundred miles! The prospect was suddenly very bleak.

The *Gauleiter* briskly produced a form which gave permission for the car to be searched on arrival. All we had to do was sign it, and we would then be taken to Iranian Djulfa to await the car. Paul and I refused as one man, although for different reasons. I had a strong suspicion that if I wasn't present, the Customs officers would pelt each other with my exposed films like paper streamers. Paul felt just as strongly that they might unwittingly do the car a mischief. And if any further complications arose—such as the car not turning up at all—we'd be in a hopeless position to sort things out at the other side of the Iron Curtain.

Our refusal annoyed the *Gauleiter* considerably. Irritably he demanded our certificates of smallpox inoculation. We said we hadn't got the certificates but—here he cut us off with a nasty ha, ha, and stomped off, telling us to stay right there. Actually we had both been inoculated against smallpox, along with a number of other diseases, before we left. Although the jabs are free, certificates proving you've had them cost money, and since our kitty was low at the time, we'd taken the deed for the word. Iran hadn't been on the agenda then. But I still couldn't see what the *Gauleiter* was getting steamed up about. After all, we were *going* to Iran, not coming from it.

I tried to read some of the magazines laid out for detained unfortunates like us. There was only one in a language I could read—the *Nouveau Soviet*—but it was such a combination of sweetness and light and hopeless colour register that it gave me eyestrain. There was also a backgammon board of sorts. I'd seen the game, or something similar, being played in Athens, but if I ever knew the rules I'd forgotten them. Rather than sit biting our nails, however, Paul and I tried to play to rules I made up as I went along. It was a very dull game, and we were almost glad to see the *Gauleiter* reappear dragging a woman doctor with him. We tried to explain about the previous jabs. But how could we have been inoculated if we had no certificates? It wasn't worth arguing, so we rolled up our sleeves, and the *Gauleiter's* head jerked at each scratch, as if he'd have made them deeper. He was somebody to watch carefully, but not from choice, so we drifted out to have a look at the shunting trains buffeting each other about. We were already falling into a slow rhythm of living, and we watched the shunting quite happily for an hour before strolling in for lunch.

Chicken wasn't on—I must have had the last one—but I made a pretty show of hesitation before ordering the only possible dish, *shashlik*. It couldn't be worse than the chicken and, in fact, it was considerably better, at only a quarter of the price. After lunch we both felt strangely sleepy. Wild thoughts. We'd been injected with a soporific and we'd wake up in Djulfa, Iran—I'll have that woman struck off the register—let's get out into the air. We took our coffee out on to the platform, and the djinn hurried after us, flashing his gold teeth, with chairs and a table. Long-stifled ambition flared in his eyes. We were going to create a new fashion, a new focus of Azerbaijan society. The platform would be stiff with the wits of Ordubad and Nakhicevan.

But it wasn't easy to create the atmosphere of a terrasse. True, the station façade of pink and white and marzipan-green gave us a setting which wasn't altogether unworthy of the Promenade des Anglais. But we were flanked by two hideous, aluminium-painted statues of Lenin and Stalin, who were cutting each other dead and staring across the sidings at the hot mauve hills immediately in front of us. A huge honking Diesel carried on some heavy courting with an even larger loco, which was steaming passionately. The crackling loudspeaker gave out an endless song by an anguished eunuch. We decided to go for a stroll in the village.

Intuition suggested that this would not be officially approved, so we slipped quietly out of a side entrance. There was a minute park—a gritty cartwheel of baked earth about thirty yards across with a whitewashed frog sitting on the dry, cracked bowl of a fountain, and a couple of benches insufficiently shaded by some desiccated locust-trees. A group of men were playing the game we'd tried to play; my rules had been much too simple. *Nahrt*—as it is called in Azerbaijan—is a game for two players and any number of onlookers. A rubber consists of three or four games of increasing complexity of disposition and types of moves of the draughts. It is always played with great speed, panache and, above all, noise. Each throw of the dice brings groans or shouts of triumph. Each move starts an argument among the fiercely partisan onlookers, who occasionally intervene with force to stop their champion making an idiot of himself.

We were invited to play, but it was like a grand master of chess challenging a schoolboy, and we excused ourselves, saying we had to get on with our tour. Not that there was much to tour. The village consisted of a couple of rutted, dusty streets dotted at intervals with faded pink houses. The afternoon lay still under the weight of the sun, and the sprayed lances of tubby palms were etched, stiff as iron, against the flat glare of the walls. A solitary, shawled woman was moving in the heat, her shadow like a black serif at her feet. One hand on hip, the other steadying the pot of water on her shoulder, she hesitated as she approached, then stopped and stared openly as we passed, as if we were a couple of giraffes ankling fastidiously down the street.

The main street was the one leading straight to the river and the bridge which crosses to Iran. A man in a crumpled uniform of khaki drill froze in the act of picking his nose and looked at us speculatively. Before his speculations ripened we moved off as casually as possible, away from the river. Outside a wooden building which looked as if it had been leaned on heavily at some time, there was a notice chalked on a blackboard. I made out 'Kino' and the fact that a film was being shown that evening, and I was moving my lips as I worked through the title of the film when a man said, in an accent I can't reproduce, 'Aimez-vous la musique?' I said we did, and we were invited inside.

I thought he might be running the film through and wanted company. I could hear a wild music skirling faintly beyond the door, but when he opened it we were right in the middle of a spontaneous session of folk-music. The room was full, but nobody paid any attention as we sidled in. All eyes were on the musicians—a plump, unshaven man whose left hand quivered and darted along the nacre-inset finger-board of his instrument, drawing from it a pure nostalgia, sometimes piercing, sometimes savage, which was driven along by the thrumming and pinging of a drum under the snapping fingers of a thin, serious boy.

There was no applause, no requests for songs from the audience, who seemed to be as knowledgeable, as integral a part of the whole thing, as the musicians. The taut atmosphere which built up during the music relaxed into quiet chatter, a little laughter while the man re-tuned his *tahr*. (*Tahr* is the local name for this plectrum-played instrument, a kind of wasp-waisted mandolin with a goatskin sounding-board. The Russian word is *skripka*.) Then there were songs from the women, who stood up gripping chair-backs like worshippers giving testament, and the tension rose and fell, rose and fell. Although I didn't understand a single word I could feel the power of the music generating a corporate possession, an excitement as fierce as a revival meeting. But I would guess that the songs were nationalistic rather than religious, harking back to the rare, precarious periods when the country was its own ruler.

The climax came when a very old man was moved to sing. Sitting in the classic folk-song pose, astraddle his chair and with one hand cupped round his ear, he sang, eyes screwed shut, with a power which shook his body. His thin neck became ropy with veins as he swept downwards in a final plangent cadenza with the breath-control of a flamenco singer. And that was it. The *tahr*-player hung up his instrument the boy unclamped his knees from around the drum, and everyone was standing up, all tension finally released.

The very old man asked my opinion of his singing. The tone of my 'Harosh!' seemed to satisfy him. I decided to come back in the evening and see the film in case there was another music session afterwards.

We slipped back into the station as quietly as we had gone. Nobody seemed to have missed us. The platform was already full of villagers chatting and strolling up and down as they waited for the daily train from Erevan. They weren't expecting anyone, and only a few of them had anything to sell. It was simply something to do. When the train came in, the people bustled about feverishly. When the train went out they stopped bustling as if a current had been switched off, drifting away like mourners, no further excitement for the day in view.

But wait. I didn't know what time the film started. Maybe they were all going to that. Dinner became secondary and we followed the peasants out through the main entrance. Much too confidently. We hadn't gone five yards when we were collared by an armed soldier and taken back to the *Gauleiter*. He laid on a great exhibition of military dudgeon, stalking up and down in his gleaming, brown jack-boots and blue breeches as he threw the book at us. Apparently we'd broken most of the rules in it, since the village was strictly out of bounds, and we would in future confine ourselves to the station. Otherwise certain steps would be taken.

I suspected that we were becoming an embarrassment to the *Gauleiter*, and he was therefore trying to make us so screamingly bored that we'd beg to be taken to Iran. Further pressure came from Grey Trilby, who sent for us as we were toying moodily with some *shashlik*. We were told to move our stuff out of the room to make way for a woman who had arrived on the train. We were also told to settle accounts with the buffet proprietor. By this time, Paul and I had got into the habit of airily waving aside the bills, and telling the djinn to add it all up when we finally left. The waving was not as airy as it looked since we had very few roubles left. I asked Grey Trilby about changing traveller's cheques. This was possible in Iranian Djulfa, he said, but here in Soviet Djulfa only pounds sterling could be changed. He was quite unmoved when I explained that our total stock of sterling was two pounds.

This anxiety to get rid of us made us even more determined to stay until the car arrived. Maybe they'd already heard that it had been stolen *en route* and wanted us out of the place before we could lodge a legal complaint. We went back and finished our congealed *shashlik*, and wiped the expectant smile off the djinn's face by telling him to put yet another meal on the slate.

A lonely walk to the far end of the platform to think. The station was now deserted except for a single engine shunting in a distant siding, and whistling to keep up its spirits. The echo from the hills was lost in the still-wailing loudspeaker. In the pauses between songs, a studio clock ticked deafeningly—the fast, tinny tick of a cheap alarm clock.

October 3

There seemed little point in bouncing out of bed, so I didn't. The lie-in developed into a levée, Louis Quatorze style. First the *Gauleiter* stamped in and rapped out a trick question.

'Iran—yes or no?'

'Has the car arrived?'

'No.'

'Likewise.'

He made the floor-boards bounce as he went out. I had hardly turned over when Grey Trilby entered to announce a change of party line on traveller's cheques. A little man shuffled in behind him with an attaché case of roubles. I had never had to sign a cheque in bed before and found it decadent, slothful and wholly delightful.

Over breakfast we tried to plan the day which stretched ahead in a sunlit vacuum. The first problem was how to give the day's meals an illusion of variety. After a breakfast of boiled eggs (not so much boiled as briefly baptized in hot water), the choice was narrowed brutally for the remaining meals. There was *bortsch* or there was *shashlik*. Once a day is enough for either of these, and the choice is simply which one to have for lunch. The other then becomes dinner. We decided on *bortsch* for lunch with a slab of goat-cheese.

Dinner, then, was *shashlik* and to take off the curse we gave an advance order for *blinchiki*. As expected, the djinn started some nonsense about the humidity not being right for *blinchiki* but he suddenly became one large servile smile when we paid our account in full. The *blinchiki* would be ready whenever we wanted them. That was the menu fixed. What else? There were the trains, of course—one from Baku at three and one from Erevan at eight. They would absorb half an hour each, say. Of course, there was always reading. Except that I was getting through my books too quickly. And writing. Except that there was very little to write about. I squinted up at the brazen sun for inspiration, and my worries were over.

My swimming trunks were in the car along with the sun-cream, and I had to improvise with Y-fronts and a bottle of almond oil. At one end of the platform was a plot of scorched grass, half-concealed by a straggle of bushes and littered with tired scraps of paper and the crumpled tubes of *papirosa*. But once I was on my back, the tatty plot, the station, Djulfa itself slid away, and I was in the mindless red-veiled world of the sun-worshipper. I was brought back to earth at intervals by the insect life. Hornets whanged past frequently. The flies on the other hand all dropped in for a taste of almond oil, leaving tiny red marks on my skin. These flies had the stupid bravery of samurais and preferred death before dishonourable flight.

Their cousins in the buffet were much more sophisticated. They were always thick on the tables, but scrambled like a fighter squadron at the lift of a finger. I once poked my head into the kitchen (I was trying to explain how to boil an egg), and saw fly-papers hanging from the ceiling like bats in a cave, each one an overcrowded mortuary, thick and black as a slab of currants. And this was October. In summer the fly must take over in Djulfa. But the sun was glorious and as long as the hornets didn't become unpleasant I was staying where I was. Then I turned on my stomach and I saw the ants.

Even the hornets would have had trouble moving me then. Ever since I was small I have been fascinated by ants. These coppery scraps of insect intelligence are like atoms of pure energy, the quintessence of drive as they push their beautifully articulated bodies to the limit. Being short-sighted I have almost microscopic vision at short range and, with my nose almost touching the ants as they hurried through the grass jungle, I could appreciate the exquisite engineering of their legs, the elegant jointing in their armour. Although I can't give them their proper names, I noted at least three Azerbaijan species. There was a tiny cinnamon-coloured tribe, so frail they were almost translucent, who darted up and down the grass-blades like crumbs of amber; a brown ant, medium sized, which hunted in packs; and a huge black beast which travelled fast and alone, its abdomen cocked menacingly.

The cinnamon ants trusted to their nippiness to keep out of harm's way and froze if a shadow fell on them. The brown ants seemed fearless, and were foraging hard. A millipede undulated innocently into a pack of them, and they jumped him like a rush-hour crowd hitting a tube train. A tense tug-of-war developed, with the millipede hanging on grimly against the pull of half-a-dozen ants until more ants came racing over as if a bugle had sounded. Then the millipede hadn't got enough legs, and it was soon being half-dragged, half-carried towards the nest, its shiny button of nose waving desperately at the air.

I would have thought, if only because of its size and vicious, ebony mandibles, that the black ant gave way for nothing among the grass roots. But I discovered that it travelled fast to avoid trouble. I found this out when one of them ran on to my stomach. When it realized that the ground had gone strangely pale, it stopped. I didn't like the look of the nervously wagging abdomen, and I knocked it off with a flick which stunned it for a few seconds. But in that short time is was discovered by brown ants, and when the black ant came round it was following the one-way trail of the millipede. I could almost sense the dawning horror as the big, glossy head swivelled from side to side, and then the black ant was fighting with desperate panic for its life. But the brown foragers didn't give up when they found that the big beast wasn't dead at all. They piled in like terriers on a bull, being flung off but landing on their feet and boring back in immediately.

The black ant caught one, two of its tormentors and squeezed the life out of them with quick, steel-plier nips. But, rapid as they were, the executions were a waste of time, time which allowed the other ants to jab and probe for the gaps in the armour beneath the body. A stand-up battle could only have ended one way. The black ant seemed to realize this, and began a lumbering trot, each leg weighted with one or two brown ants. Rushing blindly through the grass, it finally brushed off all but a couple of the brown ants, and it was their turn to panic when they found they were all alone.

By this time the big ant could have stopped and finished them off, but it never slackened its pace, and didn't even notice when the last ant fell off. It was a very scared black ant indeed, and I couldn't say I blamed it. Those brown ants were really hard cases. When I looked back at the scene of the fight they were already dragging their slain comrades towards the nest. And I don't think there was any heroes' burial in mind.

I overdid the watching a bit. When the Baku train pulled in, I couldn't focus on it properly, and my back was beginning to glow hotly. An armed soldier sprinted across my plot, throwing me a brief surprised glance as he ran to his key position at the now-locked side exit. I pulled on trousers and a vest and took my place among the crowd extras on the platform. My beachcomberish rig didn't attract the slightest attention. Not surprising, since usually about half of the passengers who get down to stretch their legs are wearing lurid pyjamas. It's a comfortable way of travelling in a hot train besides keeping suits uncrumpled.

The pyjama'd peacocks are the stars, and the whole scene revolves around them. If they want to buy fruit, there is a line of villagers squatting beside pails of grapes and kerchiefs of peaches. A kiosk is open to sell them sweets or newspapers or even to send a telegram. The drinking fountain, switched on half a minute before the train arrives, gushes liberally to fill their water-bottles. And, of course, they are protected from dangerous temptations by a line of soldiers.

I bought a bunch of grapes, washed them under the fountain and strolled about as an auxiliary to the pyjama brigade. The *Gauleiter* was trying to steal their limelight by rushing from one end of the train to the other, bellowing orders to the driver, the guard and the villagers who were unloading supplies for the buffet—cases of beer and soda-water, a side of sheep and jars of pickled cucumbers. I recognized these villagers and they recognized me; we had listened to music together yesterday. But only one—the French speaker—gave me a brief nod before hurrying on. When the *Gauleiter* was about I was clearly an unsafe person to know. It was understandable. If he caught them hobnobbing with foreigners, he might easily forbid them the station—if nothing worse—and they would then be cut off from the hub of the village, the life-line with Baku.

The passengers climbed aboard, followed by the soldiers closing in like sheepdogs; the fruit-sellers picked up their buckets and scales; the *Gauleiter* did a last pompous march down the platform, and the train rumbled off unhurriedly. As the last carriage clacked past, the fountain died with a strangled sigh, and Djulfa returned to arid boredom. I returned to the ants.

The scrawny bushes were rustling in a cool breeze, and their shadows had already claimed more than half my plot. Further sun-bathing was impossible, so I sneaked out of the side exit and into the park to watch the *nahrt* game. Dust spiralled thinly about the legs of the players, and the rattle of the dice was echoed by the brittle, black pods hanging from the trees. The *kibitzers* were as mercurial as children, changing without warning from intense seriousness to horse-play—a rough, rustic horse-play of thumping and shoving, which everyone enjoyed tremendously. As the light faded, the players and the *kibitzers* all leant forward until their dark faces fused into a dusky backdrop. And when the last counter was slapped down with a triumphant crack, the backdrop shivered with huge laughter, gold teeth glinting like nuggets of iron pyrites in a coal seam.

For lack of something to do, I went and plagued Grey Trilby to put a call through to Tbilisi to see if the car had left there, and also one to Moscow to check if the Albanian visas had been dispatched. He waffled uneasily as he explained that a call to Moscow must be booked a day in advance, and quickly changed the subject by telling me that we had been moved back to our old room. I knew he wouldn't make either of the calls, but at least my demands disturbed him. Not a soul got off the Erevan train, and the crafty old djinn left us dinnerless by closing the buffet early. Some people will do anything to avoid preparing *blinchiki*

153

—but he would make them tomorrow if I had to stand over him while he did it.

Dinner was now a simple affair of half a bruised peach each. A shunter with a grudge was shaking the earth with clangorous wallops, each one setting off a chain of clanks receding to infinity; Paul was nursing a wasp-sting and brooding about septicaemia, amputation and death.

October 4

The first item of interest was that I was stung by the same wasp. I was trying to sneak a photograph of the platform through the heavy bars on the window when I put my elbow on the beast. Retribution was crushing, and I left the body on the window ledge, like a brightly jerseyed Admiral Byng. The second item was the rebellious state of my guts; I mustn't have washed those grapes very thoroughly. My frequent walks along the platform often finished as sprints. Third item was that I seemed to be going slightly native. I descended to breakfast in a vest. Never even thought of putting a shirt on.

Also decided on a revolutionary change of menu—*shashlik* for lunch, *bortsch* for dinner. I added that we would take our valuable custom elsewhere—Iran, for example—if he shut early once more, and that, if *blinchiki* were not on at dinner, I would have him staked out near the brown ants with jam on his head. The jam available, a runny preserve of prunes, was weighed like caviar when you bought it, and came almost as expensive—but I think I convinced him that I was a desperate man about my pancakes.

When I settled down for some sunbathing, word seemed to have got around among the brown ants that I was the great white mountain that threw food. Some of them were waiting about like cricketers on the boundary, and when I flicked off a stupid fly it was fielded beautifully and probably never knew what bit it. The ants and I were soon having a great game, with me driving flies all round the wicket and the ants racing to cut them off before the boundary. No ant ever actually caught a fly in full flight, and I carried my finger, so to speak, through the match.

My early irritation at being stranded had disappeared completely. I don't know if this was true philosophical acceptance or merely the indifference of the lotus-eater, but the pulse of events now seemed pleasantly unhurried rather than sluggish. *Was* I in the first stages of going native? I know that when I heard the fountain start its extravagant splashing, I rose without thinking and was waiting with the fruit-sellers when the train from Baku steamed in. And although I didn't lend a hand, I instinctively followed the locals into the buffet as they trundled the daily consignment of crates inside. In this way I found out why there was rarely any beer available in the evening. All the helpers got perks —a couple of bottles of the weak, cloudy beer still warm from the train journey. Their friends also crowded in, and more beer was ordered—in half-dozens or even crates—and soon a serious session was under way.

Following the local custom, I sprinkled salt in my beer (it couldn't make it taste worse, and it might settle some of the floating matter), and bought a plate of cold, boiled legumes from a man going from table to table with a sackful of them. They looked like a pea-sized chestnut and tasted of lentils. These, plus the salt, increased the thirst effectively, and all the beer was finished within an hour of its arrival. In case anyone arrived on the night train, the djinn tucked away a crate in the VIP room (we now boycotted this stuffy alcove and ate in the main buffet), but sometimes even this must be decimated by a good afternoon session. However, the beer was so weak that it was a physical impossibility to get drunk on it; you'd burst before you could get enough down. Of course, mine host had a couple of bottles of 3-star Azerbaijan cognac gathering dust on a shelf, but at five roubles for a small bottle they could stay dusty.

No, on second thoughts I wasn't going native. I was still far from understanding how the locals put up with their lot. The station was their club, their pub, their high life, and yet they were checked in and out of it by soldiers. Once inside they could choose between bloating themselves with near-beer or sitting in one of the hard pews in the waiting-room surrounded by notices forbidding smoking and spitting and a couple of grisly posters showing the symptoms of trachoma. Very few villagers would ever travel to Baku or Erevan, but the station must represent escape to them. Their home life could hardly be appetizing: the women were nothing to shout about when young and something to avoid when old; the gastronomic peak was iron-sinewed chicken; *nahrt* took the place of religion. And the climate, delicious now, must be a fly-blown hell in the hot months. The only advantage was the scarcity of work, which left a man free for the important business of talking with his friends.

That night we got our *blinchiki*, but when they arrived they were as cold as lettuce leaves.

IN A COMMON MARKET, PERSIAN STYLE

October 5

Lying in bed was difficult, but I was persevering. With the
sheet up it was too warm; with the sheet down the flies
tickled. I was musing on the daring innovation of having
bortsch for breakfast when Grey Trilby walked in, smiling
broadly, and announced that the *machina* had arrived. The
transformation was immediate. We raced out to see if the
machina was really there. Sure enough, there the old
battler was, still managing to gleam gold and green under
the dust of nearly six days' crawling travel. I was so glad
to see it I let out a yip that frightened a shunter. Paul
couldn't trust himself to speak.

Pilferers had been at work. Both rear mirrors and most of
the lamp bulbs had gone. Somebody had had a hasty
rummage in the back, and stolen a weird selection of things.
A camera, typewriter and tape-recorder had been ignored,
but cotton-wool and scissors were missing from the first-aid
chest and—most stupid and annoying of all—three films
had been stolen. They were exposed films, valueless to the
thieves but irreplaceable to me. A whole crate of unexposed
films in their cellophane was untouched. And the dash-
board clock, which had an endearing habit of swinging out
on its hinge when the going got rough, was missing, too.
It was a handsome clock with a knurled-brass, nautical look
about it, and it took me several days to stop noticing the
gaping eye-socket where it had been.

A squad of Customs men began swarming over the car
like ants on a helpless, green beetle, tugging viciously at
its innards until it lay like a disembowelled shell. After
they had discovered the last sheet of Georgian newspaper
(it was wrapped around some dirty underwear), they allowed
us to embowel the car again. It was then left in the siding
until a locomotive with a dependable card-holding driver

could be found to shunt it to Iran. While transport was being found to take us and our luggage to the border, I had a last couple of hours in the sun with the ants, flicking a lot of flies to them.

We had to see the djinn again because we had some roubles left after we'd settled our bill for accommodation. We weren't allowed to keep them, and Grey Trilby wasn't handing out any pounds sterling in exchange. But he actually handed back one of our cheques for some roubles; the remainder we had to spend in the buffet. The only possible thing was the djinn's 3-star brandy. It was terrible stuff, smelling of burnt caramel and I was glad when we finished it.

A grey, bent woman who got off the Baku train looked increasingly like a refugee poster as it was explained to her that she must also spend all her roubles. She joined us on the cramped seats of a canvas-hooded truck, clutching a pile of chocolate bars and with three large suitcases which took up most of the room. The *Gauleiter* sat with the driver, two armed soldiers climbed up behind, and we bounced dustily through Djulfa to the bridge on the Araxes river. (For this short, uncomfortable ride we were charged two roubles.) Here the gates were unlocked, and we drove on to the bridge as far as the barrier at the dead centre. Beyond the barrier the colour scheme of the bridge was different. The soldiers stepped down and stood rigid guard on either side, rifles across their chests, as if Lenin's embalmed remains were in the truck.

The Iranians were in no great hurry to come and open up. I could see a few guards at the far end of the bridge walking about chatting and smoking, and it was fifteen minutes before a sort of imitation jeep drove up to the other side of the gate. Just before getting out to meet it, the *Gauleiter* turned to me and said, 'I hope you enjoyed your stay in Djulfa.' It was said with heavy irony, but I couldn't think of a sufficiently withering reply. I could only hope that his posting was permanent. He came from somewhere well north of the Caucasus—he had a very Russian face—and another couple of years in Djulfa should take the shine off his jack-boots.

The bridge is demarcated into a Russian half and an Iranian half by a white line. Our luggage was marshalled six inches from it. Then our driver carefully placed his foot parallel to, and two inches from, the line before lifting over the bags one by one. Watched grimly by the Iranians, he was very careful not to infringe their territory, literally leaning over backwards to avoid it. Swap-overs like this could hardly have been uncommon, but not a word, not a smile, crossed the white line. The operation took place in a thunderous silence, and I could hear the light tapping of pigeons unconcernedly pecking at the planking of the bridge.

The *Gauleiter* wordlessly invited us to step across the line. I found myself judging the step as if I were going to stride over a narrow but deep cleft. I instinctively checked my balance; then I lifted my foot higher and strode further than necessary to cross the line. Stepping on it would have been unthinkable. The barrier was re-padlocked, the officers turned their backs on each other without as much as a salute, and we joggled over the rest of the bridge into Iran.

The village—still called Djulfa—was, if anything, slightly scruffier than its sister across the river. But I saw it as a different world, and it looked very good. Even the people looked handsomer, friendlier, more dapper. We were ushered into an office at the Customs, and immediately offered tea, a pleasant touch of hospitality to find in officialdom. A large photograph of the Shah when young looked down on us dashingly like Rupert of Hentzau. We stared at this in order to avoid studying too closely the military-looking maps, which appeared much too secret to be papering the walls. The old woman handed round pieces of chocolate, and we sat munching and sipping scalding tea in the fading light. A procession of officials, both uniformed and civilian, popped in and out of the office, each one flicking at the light switch but getting no result because the generator hadn't started up for the evening.

At last three men settled down at a table with our documents. A young officer and a razor-faced type in a snap-brim trilby flanked the chief official, a bowed, paper-thin old man with an aristocratic tremble in his lean fingers. He asked his questions in French, in a gentle flute of a voice. His aides preserved their stern expression as he translated to them, moving his head from side to side like an aged, silvery bird and then they all began scribbling away. It was mesmerizing to watch three hands all writing backwards. Our passports were returned with a courtly bow, several pages now looking as if someone had been testing a pen on them, and we were conducted to the guest house.

Here we found that we were sharing a room with the old woman. After a concerted protest, the proprietor moved her bed to another room, but he clearly thought we were making a lot of unnecessary fuss. The dining-room was a hideously bare place in an unhealthy green distemper, and with a refrigerator stuck right in the middle of the floor. The proprietor was very proud of it, and he produced eggs, tomatoes and Dutch Pilsener out of its interior with the gestures of a magician. Our waiter was a moronic youth who looked as if he had just finished mucking out the stables. He scorned the use of a tray, and everything he served was gripped firmly in his very grubby hands. He did use a dish to bring in a depressed omelette, but he delivered the bread like a stack of newspapers. The bread comes in large, thin wafers rather like huge chapatis (bakeries must cover quite an acreage), and I took a leaf from the middle of the stack and hoped for the best.

The old woman was a well-prepared traveller. She came in with a plastic mac full of food and washed most of it down with half-a-dozen glasses of tea. I asked some sharply-dressed bloods of the village where I could buy some cigarettes. One who spoke English asked in return if I wanted to change any currency. He assured me it was all perfectly legal—flashing a wallet with a fiver and a wad of dollars as credentials—but I had no pounds left. He must have been in a fair way of business because he gave me two packets of cigarettes.

I think the Persians must be a small race. The cigarettes are slender miniatures, and as I lay in bed, waltzing through

Erevan, Armenia. Stalin on a plinth of tufa in the park. (Presumably this statue, the biggest erected to Stalin, has now been demolished.)

Erevan, Armenia. Peasant on a pile of melons in the market

View through our barred window at Djulfa, Azerbaijan

Camel, driver and car, Iran

these in half-a-dozen puffs each, my feet stuck eighteen inches beyond the mattress.

October 6

Djulfa is not letting us go too easily. We were hoping for an early start, but this hope went down without trace in a sea of officialdom. Persian officials are clearly a power in the land, and go about their business with the solemnity and unhurried ritual of high priests. We were conducted by three officials to the railway station where five more joined them, including the silvery chairman, for a game of pass-the-passport. There was no music, but at certain given moments the person holding the passport had to write something in it. In this way we soon had another couple of pages filled. Another official entered to announce that the car could not be unshackled until the shunting fee of eight tumars was paid (which worked out at £4 for a kilometre). This is where we stepped on to a merry-go-round.

I started by explaining our difficulty to the gentle old flautist, dropping naturally into his archaic periods.

'Figure to yourself, dear sir, our impasse. We have no money of Iran to pay this good man.'

'That, it is formidable.'

'Is it possible that one can change a voyager's cheque in this prosperous village?'

'One can contrive something, that goes of itself.'

He called over a couple of big-eyed children and explained the mission. They seemed to understand, and we followed their shaven heads on a tour of the village. Through a miserably tiny market—some sacks of melon seeds and a few handfuls of scarred tomatoes with half-asleep vendors —across the hard-trodden earth of a parade ground, where a line of soldiers stood at rock-still attention, their sleeves rolled up for a shot from the surgeon, and into weaving, hushed alleys deeply silted with powder-dry dung. It was still early for the business world of Djulfa. The first man we knocked up appeared for a tousled ten seconds and smartly referred us to another man. He also came to the door in pyjamas, but agreed to dress and take us to a money-changer. With him leading and the two children bringing up the rear, we threaded in the opposite direction through the dung-deadened alleys, past high mud walls shot with the mosaic glint of straw. The money-changer turned the cheque down firmly. It wasn't even printed on the back like real money.

An hour or so later after leaving the station I was picking up the threads of the conversation again.

'I have failed to realize the cheque, sir.'

'I am desolated. Now it is necessary that you go to Tabriz to change it.'

'But the auto is still enchained.'

'It is not worth the candle to disengage it.'

'I do not comprehend.'

'Tabriz holds a holy day. The banks will be closed.'

Half an hour later, a quorum agreed that it might be possible to change a cheque and, without a murmur, took the already signed cheque we'd had returned by Grey Trilby. The date was wrong, but it did have Djulfa written on it. After a last burst of squiggling on our documents, the car was released and an interpreter accompanied us to the petrol dump. I say dump because there were no pumps; the petrol was in cans and once a can was opened you had to take the lot. By the time we'd packed and were ready for the road, it was three o'clock. The old woman was still waiting for something when we left. Customs clearance; someone to collect her; death? She looked as if she didn't much care.

To be on the move again, to be leaving Djulfa at last, was fiercely exhilarating. It was like leaping over a prison wall and seeing how dazzlingly colourful the outside world still was. The country looked like a kid's crayon drawing. Lion-yellow hills, scribbled uninhibitedly with green and red and purple, were pinned under a solid blue block of sky in which the sun really *did* send out rays. And a black train puffed white smoke as it crawled across the plain ahead of us.

We went after it like a whippet, but the lay-off had shortened the car's wind, and as the road began to climb the radiator puffed like another train. A nearby stream saved us from using our can of water to top up the radiator, and we carried on climbing at a slow grind until a soldier flagged us down. He simply wanted a lift. At the rate we were going we needed a push not a passenger, but it's difficult to refuse a lift once you've stopped, and quickly we told him to hop on the back. There was a military exercise of sorts going on, and it looked as if our man was the officer in charge by the way the soldiers along the road suddenly shot to attention as he appeared. At a rough block-house the officer jumped off and laughed his thanks. But his men didn't join in. They stood frozen, hands down the seams of their baggy trousers, faces straining up at the sky, awaiting permission to start breathing again.

The asthma the car always develops at heights began to clear as soon as we started to run down the other side of the Karadagh, and it had disappeared altogether by the time we reached Marand. This was the first sizeable town, and was as Eastern as a travelogue-maker could have wished. As long, that is, as you concentrated on the women who, with their natural conservatism, clung to their robes and veils. They milled prettily around a fountain, swaying away carrying their earthenware pots with all the expected grace. Some, with less grace, squatted by an open conduit, bashing their laundry monotonously. But the men were not in keeping at all. Firmly Western in dress, they stood about in idle groups, chatting and punching each other in the chest, or cycled around the fountain in slow wobbly circles. As we took the fork for Khoi, they bellowed an anachronistic chorus of 'Good morning'.

The first camel, although it looked completely at home, came as a surprise, and I made a photographic fuss of it. With monumental composure it presented its best profile, and looked suitably disdainful when its ill-favoured owner came hobbling over the scrub. He posed alongside alike a scrofulous Napoleon, one hand scratching busily inside his shirt. After this the camels came thick and fast; lolloping along carrying huge swaying nets of fodder which almost brushed us off the road; towering out of a herd of horses near the camp of some nomad Kurds whose wild, gypsyish children raced from the tents to yell and wave at us. Shepherds urged their flocks home with high, trilling shouts, and in the dipping sun the sheep moved slowly in a glowing nimbus of gold dust.

Driving along the narrow main street of Khoi, I had the idea that we must have got off the road and were driving through a market prohibited to vehicles. Scores of tiny shops and stalls lined both sides of the street, their peppers, grapes and melons forming framed still-lifes of jewelled colour under naked electric bulbs swaying in the warm breeze. People jammed the road from wall to wall, and we drove with them, not through them. This leisured progress allowed me to compare hotels, but there was nothing to choose between them. They all looked like flea-pits. I chose the one with the most pictures of the Shah and his new wife and heir; we might as well be bitten by Royalist fleas. Paul and I had to eat in our room, squatting uncomfortably on the beds. This was because we'd also ordered beer. If you must drink the stuff, the law states that you have to do it out of the outraged public gaze.

But you can drink tea until your eyes turn amber—and the Persians do. I found this out on a crawl of the tea-shops. Most of these were cramped alcoves so narrow that you had to pass within singeing distance of the wood-burning water geyser at the entrance. A couple of the better-class ones had enough elbow room to provide customers with *narghiles*. There is no need to order in any of these shops because tea is the only thing served. And it is served fast and almost continuously.

The waiter—often he is the proprietor as well—appears at your table as if he is about to do some sleight of hand, clutching about six small glasses of tea and with a scalloped fringe of saucers interleaved between his fingers. Before your bottom has hit the chair, he has swung a saucer and glass before you in one movement. There is always some spillage in the saucer; this you throw on the floor before lifting your glass and drinking the scalding tea as rapidly as your tongue will allow. When you finish your glass, or allow it to get cool, another one replaces it immediately. The only way I found of stopping this process was to stand up at the same time as I put the glass down and move for the door.

The most entertaining of the tea-shops was about the size of a horse-box. This one had a troubadour, who also acted as barker outside. He played a version of the *tahr* (it had the usual mandolin-shaped body, inlaid with a whole oyster-bed of mother-of-pearl), and he was also a ballad-monger and story-teller. Later I discovered that he was from Baghdad, and that his tales were told in instalments with pauses for song in between—splendid tales of moguls, viziers, thieves and princesses whose beauty dimmed the jewels they wore. His tales may have been borrowed from Scheherezade; his technique certainly was, and his audience sat as if carved, hardly daring to slurp their tea in case the hypnotic flow was broken.

The story-teller stalked up and down in the narrow gap between the two ranks of customers, his voice swooping from a dove-like throatiness to biting harangue as the tale demanded. Then he would do a theatrical about-turn, almost sweeping the tea from someone's hand with the long neck of the *tahr*, and delicately pick out the bitter-sweet introduction to a high, wavering song. After his song the last sharp notes would be allowed to fade in a well-judged pause before he picked up the thread of the story again, his black eyes glittering.

When we came to pay, we found that some soldiers who'd left just before had already paid for our tea. We hadn't even spoken to them. In fact, we couldn't speak to anybody. English and French were no use, and my attempts with Turkish straight from the phrase-book were just as hopeless. Then Ali introduced himself and his two cousins as gentlemen who wished to practise their English. This meant visiting more tea shops, although by this time I was swilling as I walked. Ali had the charm of an out-of-work gigolo and the profile of a matinée idol. By all the rules he should have turned out to be a complete villain. Instead he talked about his driving test. At first he referred to it as a bus examination, which obscured the issue for a time. He told us that he was from Teheran (I thought the charm was too polished to be locally grown), but that he'd come to Khoi because it was an easier test here where the only traffic jams were caused by people.

Even so it couldn't have been all that easy. It took four days. This stringency is in line with the Iranian treatment of careless driving—or plain unlucky driving—which is very rough indeed. As soon as there is a car accident, all interested parties—which means everyone who isn't dead—are arrested pending investigation. Guilty parties are often given long jail sentences without any nonsense about the option of a fine. I understood why pedestrians are so uninhibited about strolling about in the road. Every car-driver is sweating blood in case someone merely brushes against a mudguard.

I was drinking what I swore would be my last glass of tea for the night, and listening to one of the cousins explaining that a hard winter was judged by the number of lean wolves driven to scavenge the streets of Khoi, when a policeman came in and saluted with tremendous dash. His cap was hardly visible behind an enormous, dazzling badge, and his uniform looked as if it had been on the road with *The Student Prince*. But his English was remarkably rapid and mistake-free as he told us that tomorrow we must collect a permit to leave from the Secret Police. Maybe he put the secret bit in for added drama. At least, when I asked how we could find their undercover headquarters, he said that anybody would know.

October 7

Once upon a time I thought that the police were on my side, on the side of everybody who was going reasonably straight. I don't think this any more. My innocence stemmed, I suppose, from an idealized portrait of the British bobby, the barge-booted, large-hearted, serge-suited protector of me and mine. But for the past six weeks I have been cannoning from one policeman to another, all of them more or less nasty. And not only in Russia.

166

Take the secret police in Khoi. When we went to collect permission to leave we were kept waiting about for an hour. A slender young man with a pencil moustache and sharp lightweight suit waved us to chairs with a preoccupied air, and continued to shuffle a few bits of paper around on his desk with a frown of concentration which suggested that the fate of a nation was in his hands. When he became tired of this, he went away for a rest. I smoked and looked out on a small, swept courtyard, as bare as a billiard table. The office didn't have an ashtray, and I flicked the stub into the courtyard. Immediately a large, tawny dog bounded out and pointed at it, quivering. A soldier followed, picked up the stub, stared at me through the window, more in sorrow than anger, and returned indoors with it. Either this was tidiness on the Swiss level or the cigarette was being retrieved to be analysed for hashish or messages in invisible ink.

When the slender young man considered us sufficiently apprised of how busy and important a personage he was, he came back and made out the permits. The less weight specimens of this breed have, the more they want to throw it around. There was further corroboration of this on the way back to the hotel, when a policeman prevented me taking a photograph—a photograph of a minaret crowned with a stork's nest. Such crass officiousness can only come from a desire to push people around. I have now developed a strong suspicion of the urge that makes anyone *want* to police his fellows.

Ali and one of his cousins were waiting for us at the hotel; whatever we wanted to do or see, their time was at our disposal. I asked if I could buy a Persian lamb hat anywhere. But certainly. The bazaar sold everything. It did, too, in a sprawling, teeming nest of passages and tunnels, vibrating with noise and smells, vivid, filthy, splendid. Each trade had its own alley in the warren—the clangorous tunnel of the coppersmiths full of burnished trays and hammered bowls and deaf men; the carpet merchants' alley where passionate arguments about the number of knots were smothered and muted by the rich rugs hanging, covering every available space; the jostling, dusty square with sheep-dealers standing knee-deep in their living wares; the shoe-makers' alley, richly patterned in symmetrical leathery scales; the quiet sun-hazy yards where farmers talked slowly with millers among fat sacks, and bandy little men with dusty hair flung tall golden spumes of grain up from a sieve. An old man sat half-buried in a blinding snow-drift of wool, teasing at the hanks with a wire-strung bow which twanged like a *tahr*. A vain young man squatted against a vibrating dazzle of silks carefully plucking hairs from his moustache. The smells shifted like a kaleidoscope—leather, sheep, hot metal, spice, sweat. And always there was the smell of food, leaking from dark hovels where skewers of mutton and offal spat and sizzled over braziers, or wafting in a warm floury breeze from the open door of a bakery where women, veils between their teeth, knelt pounding dough and plastering it thinly over a convex shield before it was fed into underground ovens. The baking was a matter of minutes; customers waited for a batch of bread to be raked out, rustling like great papyrus leaves, and casually folded a warm sheaf of them over their arms like a coat.

The people were more varied than the smells. All meek-ness and modesty, the shrouded women glided along, the dark-robed older women like shadows, the pale robes like spectres. Incredibly ragged, patched old men cursed at the lean, brown kids with heads like burnt matches who dodged through the crowd cheeking everybody. Kurdish herdsmen, tasselled black scarves wound raffishly round their heads, swaggered past coolly ascetic mullahs, spruce in black kaftan and snowy turban. And eddies in the crowd indicated the position of porters crabbing along under unbelievable loads of copper pots or sacks of grain.

The hatters' alley was a line of caves where the walls were covered with the entire stock. At the best cave the owner bustled around laying out everything he possessed in lamb and sheepskin and I worked my way through them all—through nattily dented headgear all the way from Teheran, brown sheepskin flat-tops, iron-grey tarbooshes. But they were all too small. Or, as the owner put it, my head was too big. Desperately he snatched a cloth cap off the wall and, by completely letting out the strap at the back, managed to force it down like an iron band over my forehead. By the time Ali and I had wrestled it off again, my head was throbbing and I had a red weal which looked permanent.

I explained that it was a sheepskin hat or nothing, and that, if I *did* want a cap, it certainly wouldn't be one with inch-size blue and white checks. Finally we found a flat-crowned hat in black sheepskin which was quite huge and almost fitted. Before Ali had finished interpreting that it was a little tight and a little too high in the crown the hatter had whipped off his creation and was ripping it apart. In ten minutes it was all sewn up again and back on my head. Even in the cheap, rippled mirror I thought it looked rather dashing. The stares I collected as we carried on through the bazaar I put down, not to the hat, but to its unlikely marriage with a black anorak and very dirty whipcord trousers.

For somebody who came from Teheran, Ali had a disproportionate number of relatives in Khoi. Uncles of his kept popping up all over the place—a bicycle-mender in the bazaar, the owner-waiter of a tea-shop, the driver of a bus which was painted like a gypsy's caravan. I was introduced to everyone. In the case of the driver, Ali sprinted after the bus and stopped it so that I could shake hands through the window. When I suggested lunch, I wasn't at all surprised when Ali said that we must eat at his uncle's place.

If *A Gourmet's Guide to Khoi* ever appears, the entry might read—It is advisable to book at this cosy bistro and if your party is bigger than four you'll have to go somewhere else. Strictly Moslem, there is no licence for wine, of course, or food either, come to that, but the jovial proprietor will send out for *kebab* from the bazaar for you without charging corkage. Round off your meal with the speciality of the house—a *ghalyan*, referred to further west as a *narghile* or, further west still, a *hubble-bubble*.

Two types of *kebab* appeared—one in the usual cubes, one minced and made into a long wallet—on a bed of dazzling white rice, each long grain separate and perfectly cooked. When we'd finished eating, the *ghalyan* was charged with light dry tobacco and an ember placed on top. Ali got it going before passing it on. An expert smoking a *ghalyan* has an air of casual, voluptuous ease. This is deceptive. You have to draw frequently and deeply with maximum lung power to keep the thing alight. Paul and I were smoking altogether too decorously, and the *ghalyan* had to be passed back frequently to Ali who would restore it with a few bellow-like sucks. The smoke is cool, mild and has a faded suggestion of herbs. It is probably much less harmful than a cigarette—a lot of the more volatile ingredients will be trapped by the water or condensed in the tube—but the effort involved makes the lungs rasp deep down in the lobes. I tried some of the tobacco in a briar, but it's so brittle and woody that you end up with splinters in your fingers and a mouth like an autumn bonfire.

The street blacksmith had finished welding the car's broken brake-shoe when we called, and he was starting to do something about a crack which had almost parted one wing from the body. Playing up to an eager audience, he was at one moment a sure-fingered surgeon as he dribbled delicate molted bridges across the gap with the welding torch. Then he became an artist as he stood back pushing up his black goggles to see his creation as a whole. The fascinatingly textured amalgam of burnt paint and weld spatter that he produced *was* almost a work of art. (As a wing, however, it was lousy. It rattled loose again within fifty miles.)

Before we could leave for Maku there was a lot of handshaking to be done—the welder, his assistant and two unspecified members of the crowd, and then there were Ali, two cousins, and another uncle. Ali had been a great help, and we must have held up his driving test for the best part of a day, but he seemed sad to see us go.

I think he might have warned us about the sheep-dogs. They were just as fierce as the Georgian hounds, but much more persistent. They loped along behind us with frightening tenacity, and they always seemed to appear when the car was hauling uphill or slowing for a blind corner. Nor did they waste their breath on barking, and it was chilling to see them silently materialize out of the dust cloud we were trailing and start to overhaul us. I wasn't quite so defenceless as before, because I now travelled with the entrenching tool to hand. Although it was no heavier than a child's spade, and wouldn't have been the slightest use if the car had stopped, I felt better with something to heft in my hand.

There is another, less obvious danger from the dogs. They hound you along faster than you ought to go, and if you're unlucky you might meet a shepherd on a corner. If you hit him you will be in trouble. If you kill him you will be in desperate trouble. I knew that Iranians were tough on careless drivers, but I didn't realize how tough until we came across a crashed bus. It had left the road and dug its nose into the earth, shedding its back axle and wheels as it went. I found out that the accident had happened early in the morning, but there was still a large crowd of people around the bus, and policemen buzzed in droves around a couple of khaki tents and several jeeps. Apparently the driver had fallen asleep at the wheel, and two people had died in the crash. The driver had already been hanged. Legally hanged, not lynched.

For all I know the approach to Maku may be beautiful, even spectacular, when the sun is up, but it is very different on a blind, moonless night. The road runs through a strangely brooding valley, thickly peopled with tall boulders which stand humped like cloaked trolls, sometimes in quiet groups, sometimes alone and waiting with terrible patience at the very edge of the road. The silence was a straining drum-skin waiting to burst in one dreadful boom—and the rocks would then stir stiffly and begin to lurch forward. In this context Maku appears like the good fairy, although its lights only blink feebly in a tiny pattern against the dark bulk of the mountains, a pinch of sequins in a towering black wave. As we pulled up, unseen dogs yelped and barked, and their message was taken up and passed on in a retreating ripple that finished in faint lonely howls from beyond the last weak lights on the mountainside. Two hotels bared their teeth at each other across the dusty road. The two proprietors came sprinting for us together shouting, 'M'sieu—M'sieu—M'sieu,' and began quarrelling over the still-warm car like jackals.

Underneath the swinging Persian calligraphy of the sign on the left was the cramped information, 'THE PLAINBOILED-RICE AND BEST MEAT OF HOTEL NEW' which must have been painted by some passing traveller because the proprietor didn't have a word of English. The proprietor on the right was more of a linguist. He could say 'Garage', and he kept saying it. This won him the day, this plus the glutinous suggestion about the other man's cuisine. Not that his cooking was any better—or even different. *Kebab* and rice —just as plain and boiled—washed down with beer which had to be drunk quickly so that one didn't taste it too much.

Although the hotel and the village itself seemed deserted, the proprietor insisted that we climbed the steep stone stairs to our room before he would serve the beer. Possibly his rival was waiting to inform the police at the first outbreak of visible roistering. Strictly speaking, alcohol should be forbidden altogether by Moslem tenets, but some casuist with a brewery must have persuaded the law-makers that beer drunk in upstairs room is not being consumed on Iranian soil.

We were allowed downstairs to drink tea, and people crossed over from the other hotel to watch us drinking it. I felt like a chimpanzee at a zoo tea-party. We were clearly expected to do something spectacular with the tea, and when we simply drank it instead of throwing it about, the disappointment was visible. But our almost human behaviour made us all the more intriguing; the watchful silence dissolved in a chorus of comment. 'At times they look almost Persian . . .' 'I do believe there are lenses in that one's spectacles . . .' 'Damn me if he isn't smoking a pipe now . . .'

A couple of the more anthropologically minded spectators tried to communicate with us, but our clicks and grunts meant nothing to them. One man produced an ICI pamphlet on plant pests and how to exterminate them. There were coloured pictures of insects and pullulating paragraphs of Persian with the odd English word cropping up. It was always the same word—a jaw-cracking insecticide presumably christened by some mad Welsh chemist. I pointed at it and smiled to show that I recognized the alphabet at least.

THE YASHMAK STRIKES BACK

October 8

We rose early, and the stone-flagged kitchen struck cold as we made a thin breakfast of tea, bread and a saucer full of pallid, acidic crumbs of cheese. The only antidote to this sort of cheerless start is movement, and we packed as if we were taking to the lifeboats. Daylight is unkind to Maku. Instead of a mysterious mountain retreat, the place is shown to be a seedy shambles at the foot of an escarpment; a grandiloquent, gold-painted statue of the Shah is carefully sited so that he is looking away from the village. Rounding on the blind side at full throttle, we left him in an impious cloud of dust and shot for the border.

A straight road across a lonely landscape was made lonelier by the black withdrawn figure of a holy man trudging along. The hills lay quiet under the all-seeing gaze of Ararat. It was the first time I'd had a clear view of it since Armenia. In some inexplicable way the Turks seem to keep the exhibition rights to themselves, and the full impact of Ararat is withheld until you are through the Customs and on Turkish soil. Customs were comparatively easy—a mere one and a half hours—but it might have been a great deal longer. The Iranian Customs demanded proof of smallpox inoculation. A large yellow vehicle with 'Quarantine' on the side waited for the unscratched and it takes ten days before one is let out of this medical ghetto. For the first and last time I actually felt grateful to the Djulfa *Gauleiter*. The efficient swine had provided us with bits of paper which recorded our forced inoculation. I had a sickening suspicion that I'd thrown mine away as useless, and I spent a bad ten minutes rooting in my anorak pouch before I found it.

Before quitting the Customs I asked an official sitting beneath a faintly neanderthal bust of Ataturk about the possibility of climbing Mount Ararat. I didn't really want to climb Ararat so much as to meet the mob of Kurdish con-men who haunt its slopes. These villains make a good living selling bits of gopher wood guaranteed to come from Noah's Ark which, according to legend, came to rest on the summit. Obviously the Kurds were well aware that, although nobody believed them, very few could resist buying a fake which provided such a great story. Not me, certainly.

But I didn't climb Ararat. The official said it was necessary to obtain permission from the military commander of the zone, and when I asked where he might be found, the official's hand waved largely at the horizon. It was too big an area to search—or at least that's what I decided after a closer look at Ararat. It rises modestly enough—nothing fang-like; more like an old molar—but it rises for a long way, long enough to make its 12,000-foot consort look like a slag heap, and high enough to hold a perpetual spider of snow through the baking summer.

Agri left little impression on my mind, but my stomach remembers it with gratitude. The staple diet of the country, *kebab* and rice, palls very quickly. The rice part was becoming particularly boring, and I slumped down in a small restaurant dully anticipating another unexciting instalment of the cereal. The proprietor was a man of few words, none of them English, and sensibly cleared the language barrier by leading us to the kitchen. And here was treasure. Jostling for position on a huge range were pots and pans and skillets, simmering and bubbling through the whole savoury spectrum of stews—and vegetables! I'd almost forgotten there were such things, and I dithered indecisively over peppers, tomatoes, aubergines, stuffed vine-leaves and beans. I ended up with a bit of everything, which was rather a lot.

Afterwards, I was certain I couldn't eat another thing for hours. Wrong again. Soon after leaving Agri I was eating dirt in large amounts. The road was softly blanketed under inches of fine, floury dust, which leaped into the air at the slightest disturbance. Once airborne it showed no inclination to settle, and hovered more like smoke than dust. It sprang up tree-high if the air sighed; even a dainty-footed mule trailed a gauze of it behind. Any passing car towed a dense white cloud a quarter of a mile long, but cars were rare. We bowled along ahead of our cloud through hills like cones of buff blotting paper, which here and there had soaked up chemicals from below—the damson stains of permanganate, pale powdery greens of copper, sulphurous browns mingled with subtler patches of rarer earths in the elusive colours seen in watered silk.

I noticed the crawling pall of dust from a long distance away. When we got closer I could just make out a thundering convoy of army trucks. Closer still, the dust began to darken the air itself. Then we were abruptly swallowed in dense, hot fog, and all that could be seen was the water-wheel-sized tyres of the truck in front, shovelling smoking dust at us like excavators. With such low visibility I didn't blame the drivers for hogging the middle of the road, but it meant we had to mark time, choking behind each truck until there was enough space to ease past. There was no hope of seeing anything approaching, and overtaking was a blind act of faith. Our faith was tested eight times before we reached the head of the column. We had been riding in the fog for nearly two hours.

My eyes grated at every blink. The handkerchief I'd worn bandit-style over my face had been useless. My mouth and nose were coated with mud, and my lungs felt like egg-timers. When Paul and I could see each other again there was a stunned second, followed by croaking laughter. We looked like clowns after a flour battle—white faces with ashen lashes framing ferret-red eyes. Grizzled prospector-like beards were mismatched with powdered wigs, and our clothes were so thickly silted-up that the folds in a sleeve looked like a terraced hillside.

Looming out of the cloud we must have been quite frightening, and the two jeeps acting as outriders to the column spurted ahead nervously at our appearance. But after we had edged our way past the trucks, the road looked as wide as the M1, and we overtook the jeeps easily. They had had it much too easy, toddling in front of us in the sweet, bright air without caring, or perhaps even knowing,

176

about the gritty hell they were kicking up behind. There was a savage satisfaction in watching them slow down and grope for the road as our dust-plume twisted in rich, soft ropes from our wheels and boiled over them blindingly. Let them eat dirt. And that went for the truck-drivers, too, who had already switched on their headlights to cut through the murk.

This uncivilized attitude didn't last very long, and we charitably pulled ahead until the column had become a curling, creeping cloud in the distance. As we rounded a bend, the last view of the convoy was almost beautiful as the dipping sun turned it into a rose-edged mist.

When we reached Pasinler we were fairly hungry, very tired and absolutely filthy. At this moment, a bath took priority over food, bed, everything. At the first ramshackle hotel we came to we threw down our overnight bags in a twin explosion of dust, and demanded to see the ablutions. The establishment consisted of a spit-and-sand tea-shop, with a corridor of malodorous cells at the rear. The demand made no impression at all on the owner, who seemed to be a low-grade idiot. I pressed him with increasing grimness for the whereabouts of a bath but his childish interest could only attach itself to one thing at a time, and the thing of the moment was our hairiness. He simply couldn't get over our beards, and he crowed and clapped his hands until I thought of giving him a hard blow to try and jerk his little mind into another groove. The word 'hamaam' popped up like an ace out of my memory, but even this had little effect on his pantomime. Not that I expected to find a *Turkish* bath, but I thought it would get the idea over.

However, the word registered with one of the tea-drunkards, who had been watching us silently. He collared a small boy, gave him brisk, military style orders and, pointing at the boy, bellowed 'Hamaam' at us. For a panicky moment I thought I'd used the wrong word, and I wasn't altogether reassured when the boy led us through the outskirts of the village to the wrong side of the railway tracks where shanty town began.

But the squat-domed building we were pushed into did

turn out to be a public bath. As we entered, the army convoy was just toiling into the village, headlights swimming smokily in the now invisible dust. The sight spurred me on, and I upset the old attendant's propriety by stripping smartly. With fierce prudery he thrust an enormous loin-cloth at me. Although the *hamaam* is strictly for men, an almost fanatical modesty is observed. I wound contritely into the cloth, slipped on some wooden slippers, and followed the old man into a cavernous room lit by one sickly bulb high up in the steamy vault. Hot water welled up in stone bowls around the walls, with shallow stone depressions by the side of them. The Turkish word for these means 'navel', and you are supposed to sit in a naval and soap yourself, occasionally swilling down with a scoop of hot water.

With my dhoti traipsing wetly around my shins I pro-gressed into a larger, even dimmer room where steps led down into a warm plunge bath. It was big enough to dive in but the main sport was a kind of aquatic wrestling, the idea being to make the other fellow swallow as much warm murky water as possible. The dome rang with the sound characteristic of swimming pools everywhere—a compound of the baying of muscled extraverts and the cries of the drowning. The only thing missing was the whiff of chlorine. The water needed more than a whiff. It was opaque enough to make your hand disappear six inches down and, after swallowing a half-pint, I rejected any idea of joining in the wrestling. When they empty the pool I imagine the local farmers outbid each other feverishly for the deposit of rich alluvial mud. I managed to remove most of it with another swill in the outer room, where the attendant waited with a dry loincloth. This was whipped on with becoming sleight-of-hand, while the old man wound a towel around my head and another over my shoulders.

The *après-hamaam* was invented by a hedonist of genius. Tea is brought as you relax on a bench, cooling gently under the towels, and you sip and smoke and think slow, warm thoughts. I felt too lazy to laugh at the comedy turn on the opposite bench—a couple of peasants, dark faces

178

set on pale torsoes, who were struggling to untape their long, baggy underpants without offence.

It was surprising and touching to find that the small boy was waiting outside to guide us back. I don't think he was concerned with our safety so much as with his strict orders to see us to and from the *hamaam*. Later I found that this unquestioning obedience is common in this part of the world; any adult wanting to send a message simply commandeers the nearest child.

Although our small boy tried to lead us back into the idiot's tea-shop, we tipped him with a handful of kurus, and hurried past to a place which had intrigued me on the way in to the village. It was a long low building blazing with lights. A large sign outside said 'Gazino'. Ever since I'd caught sight of the word, improbable translations had been running through my head. A den where you gamble for petrol . . . a well-appointed sherbet parlour . . . a gazebo for albinos . . . a strip-club in-the-round.

Fact is often considerably duller than fiction. The place turned out to be an officers' mess. I prepared to make an apology and retreat, but I never got the chance. Our obviously foreign faces drew an immediate, only slightly more sophisticated response in the *gazino* (which translates, I suspect, as 'canteen') than in the hotel. I now know how a circus feels on arriving in a televisionless village.

Chairs were forced beneath us, a table placed before us and we were then surrounded by smiling officers who seemed content just to look at our hirsute faces. I tried a couple of linguistic leads without success, and then returned to smiling back steadily. I was saved from a permanent rictus by the arrival of an officer who spoke good French. He started to interview me briskly, translating my answers for the benefit of his eager comrades. When he asked what my first impression of Turkey was, I answered truthfully, 'Dusty.' Then he asked what we'd like to drink and I said, unthinkingly, 'Beer.' Consternation all round. Where was beer to be found in a Moslem garrison?

Luckily there was a decadent beast in the barracks who had a couple of bottles hidden in his locker. These were produced with such a flourish that I knew they were the only two beers in the garrison, possibly in the village. Although I had a hard-won thirst of the kind where the first two pints don't touch the sides of the throat, I had to ration myself to a polite sip every five minutes.

The French-speaking officer kept up a steady stream of questions about Russia, about England, but mostly about Turkey—Turkish roads, Turkish food, and what did I think of the recent row with Egypt over the Syrian *coup*? He said he was a civil engineer, but he'd make a much better TV inquisitor. An hour and a half later his questions were still coming, his listeners still attentive—most of them anyway. Paul was unashamedly asleep. I thought we'd better go before he started snoring. We shook hands all round twice, and shuffled back to the hotel, aching with tiredness.

Unfortunately we ordered a glass of tea before retiring, which gave the joker of a proprietor a further chance to exercise his delusions. He had developed two beauties about us. One, that I was a priest of some sort; two, that Paul was a penknife salesman. At the risk of doing English clerics a grave disservice, I let the first notion ride, but we couldn't even grasp the second one for a long time.

The little idiot kept making a weasand-slitting action, pointing at Paul and then bringing out a grubby bank-note. As far as I could see he was inviting me to make away with my travelling companion, and we'd split whatever we could raise on his pitiful belongings. I thought it was in poor taste to suggest this while the travelling companion was sitting at the same table. It still came as a miserable let-down to discover that he was not a villainous inn-keeper but merely a Boy Scout manqué.

October 9

The fleas fed fiercely through the night. At first light—almost—I threw off the old blotting paper that passed for a blanket, swung my hotly measled legs on to a floor dank and shiny with dirt, and collected a chipped enamel teapot of water to wash with. I couldn't help wondering if a real thieves' kitchen could have been worse.

The French-speaking officer had strongly urged me to visit the ruins of something or other above the village before leaving for Erzurum, so I started out of Pasinler, bandoliered with cameras. After fifty yards I stopped. I realized that I didn't remember whose ruins they were, what period, or even the exact whereabouts. Also, the bony hillside was already glaring under the sun. I decided I wasn't such a big ruin man. People were my forte; I would photograph the children of the village. There were plenty of these about.

The trouble was that none of the kids was sufficiently indifferent about being photographed. They either crowded up to the camera, as lens-hungry as starlets, or they ducked and raced for their mothers' aprons. Small girls, with tightly scarved heads and overskirts above long trousers, scampered smartly out of focus, looking ludicrously like mill-girls with their bloomers falling down. But the school-going classes, dapper in black smocks and snowy Eton collars, jumped smartly into ranks as soon as I turned the camera in their direction. With their brief-cases held rigidly at their sides, they looked like a convention of Puritans.

Our information on Turkey contained some rules about travelling through militarized zones: 'Don't wander off the road. Stop when spoken to by anyone with a gun. Most important, report at Pasinler for an escort through the militarized zone as far as Erzurum.' The snag about the last rule was that there was nowhere to report to and not a sign of an escort.

Frankly, I'd have felt easier with an escort. I had the strong impression that we were there on sufferance, poaching on land laid aside for manoeuvres, and that if we got through without a shot across our radiator we'd be lucky. There was some tactical exercise going on, a brigadier's brain-storm to keep the lads on their toes. Knots of Turkish soldiers stood around guarding nothing more important than a communal fag, and conscripts wandered lackadaisically along the skyline, blithely unaware that they had been cut to ribbons under a withering cross-fire of machine guns.

This casual attitude lightened the atmosphere a little. The only real danger was that a bored recruit might toss a smoke grenade up our exhaust for laughs, and we kept moving briskly. But I didn't find the real reason for my uneasy sensation of vulnerability until I looked behind. The startling thing was that I *could* see behind. No dust. I should have been grateful to the engineers who'd metalled the road-surface and made the ride to Erzurum smoother and faster, but the parting from that comfortably obscuring veil of dust should have been done more gradually.

We had no intention of staying in Erzurum any longer than it would take me to post the films which had been piling up ever since Helsinki. Then on to Trabzon and a dip in the Black Sea before dinner. At least, that was the plan. I stepped briskly into the post office, left arm cradling a pile of packets of monochrome, right hand clutching a bunch of colour films all in little yellow bags. There was no excess verbiage in the exchange. I dumped the films on the counter and said, 'England.' They were pushed back at me with an equally laconic, 'Railway station.'

When I tracked down the pertinent official at the station, he was quietly dying of boredom in a dusty office, and he seized on my precious packets as a Mahomet-sent means of killing time. After being forcibly restrained from checking that they actually did contain film, he weighed each packet with impassioned accuracy, and entered each result, to three decimal places, on a long grey form. Only then did he decide that it would be safer if the packets were parcelled into a couple of larger packages.

Paper was the difficulty. The miserable scraps of stuff he dug out of his desk were obviously useless. They were like starched fragments of workhouse blanket, and cracked rather than folded as he tried to wrestle them into something resembling a parcel. The end-products of his work—nobody could have called them parcels—were depressing failures. To give the man his due, he wasn't altogether satisfied himself, and he went off clicking his tongue. He reappeared with some of the most *biological*-looking paper I've ever seen—irregular mosaic-shaped pieces that might easily have been taken straight from the jaws of a gang of wasps. But at least the stuff was pliant, and, with liberal dollops of paste, the man had soon softened the brutal outlines of his original packages. Although they weren't models of neatness, I was willing to let them go, but at this point the creative aspect of his task carried him away. He slapped on more and more sopping leaves of paper and wound a lot of string around, quite at random, until the packets had metamorphosed to monstrous, misshapen pupae, all sweating glutinously. Then he decided that everything would have to be weighed again.

When it was all over I came out to find Paul under the car's bonnet, surrounded by spanners, various oily parts of car, and inquisitive children. The towers of Trebizond were not for us that night, I could feel it.

Paul said that the fault lay in the electrics. It sounded like an arcane, medieval science, but I was taken on as unskilled labour. The dynamo was removed bodily—a long business —and some pious adjustment made. The dynamo was then replaced, and I held a screwdriver and an adjustable spanner, trying to form a mystical bridge for the current while Paul started the engine. Invariably, the volts ignored my bridge and jolted to earth through me.

Paul insisted that this was a good sign but I found it very hard to agree. It was five hours later when he decided that the car would have to be taken to a garage after all.

The garage was an ironic couple of hundred yards away. Here the last feeble hope of quitting Erzurum died as the owner-mechanic waved an overworked hand at several lorries —huge, stricken beasts with the mute appeal of sick elephants. While Paul was trying to jump this suffering queue, I went off to book us into an hotel. Incredibly, most of them were full, and I was lucky to find room at a mouldy barracks of a place with beds like rag-bags and a stench of sewers along the corridors that took you by the throat. It was called the something *Palas*, which suggested that the hotel-keeper had a sardonic sense of humour. He certainly had a firm, if unethical, grasp of the law of supply and demand, and asked a ridiculous sum for staying overnight. My attempts at bargaining only deepened his thin smile, the smile of a snake regarding a frog.

When I went to collect the luggage from the car, I was in no mood for further swindling, and the *fayton*-driver I flagged should have sensed it. The *fayton* (from phaeton but, like many words, phoneticized when it was borrowed) is the taxi of Erzurum—a razor-boned nag pulling an over-upholstered carriage. The driver often stands up and lays about him with a whip but the horse rarely obliges with a gallop. The result is that the driver is forced to get his kicks by overcharging whenever he can.

I had been told by some well-wisher that, for a reasonable ride, 150 kurus was a fair charge. The trot to the car and back again was hardly long enough to furnish a BBC sound effect but I gave him 180 kurus to show that princes still walked abroad. Halfway through waving away his fulsome blessings I realized that he was actually cursing, and inviting the passers-by to witness my meanness. The idea is that the foreigner stands there mutely uncomprehending until he becomes so embarrassed that he forks out more money to escape this emotional blackmail. But when I started to shout back, much more loudly, it was the driver's turn to be mute, uncomprehending and, finally, embarrassed. His indignant expression melted into a nervous grin of conciliation, but I kept shouting at him even as he clopped away in full retreat. I think I even embarrassed the crowd.

The hotel-keeper was one of the crowd, and he eyed me with a new respect mingled with suspicion. I felt much better, and went off to the *hamaam* whistling. This was quite luxuriously appointed and had a private disrobing room, masseur and foam-bath expert. Strictly speaking, the masseur was more of a sandpaperer. He draped me on a wooden dais with a block under my head, and started rubbing the corners off me with a black glove apparently made of emery-paper. A frightening amount of my skin came off, and when he swilled me down I felt as sensitive as a peeled shrimp. The foam-bath man appeared with a linen bag like a half-size pillow case. This must have had soap inside because when the man slopped a little water in, swiftly closed the neck, and pressed on the air-filled sack, foam billowed out through the linen. In no time I was as snug as a grub in a blob of cuckoo spit, but I'd hardly begun to enjoy my insulation when the man sluiced it away under a numbing succession of bowls of warm water. A strong anti-voluptuary, I think.

They ordered things differently in the disrobing room. With a fresh loincloth and swathed and turbanned in towels, I was lying back taking the first deep, shuddering drag at a cigarette when a white-jacketed attendant eased in with a tray and proffered tea with a respectful murmur of *'Effendi'*. And nothing sounds quite as respectful as a murmur of *'Effendi'*, even though it means simply someone who can read and write.

October 10

We take the road for Trebizond.

I had to write that, even though the sonorous name of Trebizond has long since been crassly changed to Trabzon. The power of words being what it is, the place *looks* like a Trabzon. Still, it was worth going there for the journey, a ride of vivid contrasts. From the arid grittiness of Erzurum we wound up to dank, cloud-filled mountain passes, and then descended to a balmy evening of gentle rain by the Black Sea; from buzzards wheeling in a hard, pale sky to bats jinking in a feathery dusk; from beer and stuffed peppers to fish and bad champagne.

There were two mountain passes to cross—an 8,000 and a 6,000 footer—and I assumed that the first would be the tough haul. But you never can tell about mountain passes, not even when you're on them. What appears to be a mild incline can have the car coughing, and the next minute it will sail up a wall-of-death stretch without the slightest trouble. Perhaps it's cars you never can tell about. I couldn't; not about the Alvis. It breezed up the side of Mount Kopdagi like a distance thoroughbred, and it was more or less a courtesy stop we made half-way.

Yet is was a stiff climb. I was doing some nature study on the dwarf thorn bushes when I saw a lorry far below us fighting its way upwards so slowly that I had to keep watching it without blinking to make sure it was moving at all.

The note of its tortured engine came clearly through the stillness, and two eagles were planing a thousand feet up waiting for it to die. We didn't make the mistake of letting the lorry overtake us. When it lumbered around the bend just below us we shot up to the top of the pass and started the long sweep down to the apple country around Gumusane.

And what apples they are—firm, glossy fruit bigger than your fist, with a bite as crisp as celery and a clean, acid tang underneath the sweetness. The locals are so proud of them that they never consider taking money in exchange. When we stopped for something to eat at a small *lokanta*, the proprietor immediately piled our table with apples until it looked like a Cézanne painting.

The other customers, who all seemed to be wearing moustaches and rudely tailored sheep-skin jackets, were not so forthcoming. The rumble of chatter tailed away as they lowered their loaded forks and stared at us unsmilingly. The ones with their backs towards us scraped their chairs around and joined the silent barrage. They looked like a photograph of a Partisan group—and just about as impossible to outstare. A single smile would have made all the difference, but Turks, as I discovered, don't smile easily. I took this silent hostility at face value, but it turned out to be simple unvarnished curiosity.

The wine broke the ice. From the bar and casino section of the phrase-book I had slowly enunciated an order for a bottle of dry, white wine. The waiter went off at a fast shuffle, and came back with a bottle of red wine as syrupy as prune juice. Pointing out the relevant phrase for his rheumy eyes and repeating 'sek' despairingly had no effect. Then the clients rose in a body and came over to help. I was politely relieved of the phrase-book and it was passed gravely from hand to hand, often the wrong way up. They went through it thoroughly, from 'Useful Expressions' to 'Parts of the Body', with little clicks of the tongue which sounded disapproving but might easily have been the opposite. In fact, not one of them could read, but the printed word had a tremendous fascination for them.

One patriarch was for some reason determined to buy the book, and kept thrusting a talon full of grubby notes at me. At the same time there was a steady rain of questions. One that I recognized, 'Are you German?' I must have answered half a dozen times. It wasn't that the questioners disbelieved me; they simply wanted to repeat the delight of getting an answer in Turkish.

When I unzipped the pocket of my anorak and produced a gas lighter to light my pipe, curiosity reached new heights. I never got a chance for a second light. The lighter was swooped on and passed around with more tongue-clicking (it must be approval), being flicked on and off much too close to the luxuriant moustaches.

The patriarch, perhaps made desperate by his failure to buy the book, suddenly plunged his hand into my still-open pocket to see what other treasures I was keeping back. Among the stubs of Intourist tickets, lumps of sugar, stamps, ball-point pens, dog-eared postcards and deliquescing Horlicks tablets he found my penknife. It's just a nickel-plated smoker's companion, but it was handled like a gem of the sword-maker's art.

Having exhausted the possibilities of my pocket they crowded around the car as we were leaving, all laughing and joking by now. One of the men stopped a lad passing by with a mule, emptied half a pannier of apples into the front seat with us, and sent the youth on his way with nothing but a lordly dismissal.

Full of apples and wine and feeling unusually hopeful about my fellow-men, I looked with keener appreciation at the country, which had become lush. The road ran through curving avenues of glorious birches—slender silver trunks sweeping up into shimmering masses of lemon-yellow leaf—and kept company with a quietly spoken stream, cool and green as a grape. Fat cattle paddled in a meandering river so shallow that a train of ox-carts, mountainous with fodder, forded it without drowning the squeal of axle-trees. A cubist cluster of houses swung past at the end of a long, dusty thread of track, each flat roof tiled with ripening cobs, white boxes with lids of beaten gold.

Abruptly as a film, the scene cut from a lazy, hazily golden Asia to a dank, Nordic mountain. This is the Zigana pass. The sun, flaming on saffron and scarlet bushes was snuffed out sharply as we met the forest covering the mountain, and the road began to lurch about blindly in an exhausting series of twists and turns.

We snaked our way upwards through cool colonades of pines, and as we got higher the branches began to trail banners of smoky mist. Then we were in the dim, cold heart of the cloud that had bedded down on the mountain for the night, and the noise of the engine lost all bite and resonance. The cloud had slipped like an eiderdown, which meant there was a lot more of it hanging down the other side. When we finally burst into clear air again, it didn't seem fair that the sun should have already given way to black night.

All the way over the pass there hadn't been sight or sound of another vehicle, but now we began to meet lorries, first in ones and twos, and then a whole string of them. Their undipped lights blazed at us as they shuddered upwards. Not that we objected; anybody driving a ten-ton truck up a cork-screwing mountain road on a pitch-black night is entitled to blazing headlights. In fact, one might assume they were obligatory—as long as one doesn't forget the non-conformist. We did, and nearly plastered ourselves all over the radiator of a juggernaut being driven solely by the light of a cigarette.

For a long time after the trucks had passed, I could see their lights moving like glow-worms against the hulking darkness of the mountain above us. Then we turned the flank, and we were in unrelieved blackness again with nothing but our own noise for company. Occasionally the headlights picked out a little knot of veiled women trudging home under heavy loads of wood.

As we got lower, we began to pass through one-dog hamlets. There was usually a doorway streaming out light —the solitary tea-shop, perhaps—and the glimpse inside was always the same snapshot of tables full of men tired after a heavy day's talking. The unfamiliar engine note brought some of them to their feet, and as we swept through the bar of light, briefly illuminating the green of our coach-work, they all summoned their remaining energies and gave a hoarse shout that rattled the tea-glasses.

We rolled on through a velvety evening that became balmier with every yard we dropped. And so to Trebizond, spangled under a warm, soft rain drifting in from the Black Sea, where we ate a large, unrecognizable fish and drank champagne which had a bouquet like a dry cleaner's.

October 11

Locals are liars about their own town. Either they think it's a dump or they think it's a paragon, and both views are usually wrong.

Mehmet definitely belonged to the second group. I was taking a breath of air on the charcoal-black beach, tentatively biting my tongue which had apparently changed into suède overnight. I was also trying to take a photograph of two sturdy women at the water's edge. They were belting the daylights out of some dispirited washing, but every time I moved into range they gave me dangerous looks and turned their mare-like haunches on me. Mehmet appeared suddenly at my elbow, and explained that they were stupid, ugly women and just a waste of sir's film. Fortunately, this was said in German, otherwise Mehmet might easily have taken a belting along with the washing. Did he know a better subject for my camera? Oh yes, there are so many things—short pause—the mosque of Aya Sofia, of course. I explained that I didn't have much time. (We were intending to make a reasonably early start to get as far along the coast road as possible.) Natürlich the mosque was no distance at all. Mehmet himself would show me.

It was, in fact, outside the town altogether and a good forty-five minutes' forced march away. At last Mehmet pulled me to a steaming halt on top of a grassy hillock, and announced 'Aya Sofia!' And there it was, completely smothered in scaffolding. Even after demisting my glasses I could make out only the vague outline of a dome. I did manage to get an idea of the silhouette by focusing somewhere beyond the fuzz of poles and sprinting sideways. The token hammering which a gang of masons had started up as we appeared began to peter out raggedly, then stopped altogether. The men laid aside their chisels in wonder, but kept their hammers handy as I loped lightly over the turf.

Inside, the mosque was a shambles, the floor almost impassable with rubble, the plaster pocked or chipped away in great islands except right up in the domes where faded, patchy murals still stared down palely. Mehmet assured me that the mosque was simply being repaired. He was becoming nervous about my reluctance to take photographs, but my German wasn't up to explaining that shots of scaffolding and before-scenes of interiors had only a narrow appeal. To please him I decided to waste a few shots on the mosque, but as soon as I lifted the camera the masons leapt up in a rigid, smiling group, arms folded, feet resting on blocks of stone. Convinced that every photograph should have human interest, they followed me around, moving in tight formation and hitting their pose with the speed of professional models as soon as I glanced at the viewfinder. Mehmet, as the organizer of the treat, was always in the middle. Aya Sofia appears on my shots simply as background to several uncannily identical group portraits.

When we started back, the morning had somehow slipped away, and the pavements were awash with Eton-collared schoolboys going home for lunch. My camera excited them as it does all Turkish males. A bow-wave of magpied kids broke before us, dancing, grimacing, trying to produce an expression worth capturing, and a bigger horde of hopefuls skipped along behind. We stopped by a cemetery to try and get a taxi. I turned my back on a chest-high sea of cheeky grins to photograph the slim, knobbed tombstones sticking up at all angles like the handles of deep-driven daggers. But the lads were in among them like quicksilver, striking Edwardian stances, arms flung around both tombstones and other schoolboys indifferently. Mehmet flailed into them with his cap as if they were flies, and, neatly modulating the last swipe into a courtly flourish, waved me into the taxi he had flagged down.

The heartbreaking thing about people like Mehmet is that they appear to have so little to do that you feel you are depriving them of a pastime by leaving. I muttered 'Auf wiedersehen' to him almost guiltily, although I was delighted to wave goodbye to Trabzon. Few things are as powerfully depressing as a seaside town on an overcast day off-season. One of those things, in this particular case, was the road leading out of the town—a black snake following a blacker beach bordering a sullen, pewter sea melting into a leaden sky. The surface was a treacherous mud that frequently became a quagmire, hiding ruts and fathomless pot-holes. It was narrow, too, and we sloshed along behind a vast lorry without a hope of getting past. Until the lorry slipped.

It was negotiating a steep bend with ponderous dignity when the huge rear wheels began to spin, at first in nervous bursts but soon in a flat-out, desperate dog-paddle to find some solid ground below the mud. The rear end began to slew steadily towards the edge of the road, which hung over a straight drop of twenty feet on to the beach, but the driver kept his foot down, knowing that once he stopped he would never get started again on the slope. One tyre of a double-tyred rear wheel had moved out over the drop spinning in free air, before the driver slammed on his brakes. It was much too late, but somehow the lorry stayed put, even with the load of bags of cement pushing the over-hanging corner down until the massive body was twisted like a match-box.

Three men shot out of the cab, furiously tying ropes to various parts of the lorry and racing up the bank to tie the other ends to trees. As occupational therapy it worked very well, but as a serious attempt to anchor the lorry it was pathetic. If the lorry decided to go—and nothing looked more certain—the tatty, old ropes would part like stamp-edging. This got through to one of the men; he ran off and returned with a stout wire cable and a gang of excited villagers.

Everyone immediately sized up the situation and came to a different solution. Furious arguments erupted as orders and counter-orders met head-on. Suddenly I noticed that the cab wasn't empty as I'd thought. The driver was sitting grimly behind the wheel, foot on the brake, waiting for someone to do something. But at this excited point both he and the lorry could have slid over the edge without attracting much attention at all.

After several minutes of bickering, some iron man got the mob under control, and soon there was a chain of villagers unloading the cement bags while others were hauling the attached cable taut around a tree. When everything was going so well I should have known better than to bring my camera out. Immediately the unloaders dropped their sacks and formed into the familiar group. When the hauliers saw what was happening, they let go the cable and joined the group. With only half the sacks unloaded and the cable sagging uselessly, another, even fiercer, argument broke out about who deserved positions in the front row. The lorry driver swivelled, and peered through the rear window in desperate appeal. At least I think that's why he turned round but it's quite possible he didn't want to be left out of the photograph. I put the camera away before the accident became a tragedy.

Paul was commandeered to drive a messenger on to the next village, where there were supposed to be some powerful bulldozers working on the road. He came back leading a couple of spidery yellow machines which looked highly inadequate. They strained away, shuddering with effort, to try and drag the lorry back on to the road. When *their* wheels began to spin and crab towards the edge, I reached for my camera again. But it was discovered that the lorry-driver still had his foot on the brake from force of habit. He was persuaded to transfer his foot to the accelerator and, after a terrifying last spin that eroded most of the overhanging edge, the lorry lurched back on to the road.

Although there hadn't been a dull moment, I had plenty of time to regret the two hours' hold-up as we pushed on to cover the ninety muddy miles to Giresun before dark. It was a nerve-scraping ride on which everything seemed to be hostile—the country, the road, the kids. Especially

A ford near Diyadin, central Turkey

The hat-seller at Khoi, Iran

View from the fish market, Istanbul

the kids. Gangs of grinning little monkeys, with heads razored down to the bone, were waiting around every bend, and they shouted uncouth gutturalities, skipped just ahead of the wheels in the hope of causing a skid, shot water from hollow sticks, pretended to throw stones to make us duck, and then really threw stones when we stopped ducking. One lovable little tot up in a tree, combining prodigious effort with superb timing, managed to pee on us as we passed.

On our left the hills loomed over us, never retreating far enough to let us breathe, sometimes advancing to try and bully us into the sullen sea on our right, a sea which didn't look like the sea at all, didn't even smell like it. Nor were the villages the clean, salt-scoured places one expects by the sea. Instead they were more liking mining camps— brawling bottlenecks of buses, lorries and people noisily milling around in black liquid mud.

I was keeping a ravenous eye open for anything resembling a restaurant, but the smoke-filled shacks I saw stopped my salivary glands in mid-flow. When I finally saw a *lokanta* looking as clean as a polished apple I thought it was a hunger-induced delusion. The proprietor almost tripped over himself welcoming us inside, where the smell of cooking was wrestling with the smell of plaster and newly-planed wood. The spectacular cleanliness was explained. It was a brand-new place and, in fact, we were the very first customers.

The owner apologized for the lack of a menu, which I thought was charming since there was only one dish available—a large pan of stew simmering on the stove. Protocol, however, was strictly observed. We ordered, he wrote down the order while congratulating us on ordering the speciality of the house, and then solemnly presented the order to the cook, who was two paces away and had heard every word. The service was tremendous. The cook catapulted across with our dishes and the owner watched us as if he were trying to mind-read our next order, occasionally breaking off to swing wildly at the kids gawping at us from the door.

There was no sign of anything in the sweet line. When I hesitantly suggested cakes, he collared one of the slower kids and sent him off to some patisserie. The child returned with a couple of buns so leathery that they were unbiteable. The owner was terribly upset, and he was further desolated when he couldn't procure us any coffee. The tea we settled for might well have been brewed with his scalding tears.

Giresun looked duller than Trabzon, but there were delights in store. The first was the name of the hotel—Kristal Palas. Here I found that not only was there no hot water but that all bath-plugs were missing. The hotelier listened with raised eyebrows to my complaints, and suggested that there was a cold shower for people who carried cleanliness to such lengths.

The second delight—undiluted this time—was Mr Kramer. By the time I'd had my Spartan clean-up, the hotel restaurant was shut. Everyone seemed reluctant to disclose the whereabout of a restaurant until a large, imposing man, who had been watching us for some time, came forward and said he would take us to Mr Kramer. It wasn't exactly a command. More like a princely invitation. We said we'd be only too pleased if Mr Kramer was in a restaurant. But of course, Mr Kramer always ate at this hour, and he would be delighted to see us. Mr Kramer was a white-haired little man, with a most self-effacing manner. But he was clearly a power in the place. A raised finger, and extra chairs were whisked to his table. A rattle of Turkish, and the cook, preparing to go home, was set to work to grill some fish for us. Apéritifs were not forgotten—slim tumblers with four fingers of *raki* apiece—and a jug of ice-water appeared. I went at it carefully. In places where hard liquor is officially or religiously frowned upon, it tends to be pretty brutal when it does appear. The soapy opalescence when the water hit the *raki*—and the smell—put it into the anis family. A pretty uncouth country cousin, mind you.

More people dropped by to pay their respects to Mr Kramer, and were persuaded to have a drink, too. I noticed that they all took theirs neat, and I followed suit. It was like breathing in a mouthful of annoyed bees. I quickly lowered my lips, which had gone all Congolese, into a glass of water, and hoped nobody would notice how long I stayed under. I needn't have worried, because everyone was hanging on the words of Mr Kramer. They were worth hanging on, too, because he was in marvellous form, pouring out a quiet stream of urbane, witty talk. He did it in English first for our benefit (excellent colloquial English with barely a trace of accent); then for those who hadn't got it he swiftly translated into Turkish and, for one man, French. He did it all easily, without a trace of pedantry.

When I complimented him on his grasp of languages, he parried modestly by saying that his native German was deserting him. Originally from Zürich, he had spent fifteen years in England training and working as a harbour engineer. For the last fifteen years he had been advising on harbourworks in and around Turkey, and he said that he now thought in Turkish. But nobody ever struck me as being so much a European—that ideal, almost mythical European, the widely-travelled polyglot who is at home wherever he happens to find himself, the eclectic who wears his civilization as unostentatiously as his well-cut suit, who is never embarrassed, rarely shocked, and who shows boredom only by intention.

October 12

Achmet Bey, the large Turk who introduced us to Kramer, had warned us to look out for a dangerous bridge on the way to Ordu. The trouble was that there were a lot of bridges, and they all looked dangerous. None of them consisted of more than a few casually-dropped planks with a further two laid on top, an axle-width apart, as a gesture towards safety. Planks is really a misnomer. They looked more like off-cuts from a veneer factory, and if you hit them at anything above a walking pace the whole bridge whanged about like a cane. Achmet Bey was right though. There *was* a dangerous bridge. It had a great hole in the middle, and there were crowds of people at either end waiting for somebody to drop through it. To their disappointment we took it carefully and safely.

The road itself looked more like an example of trench warfare than a highway. Before stepping out of the car, it was advisable to prod around and find bedrock. When you got back, your feet were the size and weight of diver's boots with mud. Leaving Ordu, the road suddenly went on a spree of smooth macadam, but after a couple of kilometres the money ran out and we were back in the trenches again. Once, the road petered out altogether in an appalling wasteland, torn and rutted by the savage spoor of bulldozers and giant excavators which lay littered everywhere, slumped awkwardly, making frozen gestures at the sky as if they'd fought each other to the death in the mud.

Finally the hills retreated to a smouldering blue line on the horizon, the road shook itself straight, and there was a heart-swelling moment when we got up to fifty miles an hour. But not for long. The main street of Samsun was pocked with pot-holes like moon craters, and an obliging traffic policeman diverted us to some bigger and better ones down a minor road.

We thought he was being perverse until we found that the main square was jammed solid with a political meeting. Apparently the country was going to the polls the next Sunday, and the newly-formed Justice Party was trying out its strength. When we managed to edge our way round to an hotel, I went up on the roof to sample some Turkish oratory. Although I didn't understand a word, the speaker sounded a bore, and he was attracting little applause. Then the rain came. Umbrellas flowered blackly and floated away in rivers, and in less than a minute only a tight phalanx of the faithful remained in front of the speech-maker. On his showing, the Justice Party was going to drop a few deposits.

Kramer wasn't so sure about this. (He was visiting Samsun harbour, and we had arranged to meet for dinner.) He thought that the Justice Party might attract the voters who used to support Menderes and his Democratic party, which had been dissolved since his execution. This would be a bad thing because the Justice Party was newly formed and didn't have enough experienced men to run the country. But Kramer was much too urbane to get over-heated about politics. He looked at people and their affairs with the clear dry eye of an anthropologist, and reported on them with wit. He told us one story about his meeting with two patriarchs arguing in a tea-house, apparently about a mule. The owner boasted that she could carry sixty or seventy kilos, but the other old man dismissed this as feeble. He had seen ones which could cope with a hundred, nay, a hundred-and-twenty kilos. When they moved on to other attributes, Kramer realized that he was overhearing a marriage bargain, and that the 'she' was the bride-to-be. The load-carrying power of a wife is important to these bone-idle men, and they discuss it with high seriousness.

Sociologically speaking, Turkey is simple to stratify. There are the working classes; then there are the men. Apart from Westernized types in such disaffected pockets as Ankara and Istanbul, most of the men see nothing wrong in grinding the faces of the women. The sad thing is that the women seem to agree.

Ataturk gave them the vote, took away their *yashmaks* and abolished polygamy. Considering that nobody had agitated for any of this, it was a handsome step to emancipation. But it never happened. The women didn't advance an inch. Ataturk had hardly cooled in his tomb before they put their *yashmaks* on and started to share husbands again. They haven't yet managed to get rid of the vote, but they can always abstain.

Being wife number two is no great bargain, even from the security point of view. The only binding marriage is the civil one, which is duly recorded at the town hall. But, if a man wants to increase his labour force, he quietly takes a second wife, Moslem-style. As soon as she ceases to be worth her keep, she can be divorced just as easily.

The restoration of the *yashmak* is even harder to understand. Even the flimsiest variety must be irksome in summer. It is postulated, of course, that the male is more excited by what is concealed than by what is revealed. The result of this deprivation is that a Turk becomes feverish if he glimpses any part of a woman. Her face, her hair, even her hands are regarded as stimulating. A well-brought-up girl from the country still hands her money to the bus conductor through the thickness of her shawl.

October 13

If you're travelling in an open car, the weather determines your whole mood. After being exposed to the elements for a few thousand miles, I had become much more resistant and, at the same time, much more sensitive. Far from being leatherily indifferent to the atmosphere, I could register a change in temperature with clinical accuracy; could sense coming rain long before the first spot starred the windscreen. I suspect I was sensitive to barometric changes, too, because my spirits rose and fell noticeably.

For such a nervous meteorological intelligence, the run from Samsun to Ankara was almost painful in its variety. It started off in Samsun, with a hard, unveiled sun striking splinters of light out of the black sand and making the Black Sea look, for once, like cleanly glinting brine instead of an oiled pewter tray. The sun stayed with us until we had finished the slow climb on to the plateau, long enough to get my left arm sunburnt. The dust began to smoke hotly off the road, but the pricking of my thumbs indicated rain soon. A quick stop at the pits to whip up the hood and side-screens, and resume sweaters. It had to be quick because we had fought past a couple of fast lorries throwing up the dust, and we were not intending to get boxed in again.

When the rain came it was hard and cold as iron, sweeping across the plain like a scythe, sucking a keen, slanting wind after it. The onslaught was mounted in waves, and no sooner had the windscreen wobbled itself free of water than I could see the next cloud in the convoy racing towards us—low, fast, trailing a shaggy curtain of rain. The storm took a long time to spend itself, but gradually the intervals became longer, the scythe strokes less fierce. It was near the end. . . . A last, slow, artistic stroke of the blade brought a mere flicker of rain. At this point the sun bounded out like the demon king, and I was suddenly blinded by the most brilliant rainbow I have ever seen.

There was no coy build-up to visibility, no tremulous suggestion of water-colours. The rainbow sprang out of the ground less than a hundred yards away, a perfect double, with the outer one burning almost as fiercely as the inner. The colours had no half-hearted translucency about them. Hard and sharp as jewels they completely blotted out the red earth of the fields behind them. And the arc curved through more than the accepted semi-circle, bending like a Tartar's bow until the horns dug into the soil and the blaze was quenched abruptly.

The rainbow was the high-spot of a day which wound up with a miserable series of things going wrong with the car in increasingly dirty weather. Neither the temperature nor the light really picked up again after the storm, and the air developed a numbing bite as a precocious dusk began to drop. A tyre blew, and by the time this was fixed it was lighting-up time. Easier said than complied with. The rear-lights flickered briefly, and then died with great finality (possibly something to do with the posture of the battery, which had broken its support and was temporarily held on with flex).

The headlights worked, but didn't seem at all inclined to stay in one position. Without warning they would deliberately go cross-eyed, concentrating their light into a useless pool about ten feet in front of the wheels. Or, for variety, the off-side light would swing like a searchlight to the opposite side of the road, while its neighbour would almost revulse with a sharp attack of wall-eye.

Turkish transport cafés are rarities. This was one good reason why we had to visit the specimen that loomed out of the dusk, a rambling place looking like an unpruned seaside chalet. (The other reason was that we were cold.) In the middle of the room a huge black wood-stove crackled and glowed, and sparks fell out of the gaping joints of the stovepipe which elbowed indecisively along the ceiling for yards before departing. The clients were clustered around the stove, as near as they could get without smouldering.

Nobody was bothering with food (I don't think there was any), but two waiters were kept at full stretch racing back and to with glasses of scalding tea.

The plaster-board walls were covered with photographs of lorry-drivers. Leading this regiment of snapshots was a portrait of the latest saviour, General Gurcel, black eyebrows bristling against a flapping Turkish flag. Ataturk, of course, appeared in various guises—the pomaded sophisticate in evening dress and opera cloak; the thinker, stalking broodily across a rocky landscape, incubating deep thoughts under an astrakhan hat; the man of action in a nattily tailored uniform and casually holding a glove and a cigarette.

It took will-power to leave that stove. It was warm and sputtered soothingly, and Ankara was a long, cold ride away. If we'd known how long and cold, the stove would have won outright. Five minutes from the café we ran straight into a solid blanket of fog, a refrigerated blanket. Easing through it, the engine sounding like a muffled drum, I was soon numb, dumb, and cold as a fish-finger. After a decade or two, waiting for the warm rush of blood which would indicate the body's resignation to overwhelming cold, I idly wondered if I'd have to be buried sitting up, frozen solid.

When the headlights seemed to fade in pulses, I thought my eyes were beginning to go. I settled down into a more comfortable dying position, with my head resting on the door. In this posture I noticed the red glow of the rearlight shining beyond the running board. But the *rear*-lights weren't supposed to be working. And if they had come on again they were shining a great deal brighter than the headlights. The explanation came to me in a rather slow flash.

'We're on fire,' I said in what must have been a pleased tone; burning seemed a better way to go than freezing. It was a bizarre fire. The flex holding up the sagging battery had worn through its insulation, and was shorting the battery as hard as it could go, glowing like a wire-mill. A thick rubber sheet—wrapped around the battery for some reason—was bubbling away in quite a decent blaze. Paul did a smart jackknife dive into the car for the fire extinguisher, which he'd been dying to use on something for weeks. I managed to snatch a crafty warm at the glow before it was smothered to death in foam. The night seemed much colder and darker than before. The headlights were now no more than a couple of senile glow-worms.

Some hope of survival returned when the foggy blanket lifted to a grudging ten feet above the road. Crouching instinctively under this furry ceiling we pushed our speed up to twenty miles an hour, and a little heat began to seep through the floorboards from the engine. The lorries from Ankara soon put a stop to this when they started to thunder past, sucking down wakes of mist behind them and bringing us to a dead-stop each time. I must say these big lorries are versatile. They can blind you with mud, dust or fog.

When the fog finally disappeared, we were in sight of Ankara. Winking pin-points of light pricked out the hilly contours of the suburbs; turquoise sequins on black velvet curves. But the city had been abandoned to the bleak night. Needling winds cruised the pavements, spurring on the odd passer-by, a tortoise in an overcoat. Taxis fled along wide, lonely streets. Neons stared and winked only at each other.

October 14

Ankara had an artificial, overplanned look. The feeling of slow, organic growth that gives a city character was missing; the boulevards and modernistic slabs of architecture still had the smell of the drawing-office about them. It looked more like one of the rawer American towns, but this may have been suggested by the very American-looking police—blue pants, leather wind-cheaters, snappily peaked caps, Errol Flynn moustaches. Some even wore sun-glasses, although the sun was about as dazzling as a peppermint that's been in your pocket too long.

The polls on the next day had brought on a rash of party favours. Buildings waved banners like handkerchiefs or wore them like rosettes; every other car had a flag swathed over the radiator or flapping from the aerial. Even the unflagged cars gunned along with the urgency of ambulances.

When we took a taxi to the Albanian consulate to try for a visa, the driver shot away from the kerb with squealing tyres. After racing flat out for ten minutes, he pulled up and admitted that he had no idea where he was going.

The consulate turned out to be simply a room in the consul's flat, when we found it half an hour later. But it was a waste of our time and his. As I expected, his unshaven colleagues in Moscow hadn't been in touch. Of course, if we would just fill out these forms (handing over a heavy stack), we would have visas back from Tirana just like that, zut! When pressed, he admitted that zut represented about three weeks. The taxi on the return journey went faster and charged more.

By this time it was much too late to leave Ankara for anywhere, but we left anyway. If we hadn't, we'd never have stayed at Bolu—and this would have been a pity. I liked Bolu straight away. It has kept the main road at a sufficient distance to preserve its quiet and appealing lethargy.

Unthinkingly we roared into the tiny main square. Normally our arrival in a village brought out everybody who wasn't actually bedridden, and I thought that this particularly noisy début would bring the whole population about our ears. But not a single soul bothered to come to the door; not one angry head poked out of a shutter. It was a novel sensation—one I liked. Even in the smoky little restaurant the customers hardly looked twice at our beards, and I was able to give my complete attention to a particularly toothsome tart, culinarily speaking, which was smothered in thick, buttery cream.

I went for a slow stroll to settle this, and Bolu improved with every step. Along the narrow main street shops like illuminated match-boxes splashed the cobbles with light. Narrower side-streets wound crookedly uphill in shallow steps. I followed one at random, and practically bumped into a mosque gleaming in the moonlight, a slumbering white elephant. Although I tried to walk quietly so as not to break the spell, I still sounded heavy-footed as I passed through the still backwaters of old wooden houses, the upper shuttered galleries leaning out over the street on

curving struts and narrowing the sky to a ribbon. The stalls
of a tiny market were ghostly under shrouds of sacking, but
scores of melons lay in uncovered mounds glistening coldly
under the moon.

Stretched on my plank-hard bed, I found it almost too
quiet to read, and when a dog barked a long way off under
the crisp stars I stopped reading to listen until he settled
down again.

THE GOLDEN WHORE OF THE BOSPHORUS

October 15

The rain was settling down to make a day of it as we started the winding descent to Istanbul, but at least the raindrops became warmer as we descended. Fat, weeping clouds sagged lazily all over the landscape, sitting like blowsy wigs on the hills and filling the valleys in billowing masses. When I stepped out of the car to take a photograph, the mud closed over my shoes.

While waiting for the Uskudar ferry I strolled about, but could find no sign that Florence Nightingale had ever been here when it was known as Scutari. A boy on the ferry was tripping round with glasses of tea, which had to be drunk rapidly before the rain made it tepid and weak. That's what happened to mine, but before I could collar another glass we were tying up at the very tip of Europe. The cars came off the ferry like greyhounds out of traps, and we sped along the waterfront in a tight bunch of rasping tyres and spray. To pick a route through the maze at the other end of the Galata Bridge looked difficult even on the map, and we carried on to the Ataturk Bridge which runs, with appealing simplicity, straight into Ataturk Boulevard.

Rain doesn't suit Istanbul. The Bosphorus looked like boiling lead, and sodden boatmen rowed furiously to keep off the rheumatism. The famous skyline of mosques and minarets looked like a cut-out of damp grey cardboard, and the boulevards were running like rivers.

And on this sopping day, Istanbul is dry. We found this out when we were refused beer with our lunch. At first we thought we'd run up against a local law or perhaps a holy day. In fact, the embargo was in honour of polling day, and not only Istanbul but the whole of Turkey was dry for twenty-four hours.

We'd taken a cheap hotel, since our money was getting

low, but I thought the proprietor ought to provide towels and more than two paper-thin blankets. I couldn't move him on the blankets, but he eventually threw in a towel. There *was* a hot shower, which was kept heavily locked. And those locks were not simply to keep out residents who couldn't afford the price of a shower. I could—just—but I only tried it once. The experience was almost traumatic, a Fu Manchu episode in which I spent most of the time keeping a gang of giant roaches at bay with my feet. The hotel was called, of course, a Palas.

In Taksim Square, the Piccadilly of Istanbul, the first election results were coming through on the electric placard. A highly vocal group cheered wildly at each victory of the new Justice Party—and there were quite a few. I wondered if Kramer was worrying.

October 16

At last I caught up with *döner kebab*. I had been told that this national dish was a gastronomic treat. I'd hunted it, without success, practically since crossing the border. Each time I was given some transparent excuse. It wasn't the right season, or the right day, or the right hour. I was ready to put it down as extinct when I found it with the help of Alev, a chap I'd been asked to meet by a friend of his in England. Alev was in the hosiery business, and proudly showed me a roomful of frighteningly complex machines from Leicester churning out nylon socks like colourful sausages. I was given a couple of brace before being taken to the Pendeli Restaurant in the Spice Market, a very soothing eating place in cool blue and green faience and providing impeccable service which extends to peeling your tomatoes for you.

When I hesitantly asked for *döner kebab*, the waiter brought it as if it were any ordinary old dish. He was quite right, too. It's just roast lamb. Thick slices of meat are built into a sort of large bobbin, and turned slowly in front of a brazier on a vertical spit. Portions are sawn off in slivers as the cooking proceeds. A quite acceptable dish, but it could hardly be considered worth chasing the length of a country. The sweet was much more exotic—six or seven types of tart, *bacharu*, *khedive* and so on, topped with thick cream.

Aya Sofia was an undemanding place for a post-prandial stroll. You don't have to treat it as anything in particular; once a church, then a mosque, now a museum of sorts, it has a vast neuter indifference. Between smooth columns of red porphyry stand vases of alabaster, looming above you hugely, radiating coolness. Traces of both faiths look down from the ceiling, mutually disapproving but no longer caring very much. Frescoes of Christ, the Virgin Mary and Constantine loop thinly round the dome looking reprovingly at the bold, black twenty-foot diameter shields studding the walls with quotations from the Koran. Arabic calligraphy has a remarkable emotional range. Always largely assured, many of the convex targets were like incredibly controlled action painting; some were belligerent, full of clanging shields and darting lances; some were sinuous nests of writhing odalisques; others were like the serene doodlings of a sage.

The mosque of Sultan Ahmet is altogether different. This coolly arching grotto in lapis lazuli is a working mosque. You must put on slippers outside the curtain and make certain not to come between the faithful and their worship. Their worship is silent but strenuous, and an active Moslem must be in much better shape than his Christian counterpart. I watched one man at his devotions. He arranged a kerchief on his head, and stood in contemplation before putting his hands into the cupped position around his ears like a muezzin. Then he went into a complex series of genuflexions, touching his forehead to the carpet, which lasted fully fifteen minutes. I became half-hypnotized by his intense withdrawn ceremony—this and the muted mineral shimmer of the walls and roof which throws a cool veil over the alabaster columns and the rich dark yellows and Turkey reds of the carpets. It seemed egregious to hear a guide telling his charges that this was the Blue Mosque. He went on to say that it was the only mosque with six minarets.

October 17

Istanbul has over five hundred mosques and two public lavatories. This makes it difficult to plan a route which passes the latter as often as possible. (The trots had struck again.) Tried a slow, testing-only stroll to the Mosque of Suleiman the Magnificent before deciding that walking was not good for me and giving a taxi-driver the splendid order 'The Seraglio—as quickly as possible.'

The Seraglio Palace is a rambling complex of interconnecting rooms, with the odd pavilion for dalliance set among the walks. The pavilions are now looking seedy, furnished with thinning carpets and faded cushions. But the objects in the Treasury would need a syndicate of tasteless millionaires to make a reasonable offer. Peacocktail fly-whisks with handles of gold filigree and diamonds; turban fichus which must have mesmerized ambassadors with their dazzling movement of egret-fringed stones; thrones on which every square inch is studded with huge, asymmetrical rubies and emeralds, or thickly pebble-dashed with pearls of all colours. Vulgarity on such a scale of ostentation goes beyond criticism and becomes epic.

Collecting crockery was apparently a hereditary compulsion in the Palace. A long gallery of plates and bowls starts with whole walls hung with Ming and Sung celadon ware, and runs through most periods right up to the coy stuff from Sèvres and Versailles.

The armoury gleams with the dark oiliness of helmets and chain-mail corselets, ranks of guns, some taller than a man, damascened, elegant, some massively built with six-sided barrels and triggers like boat tillers, down to cases of duelling pistols as complex as watches.

The picture gallery of sultans can be taken at a medium trot. The changes of style in dress are of interest, but there seem to be only three styles of face—hawk-nosed and fierce, heavy-lidded and languorous with lechery, or simply stupid. The impetus of my run carried me through another couple of museums which lie about for the unwary in the grounds of the palace. This headlong approach to museums is to be deplored, of course, but it does give you a couple of sharp snapshot impressions. Out of the earth-coloured rubble of eroded inscriptions and chipped sculpture two pieces stay in my mind—an austerely controlled Grecian statue of a youth in a cloak, all grave uprights, and a colossal, bestial likeness of the god Bes from Cyprus, a carving that almost bludgeons you with its primitive vigour. Hands of Epsteinian bulk hold the hind legs of an animal as if to pluck it apart. The animal's head is missing (possibly bronze) but from the ducting in the stone it looks as if water—or blood?—spouted from near the god's hairy loins.

Mummy cases abounded, a fleet of crude boats with bleached and weathered paint. I thought they were all empty, but in one a nicotine-brown skull with worn molars was perched on a tangle of bandages and, in the section walled off for the sacred cat, there was a bundle like an ancient armature winding. The most gruesome mummy seemed to be intact, until you noticed an evil, slender hand thrust like a black claw through the bindings.

Alev has lived in England, and had no difficulty in diagnosing that Paul and I were showing beer withdrawal symptoms. He took us on the underground (built in 1900, it works between only two stations like a chain-driven funicular) to Ciçek-Pazari. This is an alley-way crammed with noisy restaurants selling fish of all sorts and large glasses of draught beer. I ate everything within sight—prawns, sheep's tripe, nuts—and drank quite a fair amount of beer.

This was hardly the best treatment for my delicate condition. I felt distinctly unhappy going to bed—ice-cold feet, teeth chattering—and I knew I was in for a rough night.

When the sickly-fingered dawn crept up, I was as hollow as a gourd, and looked very much the same colour.

October 18

I forced myself out of bed (a bit late, true) on legs like pipe-cleaners, and took a double dose of Enterovioform as insurance for a walk as far as the Galata Bridge. The Galata Bridge is the main artery of the city, and most of the time it looks as if half of Istanbul is fighting a way across it against the other half coming in the opposite direction. I weaved across to the Karakoy fish-market to look at the fantastic variety of fish: tunney, gleaming like striped shuttles of gun metal, with their gills turned inside out into blood-red rosettes; red mullet rayed in rosy, nacrous wheels; slender flying fish, one wing rakishly saluting; deep-bodied thick-lipped groupers; whitebait in shoals, large ones lined up in ranks, small ones tumbled in large baskets like heaps of silver bullets. And one lean shark, elegant in pale grey, pointed its blunt nose and glaucous eyes hopefully at the crowd.

The market is quite small—just a long, low shed near the gaggle of boatmen always leaning on their oars—but it jumps with noise and smell and colour. Stallholders shout themselves deaf as they slap and gut and hurl fish from slab to weigh-pan to paper. They will tell you, and it happens to be true, that their fish is Bosphorus fish, the best fish in Istanbul. They'll also tell you the same at the other end of the bridge where the fish comes from the Golden Horn, and the men sell their fish right out of the boats. They even fry it on board, and are kept busy handing up sizzling fillets in chunks of bread to workers making for the ferry boats. But, despite its beautiful name, the Golden Horn is an open sewer for the factories, and the fish become too poorly to avoid the nets.

Istanbul is full of people who want to sell you things, and it is always a buyer's market. Not far from the fried-fish men is the Yeni Cami, the New Mosque where the steps are crowded with pigeons who do regular patrols around the mosque in whistling, rushing droves. But the pigeons are almost outnumbered by small hoarse boys hawking chocolate and blown-up plastic bags. A short step from here is the Spice Bazaar, where an army of shoeblacks squat over pedestals glittering with brass-capped bottles and plastered with lurid pin-ups. They chatter like starlings and crack the backs of their brushes on the pedestal to catch your attention as you pass.

Ice-cream attendants in the cinema do a subtler version of this by flicking a coin on the tray as they parade the aisles. There are other Turkish signals which are not what they appear to be. The clicking of the tongue is meant to express not disapproval but agreement, admiration or wonder. A particularly difficult sign to understand is the hand waved downwards violently. It looks as if you are being told to stop whatever you're doing at once, but it is a sign to approach.

It occurred to me that we were about to start the last leg of the trip without having collected any gifts for friends and relatives. Alev offered to take us round the Grand Bazaar as guide and bargainer. He was needed in both rôles. It would take a week merely to establish the landmarks in this maze of alleyways, and something like a couple of years to develop the correct approach to bargaining.

The antique section alone would be a full-time study. There is a rich, untilled look about the place which suggests that European dealers don't reach this far afield. There is little or no attempt at specialization, and busts, beads, seals, cressets, jewels, opalescent tear-bottles, relics of every cultural tide which has flowed in and around the Mediterranean—Phoenician, Greek, Persian, Arabic, Roman—are all piled haphazardly, separated only by centuries and, of course, price. Trash and treasure take their chances together, and foundry-fresh brasses jostle age-greened bronzes, while smoky old ikons hang with glossy imitations. It's a bran-tub of a market, and amongst the tourist idiocies and fakes there are some gems waiting for informed hands.

We picked up no gems. Just tourist stuff, but I think we paid the right price for it, thanks to Alev. He had the cool, disinterested air of the born dealer, and under his scornful fingers prices dropped ten, fifteen, twenty-five per cent. This bargaining is accepted as a vital part of the keen pleasure of clinching a deal. Paying the first price asked is simply not done, and only upsets the dealers. Even where there is a price-tag on an article, this is merely a pleasant fiction. There are often two prices written on it, the selling price and the cost price. The selling price can be ignored. A little haggling will soon have the article being offered at cost price, accompanied by a display of great suffering.

A lot of haggling can improve even on this, but the air of martyrdom such ruthlessness produces is hardly to be borne.

After several skirmishes and a couple of campaigns of attrition, we emerged into the evening with enough stuff to start a small bazaar of our own—a *narghile*, a silver-enlaced briar from Anatolia, a whole ironmongery of *kebab* skewers and swords, bracelets, ear-rings, cigarette-holders, a tear bottle (still containing genuine earth), a carved meerschaum, and five pairs of embroidered slippers offered at a sacrificial price by the shop-owner for the unlikely reason that he'd been born, he said, in Acton.

To wind up we went to the best sweetmeat shop in Turkey, Hadji Bekir (the Hadji means he has made the pilgrimage to Mecca) and bought three kilograms of *loukoum*. What we think of as Turkish delight bears only the faintest resemblance to *loukoum*, which is very chewy, full of nuts, and has a specific gravity like lead. I expected it to be transmuted into some still denser element before long, because packing this lot into the car was going to involve appalling pressures.

October 19

A boat-trip up the Bosphorus is a real travel bargain. For 160 kurus, about one and threepence, you are taken on an unhurried five-hour trip almost to the mouth of the Black Sea and back. The steamer slowly tacks from one landing stage to another, and each village has steeper, crazier streets than the last, with weathered wooden houses, frilly with fretwork, jostling to look over each other's shoulders as the boat swings in.

The villages nodded off to sleep as the effervescent morning light hardened into the steady glare of midday. At our furthest port of call the ship bumped gently into a quiet, bleached jetty and slid into a dreamless doze. I walked through the hot hush of the unconscious village. On a molten dazzle of water, parrot-coloured fishing boats rocked gently at their moorings. In the boats the fishermen lay where sleep had felled them on coils of rope or on the bare planks, a hand or a leg flung over the gunwale, sun-cured hairy little men. The collage of sunlight and shadow under the big plane trees was quite still; from the branches long loops of nets hung without stirring.

After my eyes had adjusted to a dark little café, I saw that there were a few insomniacs in the village. Two were playing a slow-motion game of cards. One was picking his teeth. The rest were gravely pondering whether they should play cards or pick their teeth. The waiter's eyes were open, and they were pointing in my direction, but there was no other indication that he was actually seeing me. After a time there was a faint facial spasm; he could have been willing me to disappear or perhaps twitching off a fly. I could have taken my custom elsewhere, but I wasn't sure there was anywhere else to take it. Anyway, it was too much effort. When he finally got his head off his hand and made his way to my table, he managed to give the impression of a cruelly exploited somnambulist.

The light changes in quality subtly, constantly, some-times almost while you're looking at it. When the ship moved off, the dense, gouache-like brilliance had started to thin and cool. Its angle of attack dropped, peeled away the patina of dazzle, and sliced into the glassy, green water like a knife. Ghostly constellations of jellyfish could now be seen drifting past, some no bigger than a watch, others the size of a soup plate. They ghosted beneath the surface like ectoplasmic buttons, even to the four holes, or jetted side-ways through the water, pulsing from saucer to toadstool-shape, trailing a gauzy, mellifluous ruffle.

Nowhere else does the light die so gracefully. As it lost its cutting edge, a blue shadow bloomed in the water, turning the waves from vertiginous emeralds to massive, opaque flints. A soft wind started up as we rounded the last bend. The lamps on the Galata Bridge were already lit. The bridge was black, solid, believable, but the skyline of Istanbul rising behind it was pure amateur theatre, an extravagantly unlikely backdrop painted by some doddering old romantic for the local operatic society. Too many domes and far too many minarets, all out of the same pot of smoky blue.

And the varnish had already aged, making the sky an incredible golden brown.

It must have been at about this point that I started going under to Istanbul's outrageous charm. I had been fighting it in a dishonest way—as if I'd discovered that I actually liked chocolate-box art and was refusing to admit it. There was this critic-voice piping thinly away about the crudity, the overall vulgarity of it, when an unspeakably crude, vulgar moon lumbered on. It was too much. The piping voice died away. I succumbed.

Coming to terms with your own vulgarities is always a relief, and I went for a stroll around the Grand Bazaar in a very relaxed mood. I must have been over-relaxed, because I came out with a coffee-set and a *tchibouk* so long that lighting it was a two-man operation, or rather an operation for one man and one subservient wife. I was also clutching another dangerously spiky bundle of *kebab* skewers which I seemed to attract like a magnet.

Some gourmet once suggested that the only way to get an ideal meal was to combine the specialities of several restaurants. Paul and I had a highly ambulant meal with Alev, which covered almost as many miles as courses. Corncobs for starters, fished straight out of a steaming cauldron on the pavement, wrapped in a leaf and sprinkled with crude salt. The next course came free. Calling in at a shop to buy a bottle of *raki*, I noticed what looked like a well-smoked side of bacon. Was there nothing sacred left? Taking strong waters and now eating pig. But Alev explained that it wasn't the unclean animal at all, just a cunning facsimile. Pastama is actually smoked lamb, heavily garlicked and peppered. The shopkeeper chopped off a dubiously dark rasher, and invited me to sample it. As bacon it would make a very good razor-strop. I was still chewing hard when we stopped for the third course, tripe soup with an egg in it.

This we briefly sat down to eat in a café like a steamy bathroom. Most of the floor was taken up by two enormous simmering vats, each supervised by a large man with an ankle-length rubber apron and a huge wooden paddle. The men sweated vigorously into the cauldrons as they stirred titanically, occasionally levering a blanket of tripe into view like a honeycombed mountain range being thrust into being out of a boiling orange sea.

It looked like rather a lot of soup, but to judge by the way the clients were putting the stuff away, there wasn't a drop too much. Jammed elbow to elbow at a couple of trestle tables, they fell on the bowls, just braking with the nose two inches from the brilliant, scalding broth, their soup-arms already a flickering blur. Some of them paused long enough to lace in some vinegar from a bottle in which peppercorns and smouldering vermilion pods lurked. Paul wisely omitted the vinegar, but I had to try it. It went down like a dose of fuming nitric, clearing my head in a spectacular way. In fact, the vaporized vinegar went scouring through tubes in my head I didn't know I had. Gritting my teeth, I ladled on, devoutly promising my stomach never to take on anything more adventurous than calves' foot jelly in future.

I had no doubt about the next course. It had to be draught beer, a lot of it. Before, I had judged it as potable, not exceptional, but now it was an unguent of purest amber, a long, cool poem. Afterwards, some time afterwards, the fourth course went down easily, a savoury-sweet of mussels bedded in the half-shell with rice and raisins.

Maybe Paul and I betrayed our nationality by the way we handled our beer, or maybe it was the intuition of the drunk that made the man opposite address us in English. It was very fractured English, and we prepared for another of those hopeless conversations where banalities are exchanged with appalling effort. You usually swear eternal friendship between your two countries, with blithe disregard of the official attitude, and wind up by being shown every single scrap of paper and photograph from a bulging wallet. These well-documented biographies are the last word in boredom. Fortunately this particular bore didn't seem to have a wallet, but he did have one fact that he was burning to communicate. With great gravity he told us—at least a dozen times—that he would never forget Liverpool.

Paul was closeted with the Alvis, and I was sitting in a café under the Galata Bridge waiting for a boat to the Prince's Islands. My attention was absorbed by a frieze of *narghiles* silhouetted against the hard sunlight off the water when an old man dropped wearily into a seat at my table and let one of his faded bundles fall on my foot. He apologized in German, and then swapped abruptly into excellent English. He wasn't interested in how I liked Turkey, what my impressions of Istanbul were, etc. He had his own story.

'I am seventy-three although I probably look older. I speak German and English—good English, I think you'll agree—but there is no work for me. Yet when I ask to go to Germany to teach there, the authorities say, "No, you are too old." No job, no money, no family, no State assistance. If I die of starvation nobody will worry. But if I try to die a little faster I shall be breaking the law.'

He was certainly hungry, and wolfed down the food I bought him without lifting his eyes. Afterwards his conversation seemed to be taking a more conventional turn as he asked me where I was going. But he had his reasons; he wanted to dissuade me from going to Buyukda, the biggest of the Prince's Islands, and instead take him along to another island he knew, where he promised to guide me round some appalling slums. I turned his offer down. It's not that I'm squeamish about misery, but I don't see the point in looking at a leper's sores unless you're a doctor.

A couple of hours later I was sitting in front of a lunch-table which looked like an illustration from one of those over-coloured travel brochures where everyone is always laughing like mad. In the centre, a great, glowing lobster—a pillar-box with feelers—awash in cool, stylised breakers of lettuce and ringed with an overlapping belt of sliced tomato. On the right, a tall, amber flute of beer; on the left and slightly up-table, an icy quadrant of melon—red, crisply-grained flesh studded with polished brown seeds, cradled in a waxy cusp of marbled yellow and green; in the background, the blue-green sea and blue-grey islands. I didn't stop eating until I reached the background. If I thought of the old man's hunger at all it certainly didn't affect my appetite.

I forgot about him altogether as I strolled along the quiet streets of Buyukda, lined with pointilliste-leaved trees and prosperous houses dozing behind closed shutters. There was, thank God, nothing to *see* on Buyukda; no endless acres of ruins to reduce the conscientious visitor's own arches to rubble, no monastery requiring crampons and oxygen cylinders to reach it. Actually there may well be some Baedeker-gem on Buyukda, but my ignorance allowed me to fritter my time away untroubled by the thought that I could be putting it to better use. So my stroll had a pleasing aimlessness about it. Instead of a Victorian sense of high purpose, it had an idle Edwardian dimension which was helped by the occasional *fayton* elegantly clipping past in a zephyr of ammonia. It seemed out of keeping to be belting off colour shots with a Japanese 35 mm. Really I should have been taking sepia time-exposures with a huge plate camera, all mahogany and knurled brass knobs.

The golden day flowed by unhurriedly, without incident but without boredom. Then it snapped shut like a fan, and I was on the returning boat, the sea glittering coldly under the moon. But if I looked the other way the smokily dying sun was turning the waves from the bow into masses of agate, elegantly scooped to show contours of rose, saffron, apple green and oily blue, sinuously edged with jet black.

Paul having spent a day with the car, was happy and dirty when I met him. We crossed over to Asia to have dinner with Eric and Dorin Dent, one-time regulars of 'The Lamb' pub, who were now teaching in Istanbul under the aegis of the British Council. Their flat overlooked a garden riotous with exotic flowers sending up great waves of perfume. Sweetly piercing, overriding everything was jasmine; it was barely possible to make out its pale asterisks in the dusk, but its heady smell made the night drunk. We ate by candlelight, the leaves of flame swooning at each scented gust. It was the perfect moment for the nightingale, but we had to make do with the chunnering of a refrigerator.

This refrigerator dominated the room, the table, us. Its central position had been ordained by the landlord. This is because a refrigerator is a status symbol, a sign that you have arrived. Huge, often shelfless, sometimes not even connected up, this emblem of modern living is placed where a visitor cannot possibly overlook it.

Another status symbol in Istanbul is to have your son educated by foreigners. (Educating a daughter doesn't count, and would be regarded by most people as throwing good money away.) I don't think fathers have yet got around to putting down their sons' names before birth, but there are quite long waiting lists for establishments claiming French, American, or even British influence.

Although Turkish schoolboys haven't the advantage of centuries of tradition, they outstrip even our oldest public schools with regard to homosexuality. In fact, it's so common that the lads *not* indulging are likely to be regarded as queer.

This attitude towards homosexuality isn't due to a modern, liberal way of thinking but stems from much more ancient sanctions. It's a tolerance which seems to vary inversely with the status of women. Women are more or less vassals in Turkey, so tolerance is high. If a man fancied a boy instead of his wife, it would be unheard-of for her to protest.

Normally I can last out a whole evening's talk without feeling the vaguest need to mention economics. But that night was an exception. It was the face of the little old man that did it, swimming back into my memory, a terrier-thin mask of misery. Eric explained that his was no special case; there are many people far worse off and with even less chance of relief. There is no more legislation for starvation than there is for anything else, and occasional slap-happy attempts at economic policy are criminally casual.

Some minister, for example, returns from a trip to Europe fired with the idea of building autobahns throughout Turkey. A road-improvement scheme starts off with a bang. A few miles of dusty road are given a flattering face-lift, and then the minister is removed or he becomes bored with the whole thing and starts playing off the contractors against each other.

The passion for ports, on the other hand, has lasted some time. Foreign experts like Kramer have been beavering away for years improving Turkish harbours, but there are still very few ships to be seen, and it doesn't seem to be anybody's job to attract them. The country could easily export a lot more than it does; fruit is an obvious choice (almost everything grows here without the slightest trouble), and there's also plenty of excellent fish. But this would involve erecting a sawmill to make packing-cases, or building an ice-making plant—so the ideas are smilingly shrugged off as over-ambitious. Many a European business man has bustled in with a tremendous scheme for tapping some of Turkey's abundance, only to retreat, several months later, with a sheaf of unsigned contracts.

The Turks are reluctant to say no. A direct negative is considered a sign of ill-breeding. A simple shopkeeper is allowed to utter an unvarnished 'Yok', and he does, frequently. If he's tired he may click his tongue, or give a slight backward lift of the head, or just close his eyes resignedly. But a man of any standing wouldn't dream of being so brutish—and certainly not with a gentleman who had travelled all the way from Europe to discuss business. A refusal must be couched delicately. There is a code in such matters, and it must be learned.

A Turkish businessman will say something like '. . . highly flattered you could spare the time to explain your most interesting proposition which I will certainly consider most earnestly.' The poor European takes the message at its face value, presses on enthusiastically, and winds up, utterly bewildered, exactly where he started. The puzzlement is mutual; the Turk can't understand a man who won't take no for an answer.

Things do get done, of course, but often in a weird way. The introduction of margarine is an example. It used to be unknown until, probably as a vote-catcher, the peasants were encouraged to raise their standard of living. The peasants had been getting along quite nicely on a diet of cereals and vegetables, but they responded stoutly by eating most of the eggs, meat and butter they had normally taken to market. And once they'd acquired a taste for these goodies it was a tough job getting them back on to lentils again. Meanwhile, away from the farm, people were having a pretty lean time, and butter became a rare delicacy. And so a margarine factory was born.

October 21

The last day in Istanbul. Not a happy thought at all. What could the trip home be but a tedious trek across the cold patchwork of Europe, a long-drawn-out anti-climax? I knew, without any doubt, that here was the high point— leaving Asia for the last time, butting through the glittering choppiness of the Bosphorus on the fast ferry, looking at that ridiculous skyline, that jumble of smoky pearls and amber stalagmites. It wasn't really the thought of the trek home which made me melancholy. I had simply acquired the taste for Istanbul.

Yet, although I had been there five days, I was still ignorant about the place. Suddenly I wanted to know more. Fatuously, I asked Dorin why the Blue Mosque has six minarets . . . did they hold muezzin-shouters' contests? She knew a story that was better than a straight answer. Apparently it was a mistake. Sultan Ahmet told the architect, Sedefkar Mehmet Aga, that he wanted a mosque with gold minarets. Possibly the Sultan was nibbling on an odalisque at the time or perhaps Aga's ear-trumpet was clogged with *loukoum* but the result was that the word for gold (altin) came over as six (alti). How they must have roared with laughter at their little misunderstanding eight years later when the mosque was completed. It is not recorded whether the Sultan ordered the architect's ear-trumpet to be filled with gold.

A final ride down to the Galata Bridge in a *domus*. If the Galata Bridge is the artery of Istanbul, then the *domuses* are the life-blood. The *domus* is a taxi run on a communal basis. These taxis wait at specified ranks and, like buses, they have a fixed terminal and a fixed price. Unlike a bus, however, they don't move off until they are full. That means five passengers—two up with the driver and three in the back. *Domus* means 'stuffed' and the description is apt. On a short trip to Taksim Square once I was almost extruded between two broad-beamed businessmen.

Segregation of the sexes is strict in a *domus;* no nicely brought-up woman will sit next to a strange man. The observance of this etiquette often causes chaos. A *domus* will be almost full with an all-female load when a malicious male dives in. It's like a fox bounding into a hen-shed— squawks of panic, wild fluttering exits. The driver hops about madly trying to fill the vacant seats. The fox stays put, of course, smirking at this tribute to his terrifying virility.

A word of warning about paying the driver. It is strongly advisable to have the correct amount. This may be as little as fifty kurus (about sixpence), and offering a large bill is like trying to pass the black spot. Not giving change seems to be an unwritten law among *domus*-drivers. There are also long-distance *domuses* (the Istanbul-Ankara run is quite common), and it must be very worrying trying to work out how many bills of what denominations you're going to need so as not to upset the driver. In the around-town *domus*, tipping is not expected. However, if you have to hand over more than the right fare, it's much easier simply to forget your change.

Despite the low fares charged, owning a *domus* is widely regarded as the highway to the big money. Getting hold of a car is a desperate, razor-edged venture which only real gamblers have the nerve to try. Two or three of them will scrape together enough money to cover the first couple of instalments on a Plymouth or even a Cadillac. It's no use getting a sensible European runabout; it has to be a large American job. The cash price is three or four times the US price, and the price on the never-never becomes atrocious. Even the instalments are appalling. To keep up with them, the car must be earning its keep twenty-four hours a day, pausing only briefly for refuelling. In its chromiumed youth it is run as a single-fare taxi, not as a *domus*, and the co-owners drive it on a shift system. Since there's only enough money for one licence, this is given to the day-time driver who is statistically more likely to hit something. But God help him if he does. There's no money for repairs, and if some expensive part *does* pack up, then so does the whole venture.

Another hazard is the night-shift. The night driver also works during the day, and to keep his drooping eyelids prised open for customers he often takes to smoking hashish. If he is caught without a licence *and* doped in charge, he faces a crippling fine. Even if the owners skate round all the traps, it's a toss-up whether the car becomes theirs before it is driven into the ground. Long before this it will have been demoted to hacking around the *domus* ranks. But the boys are at least in business with their own car, and if only it can possibly hold together for a little longer they'll be able to put down the first instalment on a shining, new Cadillac. . . .

We took our pre-lunch drink at the Park Oteli, which commands a splendid view of the island where Menderes was tried and hanged. Despite being a recognized haunt of spies, the hotel has a disturbingly English feel about it. The gravelled drive, the stoutly unimaginative name, the heavily panelled bar which could have been lifted from Bournemouth, an atmosphere of muffled apathy barely disturbed by the slow passage of purblind waiters—it all gave me quite a nostalgic pang. Menderes may have mistaken the apathy for quiet discretion; he had an expensive suite here for his mistress. During the trial the hotel manager remained loyal, discreetly, by keeping the suite free. In fact, he didn't let the suite again until he realized how misplaced his loyalty had been, which was when he saw the photograph in all the newspapers of Menderes hanging between two of his accomplices.

Apparently the peasants of Turkey were harder to convince. Menderes was already popular with the peasantry when he had his lucky escape from the air crash in England. This was interpreted as nothing less than a miracle and his divine stock soared. It was notched still higher by the *imams*, who told their flocks, quite solemnly, that Menderes rode throughout Turkey on a white charger every night to reconsecrate the mosques. The junta which deposed him had a very tough job to persuade the peasants that Menderes was not only human but fallible; not only fallible but dead.

The day had by now become a string of farewell performances—the last time I'll walk down here, see this, smell that. For our last meal the Dents took us to Hadji Baba. The interior was dark and cool, but only waiters and people with weak eyes ate there. Most of the customers crowded on to the vine-shaded terrace, an animated sea of faces sweating slightly with good food and loud conversation, spotlit by patches of sunlight. If you were in no hurry the place was idyllic.

Our waiter seemed to be meditating deeply on planes a long way above the mundane level of food. He had to return several times for a recap of our order, and each time he had the air of someone who had been on a long journey. The thought did cross my mind that he might be sub-contracting the cooking to a restaurant at the other side of the town. But for once the delay was welcome, and we talked unhurriedly in the honeyed sun, occasionally breaking off when a dish made a surprise entrance.

Through the leaves I could see the towering milky-blue hulk of a church dome—a Greek Orthodox church, note, not a mosque. The Turks are a bit touchy about the way this symbol of an infidel religion (*and* from a once subjugated nation) dominates Taksim Square so brazenly. It is always considered provoking when Greeks, Armenians, Bulgarians (or anyone, in fact, who took a pasting from the Ottomans) set themselves up as the equal of Turks. Especially annoying are those who are taken for Turks all their lives, only to show their true colours when they die by being buried by a papas or a rabbi. But the Turks can blame only themselves for these deceptions. Xenophobia, even of the sporadic kind, makes foreigners adopt protective colouration. When immigrants see fierce posters saying, 'You are now in Turkey. Speak Turkish!', they are liable to wind up speaking it perfectly.

Lunch finally meandered to a sticky end with cakes

voluptuously entitled 'Nightingales' Nests' and 'Ladies' Thighs'. At the end of this syrupy debauch we were taken to a tiny shop stacked with postcards all printed about 1910. We couldn't stop laughing as we dug up more and more finds of phthisic-looking couples plighting their troth or of rakehells with patent-leather quiffs snatching kisses from girls blushing under huge wigs of tow-rope. The period pornography was even more hilarious: women of an ultra-Edwardian opulence trailing cheesecloth in imitations of nymphs; standing frozen against backdrops of moonlit glens or rose-gardens, wearing all-too-obviously wrinkled tights; reclining with mountainous coyness on couches. Our ribald appreciation didn't go down at all well with the shop-owner. He clearly didn't know how to treat us. Certainly not as potential customers—and he was very surprised when I wiped my eyes and handed over a whole fistful of postcards. He counted them very slowly, examining each one to see if I'd been drawing moustaches, or worse, on the pretty ladies.

Various welcome delays cropped up to put back the hour of departure. Almost any excuse would have seen the whole thing postponed until the next day, but finally we were all battened down, tanked up, anoraked and ready to go. And when it gets to this point you simply have to go. It was a restrained departure with none of the usual glad feeling to be on the road again.

We drove quietly, without haste, along familiar streets and out to the boundary of Istanbul. It felt like an age since we had roared furiously across Ataturk Bridge in that rainstorm. We rode through a dusk as soft as silk, and out through the walls of Constantine. The moon, coin-smooth, slid behind a gauze of cloud, and the beaten silver of the Sea of Marmara was anodized in a wink. The road wound away palely through deep-shadowed villages, and distant dogs made pinpricks in the silence. The car ghosted along holding its breath, and the ashen landscape flowed past soft-edged and timeless like something half-remembered from a dream. It seemed that we might easily drive on across the whole of sleeping Europe in a night.